AF352489

Shared Governance in Higher Education

Shared Governance in Higher Education

New Paradigms, Evolving Perspectives

VOLUME 2

Edited by

Sharon F. Cramer

Preface by

Peter L.K. Knuepfer

Introduction by

Nina Tamrowski

Published by State University of New York Press, Albany

For information, contact State University of New York Press, Albany, NY
www.sunypress.edu

Production, Ryan Morris
Marketing, Kate R. Seburyamo

Library of Congress Cataloging-in-Publication Data

Names: Cramer, Sharon F., editor.
Title: Shared governance in higher education : new paradigms, evolving perspectives / edited by Sharon F. Cramer ; preface by Peter L.K. Knuepfer; introduction by Nina Tamrowski.
Description: Albany : State University of New York Press, [2017] | Includes bibliographical references and index.
Identifiers: LCCN 2016031462 (print) | LCCN 2016047976 (ebook) | ISBN 9781438467443 (ebook) | ISBN 9781438467436 (hardcover : alk. paper)
Subjects: LCSH: Education, Higher—United States—Administration. | Teacher participation in administration—United States. | Student participation in administration—United States.
Classification: LCC LB2341 (ebook) | LCC LB2341 .S44779 2017 (print) | DDC 378.1/01—dc23
LC record available at https://lccn.loc.gov/2016031462

10 9 8 7 6 5 4 3 2 1

Contents

Part I.
Evolving a Collaborative Approach Regarding Shared Governance

Preface

The State of Shared Governance in the
State University of New York

Peter L.K. Knuepfer

As the largest comprehensive university system in the United States, the State University of New York (SUNY) is a complex organization that incorporates higher education institutions including research universities, comprehensive regional masters'-level colleges, technically focused colleges, specialized and statutory colleges, and a community college system. Despite this complexity, a system of shared governance has evolved at SUNY that exemplifies the best principles of the shared governance concept, bringing together in various ways the faculty, students, administrators, and governing Board of Trustees of the SUNY system as well as local trustees of the community colleges and council members of the state-operated campuses. Indeed, there are intersections and connections across all these groups, resulting in a unique system of truly shared governance.

The Organizations

Two governing bodies represent the academic staff of SUNY at the system level. The University Faculty Senate (UFS), established in 1953 by the Board of Trustees, represents the faculty and professional staff of the state-operated campuses (the research universities, medical universities, comprehensive colleges, and the technically focused colleges) as well as five statutory colleges at Cornell and Alfred Universities (a unique arrangement in US higher education)—34 campuses in total. The Senate elects a president to serve a two-year term; the president can be reelected to a second and final two-year term. The president is not only the presiding officer of the UFS but also the principal representative of the faculty of the state-operated campuses to the central administration of the SUNY system. The Faculty Council of Community Colleges (FCCC), which was established in 1967 by the SUNY Board of Trustees, represents the faculty of the 30 community colleges within the SUNY system. The president of the FCCC is elected to a two-year term and can be reelected to successive terms without limit. Likewise, the president is the principal representative of the community college faculty.

The students of all 64 SUNY campuses are represented by the Student Assembly of the State University of New York (SA), which was established in 1973 by the SUNY Board of Trustees. The SA elects a president each year for a one-year term.

SUNY is governed by a Board of Trustees consisting of 18 members, 15 of whom are appointed by the governor of New York (subject to approval by the New York State Senate). Of significance, however, is that the three presidents of the governance bodies previously noted become members of the SUNY Board of Trustees upon election to their respective positions, in a structure that is unusual if not unique. The two faculty trustees serve without vote (but with voice); the student trustee is a voting member of the SUNY Board of Trustees.

Each campus has its own president, all of whom are appointed by the SUNY Board of Trustees. But the local governing structure differs between the community colleges and the state-operated campuses. Each community college is governed by its own local Board of Trustees, and the result is a unique governance model, whereby the SUNY Board of Trustees has oversight of some community college matters, but not all. The state-operated campuses each have a College Council, consisting of members appointed by the governor and with a student member elected by the students of the campus. The College Councils have somewhat limited authority but importantly act as the recommending authority (to the chancellor and Board of Trustees) for choosing a campus president.

The SUNY system is overseen by a chancellor, appointed by the Board of Trustees, who is located at the system headquarters in Albany, New York. Chancellor Nancy Zimpher's term of service was July 2009 through early September, 2017. Her eight-plus years as chancellor were marked by a host of major initiatives (including seamless transfer between SUNY institutions, aggressive goals for student retention and completion, an increased role for SUNY in economic development within New York, and reform of teacher education).

Interactions among Shared Governance Groups at the System Level

The structure of the SUNY Board provides a direct tie between the governing body of SUNY and the shared governance organizations representing the faculty, professional staff, and students. This has obvious advantages: the voices of the faculty and students and the perspective of state-operated, statutory, and community colleges—all are represented. This is especially important when policy issues that may impact the academic mission of SUNY and its campuses are considered. It is also important when the Board considers the appointment of new presidents, as the faculty leadership advises the voting members of the board and the prospective president on the importance of shared governance in the SUNY system. As positive as the role of the governance leaders is, it comes with a potential cost: when/if the board enacts policies that may be at odds with positions that faculty or students take, the membership on the board can be viewed as a tacit agreement with or at least acceptance of those policies. At its worst, this could be construed as co-opting the positions of faculty and student leaders. On balance, however, the opportunity to help shape policy and the direction of the State University outweighs the potential cost, at least in my opinion.

Chancellor Zimpher has established a strong commitment to shared governance. She made it a key point to include the three faculty/student governance leaders as part of her cabinet, which is composed of the senior staff of SUNY's System Administration. The cabinet meets typically every one or two months to consider and offer advice on SUNY initiatives. And the chancellor is very direct about requesting input from the three governance leaders in attendance.

Finally, the three faculty/student governance leaders are regularly invited to attend meetings of the presidents of the SUNY campuses, the chief academic officers of the campuses, the Association of College Trustees and Council Members from the state-operated campuses, and the New York Community College Trustees (NYCCT) association. All three leaders attend each other's plenary meetings (two per year for the SA and FCCC, three per year for the UFS). Thus, all elements of shared governance across the SUNY system have opportunities to interact with one another.

The SUNY Voices Initiative

SUNY's commitment to the principles of, and improvement in, shared governance is best illustrated by the SUNY Voices initiative. As Good (2017) notes, this project grew out of the Power of SUNY Strategic Plan launched in 2010 by Chancellor Zimpher and the SUNY Board of Trustees. The goal of the initiative is to strengthen the ties among the various shared governance constituencies at the system and campus levels. The project has supported annual faculty and student governance leadership institutes, special meetings of faculty and student campus governance leaders, and two major conferences on shared governance.

This book contains six of the papers presented at the second SUNY Shared Governance Conference that was held at Onondaga Community College, March 20–21, 2015, on the topic "Rethinking Shared Governance in Higher Education." Keynote presentations by Susan Resneck Pierce (who spoke on "The Shattering of Shared Governance: Why Has It Happened and What Do We Do About It?") and Steven Bahls (who spoke on "Effective Shared Governance: Creating Boundaries or Alignment?," which led to his chapter in this volume) highlighted the two-day conference, which included 21 papers and panel discussions. In addition, the volume contains four essays inspired by the 2014 and 2015 conferences, representing "Lessons Learned" from experiences with shared governance in the SUNY system.

It is our hope that the SUNY Voices conferences and the two volumes that have emerged from them will provide insights into successful approaches to shared governance. To no small extent, the success of the higher education system in the United States is tied to the success of shared governance in engaging all the key stakeholders from campuses and university systems to work together toward common goals. SUNY's commitment to shared governance across the range of major interest groups may not be unique, but it certainly illustrates how a commitment that is shared across groups can lead to successful decision-making.

References

Good, T. (2017). "Introduction." In S.F. Cramer (Ed.), *Shared governance in higher education: Demands, transitions, transformations*, vol. 1 (pp. 10–12). Albany: State University of New York Press.

Introduction

Nina Tamrowski

The second SUNY Voices Conference on Shared Governance that occurred in March of 2015 had a robust program; some of the papers presented were converted into chapters for this volume. The wide variety of topics and issues covered in this volume emanates from the larger theme of shared governance. "Shared governance" in higher education refers to *structures and processes* through which faculty, professional staff, administration, governing boards, and, sometimes, students and staff participate in the development of policies and in decision-making that affect the institution (FCCC Position Statement on the Role of Faculty in Shared Governance, 2008).

To organize our thoughts on the general theme of shared governance, I thought it helpful to distinguish between essays that touch on structure and those that focus on process. There are also two pieces herein that are centered on professional and leadership development of faculty who engage in shared governance.

In many cases, leaders of higher education institutions are preoccupied with the structures of governance. However, it is misleading to think that structures alone produce good governance. If the constituent parts of a governance structure are active and engaged participants, with accepted norms or rules of conduct, then perhaps said structure(s) will operate effectively. But certainly, that is alone insufficient to guarantee true, effective shared governance in institutional decision-making.

Several chapters in this volume focus on the structures that are necessary as foundations for good shared governance. SUNY Fredonia President Virginia Horvath and Professor Rob Deemer (who was the chair of the University Senate at Fredonia) wrote "Shared Governance—From Both Sides of the Fence," which illustrates the authors' perspectives on shared governance from two official angles: the president's perspective and the faculty senate's perspective. SUNY Fredonia was awarded the inaugural SUNY Shared Governance award in 2014, and, accordingly, their vision of what constitutes shared governance on the Fredonia campus is important and illustrative.

Conference keynote speaker Steven Bahls offered a further discussion of campus roles in his chapter, "From Shared Governance to Shared Accountability." This piece develops a case for campus decision-makers to align their institutional priorities, which then invites shared accountability for the pursuit and achievement of those priorities. The framework in Bahls's chapter centers on institutional structures (creating governing rules for board members, administrators, and faculty) and their interrelationships that can productively generate decisions on a college campus.

It can be argued that the use of task forces on a college campus subverts the authority of the governance structures that are formally charged with institutional decision-making. Authors Gwen Kay and Joan Carroll analyze a series of successes and failures of task forces at SUNY Oswego in "Task Forces: A Case Study at SUNY Oswego." Faculty members have worked to optimize their influence on these task forces to achieve established goals and maximize participation of campus stakeholders.

The second essential ingredient for developing sound shared governance practices is the existence of process. After all, structural entities don't necessarily "talk" to each other without explicitly stated processes between the governing entities. It's important to ensure that transparent processes exist for issues to move through a governance system or through a series of governance structures. Budget-making, in particular, challenges shared governance at most college campuses as many assume that this responsibility lies within the purview of the president. Yet all institutional decisions involving the use of campus funds can ultimately impact academic programs and their quality, in which faculty are deeply invested.

Professor Debra Sabatini Dwyer and Distinguished Service and Distinguished Teaching Professor Norm Goodman together with Associate VP for Budget Mark Maciulaitis offer a chapter called "The Development of Shared Governance for the Budget Allocation Process at Stony Brook University: A Positive, yet Cautionary Tale," which shares the evolution of the campus budget committee from an administratively driven entity to one with elected representatives who offer genuine input into financial decision-making on the Stony Brook campus. Specifically, the budget allocation process was revised over time to institutionalize shared governance as it relates to budget-making at Stony Brook.

Likewise, Public Administration Professor Tom Sinclair and his graduate student Chelsea Reome have written "Better Budgeting Is Good

Governance: Applying a Best Practices Framework to Public Universities' Budgetary Processes." This piece of academic scholarship examines budgeting practices among dozens of higher education institutions and finds them lacking in their inclusivity and openness. The authors review the best practices in public budgeting for local government and recommend the use of these practices in the university setting to accomplish goals of transparency and accountability that are expected in public budgeting.

Distinguished Teaching Professor Ron Labuz and Erin Severs from Mohawk Valley Community College present an account of how their campus developed a process for the creation and implementation of a professional development system. The development of this process empowered faculty as they improve their proficiency in teaching and scholarship. The consequence of this work was a beneficial outcome, both for shared governance and faculty ownership of their own development.

Co-authors Joseph Storch (SUNY Associate Counsel), Andrea Stagg (Deputy General Counsel at Barnard College), Peter Knuepfer (President of the SUNY University Faculty Senate), Martha Asselin (Interim President of Schenectady Community College), and Lori Mould (former President of the SUNY Student Assembly) present a case study on the use of a very nimble, almost quick-fire approach to shared governance on the topic of SUNY's sexual assault policy. The development of a SUNY-wide policy on sexual assault, which brought dozens of people together to create a common policy in two months was laudable. Yet the authors themselves question whether this is the best example of shared governance. This example serves as an exception to best practices in shared governance, because the typical goals of deliberation and inclusive sharing of policy language as it evolved were put aside. Nonetheless, this case study exemplifies the importance of transparency, expertise, collegiality, and common purpose in crafting an important system-wide policy.

Distinguished Service Professor Joe Hildreth shares his campus's approach to the development of a process that allows for faculty evaluation at SUNY Potsdam of their three deans. While faculty expected this role as expressed in their School of Education Bylaws, the administration at Potsdam resisted this effort. The SUNY chancellor at the time, John Ryan, endorsed the practice as a local prerogative. This empowered the Potsdam faculty and administration to work together on a fair and transparent process that has been in use since 2011. The process is described in "A Shared Governance Success Story," and the review instrument is provided.

Faculty members who are involved in governance on their campuses can attest to the leadership skills that are developed, challenged, and sustained over time and across different college administrations. The last two chapters described here offer examples from SUNY Buffalo State, which address the ways in which governance can be both beneficial and essential to faculty leadership development.

Heather Maldonado, as Assistant Provost for Academic Success at SUNY Buffalo State, makes use of Bolman & Deal's four frameworks for understanding organizations (leadership: structural, human resource, political, and symbolic) (2013). Dr. Maldonado applies these frames to the exercise of shared governance in her own experiences as a campus leader in the College Senate at SUNY Buffalo State as well as in the University Faculty Senate (the state-wide governance body of faculty across the SUNY system). Overall, she illustrates the deep value of engaging in governance as a leadership development process for its participants. Maldonado also explains how contributing to shared governance generates an understanding of institutional and systemic demands that go beyond our disciplines, departments, and research efforts.

This introduction ends where it begins: with this volume's editor, but also with the concept and practice of succession planning. Distinguished Service Professor Sharon Cramer elevates the importance of serving in governance, as well as its use as an avenue for succession planning whereby new leaders can be encouraged and nurtured into governance roles. Her metaphor of governance as a "greenhouse" is thoughtful and effective as we reflect on how governance leaders at both the campus and system level can further serve by identifying and supporting leadership among our peers.

The variety of the aforementioned essays offers a wide and deep review of how shared governance can improve the well-being and vitality of our institutions of public higher education in the State University of New York. Campus and system-wide structures and processes that are fundamental to shared governance are explored on many levels and through many topics. The benefits to individuals and campuses who value and practice sound shared governance are irrefutable.

References

Bolman, L.G., & Deal, T.E. (2013). *Reframing organizations: Artistry, choice and leadership*, 5th ed. New York: John Wiley & Sons.

Editor's Note

Shared Governance in
Higher Education Redefines Community

Sharon F. Cramer

Many members of shared governance in higher education have made identical discoveries: within governance, unexpected communities exist. Surprisingly, these communities are not limited to in-person collaborators. As this book illustrates, many who invest in shared governance in higher education never actually meet, and yet they are closely connected to each other's ideals and goals. We form our own de facto communities when we share passion, values, and commitment regarding shared governance.

Centuries ago, community was largely defined by geography. Whether the community consisted of neighbors who were within a day's walk or ride, or part of faith-based or ideological groups who shared written documents, the outreach one made or received was primarily tangible or visible. Even in death, one stayed close to those who had been in one's life; visiting a cemetery to connect with a departed loved one usually did not require extensive travel. In the last two centuries—with the addition of flight, population migrations, and enthusiasm for the unknown—geographically dispersed communities (in life, and in final resting places) became more common.

In our current century, community has again been redefined: some communities are composed of members who will never meet, yet thrive virtually, 24 × 7 × 365. And the members of our virtual community are the authors of the chapters of this volume, each of whom has been directly involved in many roles in shared governance. As readers become part of our extended community, you will find that the authors have many pertinent observations and suggestions to share. In fact, we may have more in common with our readers, and other virtual governance colleagues, than we do with our nearby nongovernance friends.

This century requires much more of those of us committed to governance. The intense and detailed requirements of governance ask us to reach out virtually (sometimes, desperately) when we seek answers to specific concerns. When help is received, we are instantly and deeply appreciative of these helpers (some of whom will forever remain invisible to us). Like other long-lasting virtual communities (e.g., the community that is enfolded by the time and space defined by *Star Trek*), the authors of this volume share unusual, vital connections to others in the governance universe.

Many communities thrive on shared values, and the virtual governance community (like the *Star Trek* community) resonates to beliefs that have always been at its core. It takes time spent in one or more of the roles within governance—committee member, elected representative, officer, leader—to recognize the commonalities that surface within face-to-face or virtual governance communities. When we see problem-solving at its best, or hear eloquent arguments, we feel the intoxicating pull toward aspects of governance to which we can relate. While within the *Star Trek* universe, members evidence commitments to exploration, and to family (biological and crew), the universe of shared governance repeatedly offers endless variations of how organizations progress toward reoccurring goals. This can include appreciation of how challenges are overcome, or how some members collaborate to propose novel solutions. We recognize a fellow governance leader's courageous and selfless acts and strive to incorporate these behaviors into our own governance worlds.

Within this volume, you will have the opportunity to learn from individuals who have, collectively, devoted hundreds of years and thousands of hours to governance. Although each author has powerfully articulated his or her own experience, emphasizing generalities from which others can benefit, we can look behind their words and see that their wisdom emerged from substantial mental and emotional investments. Without such generosity, nearly always uncompensated, their institutions and the SUNY system would be the poorer.

The opportunity to be part of the governance community is humbling. Each member knows that for every accomplishment, many invisible hours were spent drafting documents, formulating arguments, or working out political difficulties. Each member recognizes that governance cannot be done alone—it is always a shared experience. With these chapters, each author has invited you, the reader, to enter into his or her governance community. We welcome you to our worlds: let your imaginations transport you into membership in our community. Make use of what we have learned.

Note: We express our gratitude to the members of SUNY Press (Donna Dixon, Ryan Morris, and Kate R. Seburyamo) for the care and professionalism they dedicated to this volume. Dave Prout not only crafted the useful index but also provided a valuable final proofing. Carol Donato facilitated many aspects of this project. A volume is a commitment of intelligence, time and determination, and all authors rose to the many challenges over the production period—thanks to each of them.

Part I

____

Evolving a Collaborative Approach Regarding Shared Governance

1

Empowering Faculty
A Shared Governance Model

Erin Severs and Ronald Labuz

This chapter focuses on a paradigm of shared governance, which emerged via the deliberative processes of a Design Team of faculty at Mohawk Valley Community College. This group had been tasked with developing a new system for the distribution of funds for off-campus professional development. Research associated with implementation is also presented. The authors examine the background and context of both the team and its tasks. The resulting recommendations are also presented.

While unintended, the result of this implementation was the establishment of a faculty-run system that models some of the best features of shared governance. The new system involved faculty at all levels of shared decision-making and has led to faculty empowerment. This chapter, written after the conclusion of the system's first year of implementation, provides perspective, both on the complete roll out of the new system as well as on plans the All-Campus Committee has for future professional development.

Introduction

In 2012, a group of faculty was empowered to develop a strategy to allocate professional development funds at Mohawk Valley Community College (MVCC). The team was formed by Vice President for Learning and Academic Affairs Dr. Maryrose Eannace, and it was charged with (1) investigating best practices regarding professional development (and associated budgeting) and (2) delivering a proposal to change the existing professional development budget allocations process regarding external professional development. Assistant Professor Erin Severs and

Distinguished Teaching Professor Ronald Labuz agreed to co-chair the team (henceforth referred to as the "Work Group").

Professional development had always been handled with a separation between the budgets for internal and external professional development. Internal professional development was (and continues to be) handled through the programs offered by the Office of Organizational Development. This office sponsors faculty/staff institutes (scheduled three times each year), annual Core Workshops, the New Faculty Institute, and the Leadership Academy. These initiatives were not under the purview of the aforementioned Work Group. It was expected that the internal professional development would remain unchanged. The Work Group was specifically looking at the funding process for external professional development opportunities.

The existing allocations process (reflecting a change six years previous, as is explained herein) was simple: all external professional development funds for faculty were allocated to a single line in the vice president for learning and academic affairs' annual budget. However, empowering a single individual to make all such budgetary decisions does not reflect the institutional history at Mohawk Valley.

For at least three decades before the college's reorganization from departments into centers, external professional development funds had been available from three sources: departmental budgets, the Staff Development Committee budget, and (when travel or staff development impacted the college as a whole) the budget of the vice president for learning and academic affairs. The three external professional development budgets were controlled, respectively, by department heads, by a committee of the college senate elected by the college community, and by the vice president.

Several years earlier, in 2008–2009, the college's academic structure had been reorganized around individual disciplines chaired by department heads with faculty who reported directly to the vice president. In the reorganization, it was decided to change to more broadly organized centers headed by deans, with the support of assistant deans, associate deans, and academic coordinators. These centers introduced a more interdisciplinary approach to the college's programs, by grouping subject matters and faculty in new and more expansive ways.

There are now six centers:

- The Center for Language and Learning Design, which houses developmental courses, the English as a Second Language program, the honors program, the education programs, and the foreign language programs.

• The Center for Arts and Humanities, which houses literature courses and the arts and humanities programs.

• The Center for Life and Health Sciences, which houses biology, medical, and human-service programs.

• The STEM Center, which houses math and chemistry courses and all engineering and trade programs.

• The Center for Social Sciences, Business, and Information Sciences, which houses all computer science, service industry, and business-related programs.

This new organization allows for greater teamwork across the disciplines and stronger coherence among faculty as a whole.

When the reorganization into centers took place, there was no reduction in available professional development. However, it was decided that distribution of the funds previously contained in the departmental travel budgets and the Staff Development Committee budget would be deferred. All three budgets were combined into one budget line, controlled by the vice president. Three years after the reorganization, our Work Group was charged to evaluate alternatives and make recommendations regarding how Mohawk Valley should allocate the academic professional development funds.

The Work Group began with an investigation of best practices at six different colleges and universities. After spending several months completing this exploration, we discovered that none of the practices reflected the culture of Mohawk Valley.

This culture is the culmination of nearly 70 years of serving the communities of the Mohawk Valley region of upstate New York. MVCC became the first community college in the state of New York in 1953, and it has kept this tradition of innovation and progress ever since. "Building community" and "fostering collegiality" are core principles that are at the foundation of every aspect of the college. Our values statement is: "I believe in you so that you can believe in yourself." Though primarily about students, this statement can be applied (in a more general sense) to all levels of the college, in that our community works as a team, believing in, and supporting, one another.

With this culture and history in mind, the Work Group, consisting of faculty and administrators from several centers and the library, decided to recommend something completely different from the existing budget allocation process. We decided to make a recommendation to create a distinctive process for budgeting, to uniquely respond to the values and governance structure at Mohawk Valley.

In this chapter, we describe our deliberative process and share our recommendations. We also illustrate the support we received when we decided to recommend a radical shared governance approach, and the progress made thus far in the development of a process that empowers faculty.

Research and Deliberations

The Professional Design Work Group met in the spring and fall semesters of 2012 to develop ideas to create a comprehensive approach to providing external professional development at the college. The charter of the Work Group called for us to complete the following tasks:

1. Research exemplary programs and best practices at other institutions.

2. Define professional development in terms of external opportunities.

3. Inventory existing components and assets related to professional development.

4. Identify key components of comprehensive professional development for faculty and staff at MVCC in relationship to strategic and professional growth.

5. Develop preliminary recommendations to present to the academic deans and college senate for feedback.

6. Develop final recommendations, with preliminary programs and budget needs, to present to the cabinet.

We started the work by examining best practices at five colleges and universities. After discussions with colleagues at other institutions and our internal research, we decided to examine practices at Broward Community College, Clinton Community College, Monroe Community College, SUNY Cortland, and the University of Florida. During several meetings, we discussed how the research would be done and what answers we needed to find. We developed a series of questions to use in interviews with colleagues at these five colleges and universities. Different members of the group were assigned specific institutions. Key questions were:

- How does your institution define professional development?

- How are decisions made regarding funding? Is there a rubric or scoring methodology used to determine fund eligibility? How are conflicts of interest handled?

- What requirements are in place to return value to the institution, for instance, do participants have to deliver a seminar? How is that controlled?

- How is off-campus professional development tied to on-campus development initiatives?

The individual members of the group conducted the research through phone interviews and electronic mail. After the results were compiled, we reported to the group as a whole. Because the five institutions studied differed in size, mission, and state mandates, the research was both interesting and, at times, inapplicable. Some states, for example, require professional development of faculty; New York does not.

Each member of the group discovered specific features that we believed were valuable and instructive in this research. Ideas that were adopted from other institutions include the development of a matrix to evaluate proposals, the requirement that faculty share results with their colleagues, and the recognition that faculty should be encouraged to use professional development funds in creative ways. Despite these specific features, it was discovered that no one model would suit the goals and needs of Mohawk Valley Community College. Rather, after learning about best practices and discussing them, the Work Group decided to frame a unique model for our college. This was largely because the colleges researched were, in many ways, quite different from Mohawk Valley Community College.

Research institutions such as the University of Florida emphasize the ability to foster research opportunities. Smaller community colleges, such as Clinton Community College, do not have sufficient resources to develop a broad-based initiative. Some institutions, such as Broward Community

College, have tied professional development tightly to collective bargaining agreements. Other institutions have a very broad-based approach, combining, under the auspices of one office, many different factors related to professional development, including teacher awards, new faculty institutes, external travel, and internal faculty seminars.

Although none of these particular models suited MVCC precisely, the group learned from the practices of each college and university that was studied; as a result of the research, members of the group were in a better position to start envisioning a system that would meet the needs of Mohawk Valley Community College.

After completing this research (point 1 of the charter for the group, "Research exemplary programs and best practices at other institutions"), available resources at the college were discussed (point 3 of the charter, "Inventory existing components and assets related to professional development"). These included the travel and professional funds controlled by the office of the vice president for learning and academic affairs. Additional funds are available through the programs offered by the Office of Organizational Development; these include faculty/staff institutes scheduled three times each year, annual core workshops, the New Faculty Institute, and the Leadership Academy. These initiatives were not under the purview of the work group. However, we discussed ways in which external professional development initiatives and external professional development should be coordinated.

Discussions with college officers and committees directing these different programs were both informative and positive. This support was incredibly important, particularly when it came to the freedom the group had in brainstorming. Though initially there was no intention of a shared governance plan, the fact that the group was founded with the goal of getting away from a single-person top-down approach suggested that there was the potential for broader cross-campus/faculty empowerment.

Next, a working definition of "professional development" was developed (point 2 of the charter, "Define professional development in terms of external opportunities"), as well as methods of how external professional development initiatives and external professional development funding should be coordinated (point 4 of the charter, "Identify key components of comprehensive professional development for faculty and staff at MVCC in relationship to strategic and professional growth").

Professional development was defined, within the context of the reorganization, as "an external opportunity for faculty and staff to learn and grow personally and professionally, both individually and from each other." Then the Work Group discussed how to frame a plan that would accomplish two specific purposes: 1) to closely tie professional development to strategic planning; and 2) to create a plan that empowers faculty in the centers in which they teach. The Work Group was now ready to address point 5 of the charter, "Develop preliminary recommendations and present to the Academic Deans and College Senate for feedback."

Recommendations

Because the teaching professionals of the college have been organized into centers, members of the Work Group felt that a center-based approach would build cross-disciplinary teamwork within the centers. In fact, this organization into centers provided a unique opportunity to think about professional development in a new way. With the structure of centers in mind, the following recommendations were made:

1. Six professional development committees should be formed. Each of the five centers will have a committee of at least three faculty members elected by the faculty of the center. Self-nominations are appropriate. The center committees will select the chairs of their respective committees. There will also be a larger unit-wide professional development committee. This committee will consist of seven members: one representative from each center committee (generally the elected chair), one librarian (elected by the librarians of the college), and the executive director of organizational development (or the director's appointee).

2. The available annual budget for professional development should be no less than the currently allocated budget. These monies should be allocated as follows: 80 percent of the budget should be controlled by the center committees, divided proportionally (based upon the number of faculty and staff) among the five centers. Allocations of these funds will be made directly by the center committees without further approval.

   Appeals of center committee decisions may be made to the dean of the center. It will be the responsibility of the center committees to announce to center faculty when funds are available. Policies and procedures as to deadlines, semester allocations, and so on, will be developed by the college-wide committee and implemented by the center committees. No recommendations were made as to the maximum award to be made by center committees.

3. Twenty percent of the available professional development funds will be allocated to the unit-wide professional development committee. These monies will specifically be allocated for larger awards and for awards that are specifically related to the college's strategic plan. They can also be allocated for the external professional development of non–center affiliated staff members (librarians, for example). Appeals of the college-wide committee decisions may be made to the vice president for learning and academic affairs, who may direct that monies be allocated.

4. The unit-wide committee will have additional responsibilities. These include:

   - Developing policies to ensure that the center committees have been formed and are working in a timely manner. Communication with the center committees regarding policies, procedures, and other matters.

   - Developing and distributing forms and procedures to be used by all committees.

   - Developing a point system and metric to be universally used by all committees when evaluating proposals. Recommended criteria include: whether the faculty/staff member is a presenter or organizer, connection to strategic plan, relationship to the faculty member's professional responsibility and job description, whether the person making the proposal has received support recently, and the overall benefit to the college.

   - Each recipient of professional development funds will make some type of presentation or report after completing the professional development activity. The college-wide committee will be responsible for creating a repository of these presentations or reports, which may take many forms (a presentation at an institute, a written report, a presentation at a center meeting, a brown bag lunch report, etc.). The repository of reports will be publicly available. The college-wide committee will develop plans for how the repository will be kept; ideas include in written form, on Blackboard, or as a web presence.

- Revising and refining policies and procedures as necessary.

- Creating a centralized set of resources, including approved professional development proposals and subsequent reports, to be made available to applicants. These resources will make it easier for applicants to understand the funds request process and the procedures of the committees.

- Discussing and determining a thematic approach to professional development on an annual or biannual approach. The college-wide committee will work closely with appropriate college offices, committees, and the Senate to develop appropriate annual or biannual themes for professional development. This "Major Endeavor" theme may be developed in concert with organizational development. It will be the responsibility of the college-wide committee to work closely with organizational development to maximize synergies between external and internal professional development activities.

- Issuing a request for proposals (RFP) by March 1 each year. Before issuing the RFP, the college-wide committee will determine what monies, if any, have not been allocated by the center committees. Center committees will conclude their business by the middle of the spring semester, and any funds not allocated within the center will then revert to the authority of the unit-wide committee. At that point, the unit-wide committee will issue a request for summer project proposals and make decisions as to allocation of available monies for summer projects.

5. Many types of appropriate professional development activities were discussed. These include but are not limited to:

- Professional travel to conferences and seminars.

- Course development and course improvement.

- Pedagogical and technological developments in the classroom.

- Developing journal articles, preparing for exhibition in professional galleries, directing or participating in a performance.

- Maintaining or seeking licenses or certification in specialized areas.

- Creating new course materials.

- Faculty taking courses to improve their teaching effectiveness.

6. The Work Group recommends that summer projects be considered as a specific positive approach to professional development. These projects may take many forms including course design (or redesign), taking a discipline-specific class, or conference attendance, among others. It is recommended that such summer projects be funded in a limited way in the first year of operation. It is also recommended that summer projects, limited to $500 and $1,000, be directly related to either the annual/biannual themes or the strategic plan.

7. It is recommended that the unit-wide committee consider whether allocations of funds should be made on a semester basis (with specific deadlines and RFPs each semester) or if committees would meet as necessary when proposals are made. It is also recommended that no policy be constructed that would specifically limit the number of attendees traveling to a specific conference or workshop. Although it is understood that in specific disciplines it may be wise to limit attendance to one person who will then share information, there are many examples in which a greater number of people attending a conference would maximize the benefit to the college.

8. Any faculty or staff member of the college community may submit a proposal to the college-wide committee. Specifically, it is expected that the chairs of the center committees may request additional support from the college-wide committee for specific requests, as needed. Faculty, librarians, professional staff, and administration may submit proposals to the college-wide committee.

9. The college-wide committee should research and understand the current budget and make recommendations as to usage of those funds. It is recommended that among the first tasks of that committee should be an analysis of the adequacy of the

budget and recommendations for budget adjustment as needed. Because it is impossible to predict future needs without an understanding of past usage, it is recommended that the current budget be maintained until an analysis is complete.

Concerns

After development of the recommendations, the Work Group discussed potential concerns. Four concerns were prominent.

First, the plan, as recommended, did not specifically direct proposals toward the strategic planning priorities of the college. It was decided that this issue could best be handled by the college-wide committee emphasizing the importance of a connection to the college's strategic plan when developing the metric to be used in judging proposals.

A second concern focused on the potential for fluctuation of fund usage. Some were worried that professional development funds might be completely expended in one year, and then not expended fully in a subsequent year. To address this concern, it was agreed that, going forward, the Work Group monitor several budget years. This would enable the Work Group to observe that actual, rather than projected, percentages of budgeted funds were spent. As a result, it would be possible to maintain consistent funding and distribution.

A third issue included whether course development/course improvement would be a priority for funding. Although course-related activities are at times funded (such as a stipend for developing an online or hybrid class), it was agreed that no specific determination was made by the Work Group, with the expectation that, going forward, such requests would be handled on a case-by-case basis.

A final issue was whether to fund professional licensures. Some disciplines require different sorts of licensure and certification for different purposes. Respecting the belief that shared governance should extend deeply as well as widely, we decided to defer to individual center committees. Because individual faculty in different disciplines have needs for professional development in ways that vary, the center committees are afforded wide latitude in deciding what activities to approve.

Administrative Response

The co-chairs of the work group scheduled a meeting to discuss the proposal with Dr. Maryrose Eannace, Vice President for Learning and Academic

Affairs. The co-chairs had been chosen by the vice president with purpose. A young faculty member, Erin Severs, was selected as co-chair as an expression of trust in the ability of a new generation of faculty at Mohawk Valley (more than half of our full-time faculty members have been hired within the last seven years). A more senior faculty member, Ron Labuz, was selected as co-chair to offer a memory of process; he has chaired major senate committees and served as a department head for seventeen years. In his time as department head, he managed the travel budget of the department and had closely worked with the staff development committee. Together, the co-chairs offered both the experience and new vision necessary to successfully manage the committee work and then deliver a unique proposal.

Because the proposal was unexpected in scope, we shared our recommendations in writing with the vice president prior to the meeting. At this first meeting, the vice president was enthusiastically supportive. She made suggestions that were incorporated into the next draft of the proposal (having served as vice president for several years, Dr. Eannace has a unique perspective on issues relating to college process). After those suggestions were incorporated, three additional governance steps were required: advising the college senate about our proposal and asking for senate input, discussing the proposal with the deans, and meeting with and acquiring the advice of the president's cabinet. Because President Randall VanWagoner and Senate Chair Donald Kelly believe in the importance of shared governance, there was confidence that a proposal supported by the vice president and the faculty would almost certainly be approved by the president and supported by the senate. We also knew that the presidents' cabinet would offer valuable input, based upon their unique perspectives within the institution. This, indeed, was the case.

Discussions with the senate occurred during two monthly meetings of the college senate. The senate is a college-wide deliberative body with representation from support staff, faculty, professional staff, and administration. Senate members expressed their appreciation for the proposal. Their response to the proposal essentially led to one central question: Should faculty be empowered, without further approval, to spend money? Because the proposal was not being made by a senate committee, members did not vote on it, but the attitude of the senate was unanimously positive.

However, the proposal did meet with some skepticism. During several meetings with the five center deans that extended over two semesters (taking us into the 2013–2014 school year), the proposal was discussed in detail. During the discussions, we observed that individual deans responded to the proposal in different ways: with questions and concerns, with enthusiasm and uncertainty. Looking back at the process now, it is clear that the vice president insisted on a real shared governance process with the deans, just as she had with the faculty.

We realized that what took place was a true test of shared governance: everyone, at every level of authority, must know that they have had a significant opportunity to share their views and influence the decision-making process. The co-chairs were impatient to launch a great new idea. The meetings slowed down that launch, but the reality of shared governance is that contribution and deliberation take time. Patience was a key component to success of this new plan. The vice president successfully guided the proposal to a collegial place, one in which everyone participated and all concerns were addressed.

In the meetings with the deans, different types of questions were raised. For example, because we had decided to divide the budget based on center size, the center with the fewest faculty members would receive the smallest proportional budget.

Two responses were developed: First, any center faculty could access the 20 percent of professional development funds that would be controlled by the unit-wide professional development committee. It was decided that a center committee that expended all its funds could refer faculty seeking funds to the unit-wide committee. Second, as in the past with department budgets, center committees could decide to assist fellow faculty in other centers by shifting funds from one center committee budget to another.

The concerns of the deans were not parochial. The dean of the largest center, whose center committee budget under our proposal would be the largest, expressed philosophical reservations about how the process would work, how the center committees would be formed (and whether that formation should consist of both faculty election and dean appointment), whether faculty within SUNY were empowered to exercise such authority, and the value of dividing what was currently one large budget line into six different parts.

These and other concerns were discussed at several meetings; changes were made. At several points, the co-chairs discussed changes and returned to the original Work Group to seek advice. Two deans shared the enthusiasm of the vice president and the Work Group, expressing their immediate support. In addition, they offered suggestions that were incorporated into the final proposal. These included ideas about the value of different factors within the rubric.

Enthusiastic and productive discussions occurred about, for example, how many rubric points would be assigned if a faculty member was a presenter, or an officer. Discussion took place about how many points would be assigned for a dean's recommendation. These were among many different categories considered on the rubric, in addition to determining how many points were needed for approval. Because the Work Group was charged to develop an idea and not procedures, these meetings raised important questions about how the rubric would work, what it would contain, and how it would be implemented. The deans wanted to see the rubric, or at least a sketch of the rubric, before implementation. The Work Group responded with several iterations of the rubric.

Discussions with the deans became a process of shared decision-making. The final product was greatly improved because the deans were permitted the time to think, and deliberate, about this fundamental change in authority. Some of these deliberations occurred with the co-chairs of the Work Group, at several joint meetings. Other discussions occurred in deans' meetings. At the time, more than once, we asked the vice president for more speed. Faculty and the Design Team wanted ideas to be implemented as soon as possible. However, we realized that, despite the time involved, the new ideas were launched more successfully, and more productively, because of the deans' input.

The next step in generating an administrative response was discussion with the president's cabinet (point 6 of the charter, "Develop final recommendations, with preliminary programs and budget needs, and present to the Cabinet"). The cabinet consists of the president, three vice presidents (learning and academic affairs, administrative services, and student services), the dean of the Rome campus, the director of marketing and communications, the director of human resources, and the assistant to the president/secretary to the Board of Trustees. Because the proposal impacted only the faculty and staff led by the vice president for learning and academic affairs, the other members of the cabinet expressed interest in the proposal but were not directly impacted by it. President VanWagoner expressed his view that the proposal was entirely consistent with the college's core values of building community and fostering collegiality. The cabinet unanimously expressed its support. The proposal was approved for implementation in the fall 2014 semester.

First Lessons Learned

At the time this chapter was written and presented as a paper at the 2015 Shared Governance conference, we had completed our first year of the allocations process. The five center committees were elected, as were chairs of each committee. Different centers decided to have different numbers of faculty on their own committees, ranging from three to seven members. It was decided, before the year began, to create a sixth committee that would represent those individuals who report to the vice president but who would not be in a center; these include the librarians who have faculty rank at Mohawk Valley, members of the staff who work in the vice president's office, and the Office of Educational Technologies.

In developing the working procedures, the first step was to develop the rubric into a funds request form. Before the fall semester began, the original Work Group, led by two members who later were elected as chairs of their respective center committees, created a rubric. New forms were developed that required the signature of a committee chair. Offices of the college, including the Business Office, were informed that procedures had been changed. New online application procedures were developed to permit faculty, for the first time, to submit applications for professional development online.

There were stumbles. Different centers began the process differently. For example, one center was extremely successful in encouraging faculty to submit applications. That center's budget was fully expended by February. In the case of another center, the faculty response was not as energetic: fully half of the budgeted funds were not expended by the deadline of March 1. An unexpected positive outcome of such discrepancies was that one center's budget, unused, was willingly used to fund colleagues in another center. The sense of collegiality, especially among the chairs, was very positive. We also had the sense that all of us were learning at the same time. We were very pleased to see that all finances were managed effectively. No budgetary errors were made, and no expenditures beyond the given budgets of the center committees were committed.

In addition, there were unexpected successes, which were highly gratifying. In one case, a faculty member in one center applied for funds from two different center committees. His proposal impacted programs in both centers. The chairs of the two committees discussed the issue with the two committees and the faculty member received support from both committees. In other cases, faculty received support for professional development activities that were not bounded by the "travel budget" the college once had. A faculty member, for example, asked for support to fund an online subscription to take a full year of seminars in his discipline. That proposal did not fit into any professional development model previously held by the college. The proposal was approved by his center committee, establishing that a different form of professional development could now be supported.

This first year was incredibly successful, but it demonstrated certain areas in which more work remains to be done, as is to be expected in any new process. We will, in the years to come, develop a more consistent approach to encouraging faculty to participate. We will more thoroughly investigate ways in which the faculty of different centers can learn from each other. We understand that a budgetary recommendation may not actually result in an expenditure; a faculty member in one center was approved for a sizable amount of the budget of that committee's allocation (nearly 40 percent of the total), pending approval by a third party of the faculty member's application. The application was not approved and the budgetary opportunity to fund other proposals was lost.

Moving Forward

Overall, the first year of utilizing this new system has run very smoothly; however, as with any new college process, there is still work to be done to make this as efficient, judicious, and productive a system as possible. The committee chairs, whom, it was decided, would serve two-year terms in order to foster continuity and order, will work more closely in the second year, and the college-wide committee will continue in efforts of refinement and further scope.

For one thing, sufficient progress has not yet been made in organizing a repository of final reports. Quality professional development is not just about faculty bettering themselves and their practices, though certainly that is a central goal; it is also about bettering centers and the college as a whole. To this end, there has been discussion about creating an online space, perhaps within Blackboard, where faculty can post what was learned in professional development opportunities as well as posting reviews about different conferences, seminars, and other opportunities. Sharing the gains of professional development activities will allow the college to maximize the value of such activities. The All-Unit Committee will continue to discuss ways of formalizing such sharing.

All of the professional development committees can also do better in continuing to encourage faculty to take advantage of professional development opportunities. Further education about how the new system works and promotion of the value of professional development will be helpful to this end. That said, faculty—even those who chose not to participate by submitting a proposal—were appreciative that the administration ceded authority. This kind of trust and empowerment is emblematic of the environment MVCC fosters. It was not difficult to elect center committee members who were enthusiastic contributors to the deliberations involved in implementing this new system.

In addition, expanded discussions of how the year's implementation had gone led us to identify several logistical problems with the funds request form. These were brought to the attention of the All-Unit Committee in a meeting near the end of the year. Two center administrative assistants were in attendance, and thanks to their contributions, needed modifications to the form were discussed to ensure that necessary signatures are included, and that copies go to all areas that need them. It may still be possible to use a paperless system, but further work is needed in this area.

Lastly, moving forward in the longer term, it will be important to analyze fund usage center by center. Current distribution is an even division of funds based solely upon the numbers of faculty members within each center. Other methods that were discussed (and that may be revisited upon further analysis of fund usage over a span of years) are: (1) center history of fund usage and (2) center percentages of younger faculty in need of greater professional development.

Conclusion

Though only one year of implementation has been completed, the beginning has been very positive. Today, from a faculty member's point of view, the allocations process is a model of shared governance. Each year, the faculty will vote to create professional development committees in each of our centers. These faculty committees have complete budgetary control over all faculty professional development funds. They approve proposals from their colleagues and make allocations. No further approvals are required. The faculty is now empowered to make one of the most fundamental of governance decisions: spending money. There has been no dilution of the amount of funds that are allocated. The professional development of faculty is now governed, in a large part, by faculty.

This new professional development allocations process was created by faculty and, in a significant moment of faith in the value of shared governance, the ideas of faculty were respected and implemented by the administration. Significantly, the new democratic process replaced a system in which funding authority was completely controlled by one person, a vice president. The faculty voice, fostered by a decision to share governance, developed an idea that has resulted in a fundamentally new expression of shared governance by faculty. That decision required confidence, both from faculty and administration, in the opportunity for shared governance to help foster a culture of community and trust. And we have seen evidence that this confidence has resulted in authentic, meaningful, collaboration.

2

Shared Governance—
From Both Sides of the Fence

Rob Deemer and Virginia Horvath

Academic leaders today face numerous challenges, including outdated financial models, accountability to external forces, and the ever-growing number of critical decisions that must be made more quickly than ever. Shared governance, while requiring considerable commitment on the part of faculty, staff, and administrators, provides a collaborative model that allows leaders to address those challenges in a manner that is better than what any individual might achieve. In order for shared governance to be truly effective in higher education, it must be seen as an essential aspect of any major decision-making process; it must be based on written bylaws the entire campus follows; it must include trust among all parties and a culture of open dialogue among all constituencies; it must exist within an environment where leadership and service are priorities and governance bodies are diverse; it must be both goal-oriented and efficient in its planning and execution; and it must be clear about which aspects of governance are advisory and which are executive.

Introduction

Rob Deemer

In May 2012, just days after our commencement ceremony at the State University of New York at Fredonia, I sat down with our then-vice president for academic affairs, Virginia Horvath, to make some lists. Some might not consider such a routine appointment between a music faculty member still on the tenure track and the CAO of a comprehensive liberal

21

arts university noteworthy, but this was no ordinary discussion. Ginny, as we all call her, had recently been selected as Fredonia's new president, and I had recently been elected as Fredonia's new university senate chair (or in SUNY's parlance, campus governance leader), and the lists we were making were the first drafts of membership lists for several high-profile committees.[1]

That meeting (and each of the many interactions that followed) served to form a strong mutual respect between us—as individuals and as representatives of our university's faculty and administration. As we attempted to configure the size and makeup of each high-profile committee, questions turned into casual conversations that morphed into aspirational discussions. Sometimes, we had to define our terms—"representational," for example, meant different things to each of us.

We discussed many issues, ranging from how representational each group would be to how the committee charges would be developed and distributed. I initially assumed that this method of collegial collaboration was the obvious and natural way that things should be done. It wasn't until months later, after speaking with my counterparts at other institutions, that I discovered how rare it was to have such a seemingly simple and effective relationship with a university president.

The opportunity to reflect on our working relationship for the 2015 SUNY Voices conference on shared governance enabled us to articulate the experiences we had and share them with the conference attendees. By pushing ourselves to fit the completion of this chapter into our over-full schedules, we welcomed the chance to reach an even broader audience.

I. Why Shared Governance Is Essential for Administrators

Virginia Horvath

As American colleges and universities are challenged to operate under greater external scrutiny, with expectations of compliance with shifting state and federal policies, and demands for efficiencies in all operations, shared governance may be viewed by some as one of the archaic practices of a former age—as quaint as the stereotypes of faculty in tweed jackets holding forth in lecture halls full of students, notebooks open and pens poised, waiting for wisdom.

Today's academic leaders must face numerous concurrent challenges:

- The historic financial models for both public and private institutions are no longer working, as state support and endowment revenue cannot keep pace with the costs of educating and supporting students.

- With limited resources, institutions now have even greater competition for those resources—not just among academic programs, research, athletics, and facilities but in newer areas of institutions such as technology, academic support, and student services.

- Accountability to external forces—accrediting bodies, state and federal agencies, political and business leaders, funding agencies, parents—requires more policy-making, reporting, data collection, and analysis than ever.

Quite simply, the *number* of critical decisions to be made is increasing, but there is also increased expectation that decisions will be made *more quickly*.

The model of shared governance, with its more thoughtful pace and sometimes cumbersome iterations, might seem unsuitable for modern colleges and universities, which are expected to be efficient and lean. I argue, however, that more than ever, we need shared governance to have the best ideas driving decision-making, to ensure faculty and staff engagement for smooth implementation of any initiatives, and to promote and model civil, democratic approaches to leadership.

Promoting a collaborative model such as shared governance requires considerable commitment and work on the part of faculty, staff, and administrators. Unlike in corporate settings, with clear, authoritative supervisory roles and assigned tasks, reaching consensus in colleges and universities almost violates important principles of academic culture, for a few reasons:

- Academe is a culture of challenge and debate, with respect for diversity of opinions, backgrounds, theoretical lenses, and practical experiences.

- Academic culture relies on revision, as knowledge in any field relies on raising new questions and revising previous assumptions; the idea of not concluding a discussion is valued.

- And academe is a culture of individualism: faculty, professional staff, and administrators are hired for their independently achieved expertise and are often rewarded based on individual accomplishment.

Yet, there are numerous circumstances in which these cultural norms clash with institutional needs. For example, there are many institutional decisions that require people to work together *across* departments and divisions. Although some may approach this in terms of establishing a base of support or achieving *buy-in* for ideas and initiatives, I have found that the best strategy is to *build in* collaboration, from start through the end of the entire process. Experience has shown me that, time and again, this leads to a much better result than any individual or group pushing things through.

Several persistent myths about how to get things done in academe interfere with the approach of building in collaboration. These are the kinds of statements that one is likely to hear as decisions and new ideas are coming forward:

- "Let's do this as quietly as possible."

- "Let's not upset people as we're designing this project. We'll work to get buy-in when we roll it out."

- "Someone is going to have to sell this to ______."

- "It's better to seek forgiveness than permission."

- "If we ask people about their ideas, it will slow us down too much. Let's plow ahead and worry about the PR later."

- "We know what we're doing, so we can complete this project and then bring others on board later."

- "If we build it, they will come."

Those who repeat these statements are probably not malicious or arrogant: they are trying to move forward as expeditiously as possible. Yet, such cloistered approaches are likely to take longer because so many people at colleges and universities do, in fact, care about the institution and want to be included. If inclusion is not possible, opposition becomes an attractive alternative. As Alexander Hamilton once warned, "Men often oppose a thing merely because they have had no agency in planning it, or because it may have been planned by those whom they dislike."

Thinking about process or politics when a new initiative is "rolled out" is much worse than taking time early on to be sure that a variety of people and perspectives are at the table. These are the challenges for leadership: to build a sense of shared ownership, to acknowledge and work with reluctance to change, to encourage genuine collaboration, and, still, to move efficiently toward decision-making and implementation.

Perhaps the greatest challenge is an intellectual one, maintaining a state of mind that allows true dissent on an issue. If, as F. Scott Fitzgerald stated, "the test of a first-rate intelligence is the ability to hold two opposed ideas in the mind at the same time, and still retain the ability to function," administrators need to value and excel at this seemingly contradictory intellectual work. Some describe this as a capacity for ambiguity, and because administrators must make the difficult decisions, the intellectual work depends on using that place of ambiguity to make informed decisions.

I use this as my core operating principle: Valuing shared governance means genuinely believing that what is created or determined collaboratively is better than what any individual might achieve. Essential to its success are the following expectations:

- Respect diversity of all kinds.

- Ensure that representation at the table is inclusive and meaningful.

- Embrace the messy, tangled parts of democratic action—*all* the words and positions and conjecturing and arguing.

- Believe that it can be learned.

Based on my experiences as a faculty member involved in governance, as a chief academic officer, as a university president, and as a person who has been on both sides of the union table for interest-based bargaining of contracts, I have learned that specific approaches can lead to effective shared governance. The following are the principles that I use when working with the university senate, the student association, the committees and task forces, and the union leaders with whom I regularly interact.

Set a realistic timeline. Many decisions, particularly those related to policy and finances, have deadlines. Working backward from the endpoint, one can build in realistic blocks for discussion, debate, and response. Resistance is more likely—from anyone—when there is a feeling of being rushed or pressured; allowing time for reflection and response is necessary. By the same token, everyone needs to know that deliberation will not continue indefinitely, so it is essential to build in, and communicate, a timeline that shows the opportunities for input and decision-making. As a chief academic officer faced with a decision about what to do with a vacant dean position, for example, I acknowledged the short time frame for the decision about whether to search, appoint an interim, or reorganize and then engaged governance and campus input via a public meeting to announce my decision.

Work with campus leadership to identify stakeholders. In forming committees and task forces, governance leaders and administrators should consider together who has expertise on an issue and who will be affected by the recommendations of a committee. Including faculty and staff members from a variety of disciplines and divisions—as well as students and, if relevant, community members—will provide the richest opportunities for discussion and the most imaginative approaches to an issue. Building in this diversity is essential, as is a commitment to engaging those who are not regularly tapped for such roles. At Fredonia, I am proud to work not only with the cabinet but the university senate chair and executive committee in considering how to have representative, diverse, inclusive committees.

Think about opponents. Although one may see opponents to an idea as obstructive, including skeptics early in a process brings a valuable perspective to all involved—administrators as well as committee or task force members. An interest-based approach to an issue focuses on why people are opposed to an idea: the opposition or skepticism is often rooted in concerns that the institution needs to address. As Mahatma Gandhi said, "honest disagreement is often a good sign of progress," and that disagreement needs to be built into the process. "Welcome those who disagree" is a commitment I make when establishing groups to address complex issues.

Use existing governance structures effectively. Although this may seem obvious, it is often overlooked. Some of the extra work and/or task forces that institutions create would be unnecessary if administrators routinely relied more on the governance structures already in place. This means engaging cabinets, advisory committees, curriculum committees, faculty governance, student governance, boards, and other groups in formulating recommendations on issues.

When it is unavoidable, and task forces must be created to address specific new initiatives, I recommend the following:

- Consider potential members via consultation with a broad, appropriate advisory group (e.g., the governance leaders, union leaders, and administrators).

- Jointly announce the appointment of members.

- Clearly state the charge and time frame given to the newly formed groups.

I have found that task forces, even when comprised of well-intentioned individuals who have a strong interest in the task at hand, can work against shared governance. Having the governance leader and administrator charge standing committees with special tasks is more likely to result in building in implementation of new ideas and allaying concerns that special initiatives are going around established governance.

Engage people who are new arrivals and those with depth of experience. In forming committees and governance groups, having institutional memory as well as fresh perspectives can make a big difference in understanding an issue and the culture of the institution. Those who have been at the institution for a while can explain the context of previous decisions and directions, as well as the kinds of cultural changes required for a new idea to work. New members of the campus community can ask important questions (e.g., about the rationale for a certain approach used in the past). They can bring to the table the experiences they have had elsewhere or new ideas that their absence of institutional history enables them to consider. Building in opportunity for this kind of dialogue is essential.

Be transparent about the process. Administrators and governance leaders should strive to be timely and jargon-free whenever they explain the work being addressed and the timeline; if revisions to the process occur, they should be shared promptly. A website (with up-to-date content, working links, and contact options) or newsletter can also invite feedback. Ideally, interested individuals could easily see how feedback is affecting the process. Building in ways to keep the process accessible to all ensures that the campus community is given the opportunity to think about, and participate in, the issue or problem being addressed.

Provide multiple chances for input. Communication in shared governance is not one way: committees and administrators can provide regular updates and still miss opportunities to hear from others. Those engaged in considering an initiative or issue have richer ideas with which to work if they make use of governance channels, open forums, focus groups, gallery walks, charrettes,[2] online surveys, and suggestion boxes. Even including the email addresses of committee chairs in an update builds in an easy way for the campus community to express their ideas. At Fredonia, this has guided the work of such activities as inclusive strategic planning, revising the mission statement, and determining a new campus logo.

Respond to suggestions. If people are taking the time to share their ideas, effective shared governance mandates that someone (or a group) consider these ideas and respond to them. Reinforce that the committee has listened by giving credit to others for ideas or by clarifying why a suggestion was not followed. If members of the campus believe that the committee is willing to change directions or to improve the process based on the feedback from the campus, they are more likely to provide helpful suggestions. This can cement expectations for a collaborative process and set the tone for appreciative inquiry on the part of committee members and administrators.

Collect and use data. Administrators can assist governance units with timely and thorough access to institutional data, as well as approve institutional assistance in gathering new information. If groups identify the questions they need to have answered, their time can be more appropriately focused on analyzing and using the results if they do not have to collect the data themselves. Building in access to institutional resources can make governance processes function much more smoothly.

Communicate a consistent message. In addressing complex issues, administrators and governance leaders should be prepared to articulate clearly *what* problem is being addressed and *why* it needs to be addressed. For genuine collaboration, the message should also be that it is not one person's project or even one division's project if the process is working toward an institutional goal. And most importantly, leaders must not only say but *believe* that others' ideas about the project and the process matter.

Shared governance can be learned, but it takes diligence on the part of those who hire and guide leaders. Not all of those who assume administrative positions have had positive experiences with shared governance, and some may enter their roles with skepticism. One colleague who was new to our institution was puzzled when I asked her to share information with the Senate Planning and Budget Committee and the Executive Committee for their input before going forward with an idea. I was met with eye-rolling and a sigh, and there was little enthusiasm for more meetings instead of immediate action. This same colleague, however, came to see how such collaboration and communication really did improve ideas and address areas of concern. Within a few months, she mentioned to me that the ways we approached things seemed inefficient at first, but she learned how commitment to shared governance made a positive difference, with less confrontation and more shared problem-solving. As a president, I see my role not only in demonstrating my own commitment to shared governance but in expecting those who report to me to be fully engaged as well. I approach the processes and people involved with respect and guide others in doing the same.

II. Why Shared Governance Is Essential for Faculty

Rob Deemer

The achievement of truly *shared* governance within institutions of higher education is challenging. The primary challenge can be summed up as follows: shared governance depends entirely on the "sharing" between two groups of highly trained, highly motivated individuals. Such collaboration and sharing of responsibility, unfortunately, are rarely modeled or encouraged within most disciplines and divisions within academe.

Any of the following challenges to configuring a strong shared governance environment may occasionally or regularly occur on a campus:

- Governance members may lack experience in, or preparation for, service and/or governance.

- The influx of presidents and administrators who hail from outside of academia (primarily business or corporate environments).

- The lack of adequate leadership training for faculty and professionals.

- The variety of definitions regarding eligible governance representatives (at the campus and departmental levels) across institutions.

- Overreaction by administrators to any (even healthy) criticism from faculty.

- Overreaction by faculty to any new initiatives or changes to the university as a whole.

- The assumption that faculty will say "no" to any proposal, no matter how good it might be.

- The assumption that administrators will ignore any criticism from the faculty, no matter how well founded it might be.

- The assumption that administrators are more concerned with money (and, often unspoken, about their own jobs) than the welfare of the faculty or the students.

- The assumption that faculty are more concerned with money (and, quite loudly, their own jobs) than they are the welfare of the students or the institutions.

I agree with everything that President Horvath mentions about shared governance and collaboration—especially with the belief that all the skills involved can be learned. We have had several administrative positions change hands since I began my leadership of the university senate. Time after time, I have witnessed new administrators begin their tenure referencing their prior (negative) experiences with governance. They relate detailed stories about how impossible collaboration was at their previous institutions. Each time, I have seen the new administrator slowly but consistently be won over by our culture of shared governance and consultation. We take pride in what we have achieved and do not take it for granted.

The following are observations I have made over the last four years as the campus governance leader at Fredonia. While my suggestions may emanate from my position as a faculty member, many of my suggestions are geared toward administrators as well. I have discovered that as much as faculty would like to claim an equal portion of the shared governance pie, at the end of the day much of the success or failure of a shared governance system is the willingness of administrators—especially presidents and provosts—to embrace and champion its concepts and practices.

Shared governance is essential. The sharing of governance responsibilities and activities is not a luxury: all on campus should come to see it as the single most crucial aspect of an effective institution. When major decisions are made without input and consultation from the campus, the ramifications can be both disastrous and long-lasting. All important decisions should incorporate input and consultation into the process. Just as administrations and boards must not weaken or remove faculty roles in governance, faculty must not abdicate their role in governance responsibilities.

Learn to trust. Media stories are often rife with conflict between faculty, administrators, boards of trustees, students, and state and federal governments. While specific points of conflict between faculty and administration can vary widely, most issues can be ultimately traced to one insidious problem: distrust on the part of someone toward someone else. Above all else, addressing this lack of trust and working together to eradicate it must be the most important aspects of building good shared governance.

Strong collaboration cannot happen without trust on all sides. This is possibly the most difficult challenge to overcome. All parties must agree to work toward authentic, meaningful shared trust. Any governance system built on distrust will ultimately fail.

Make service a priority. Strong shared governance works when all voices are heard and fairly incorporated into the decision-making process. This can be best achieved if the expectations for campus-wide service are equitable and tangible. While most universities and colleges expect faculty to achieve a balance between teaching, scholarship and research, and service, many faculty members and their supervisors consider the service component ancillary. If governance is relegated to a few willing participants, the overall impact of the decisions made will be weakened: conflict will inevitably follow.

We have worked especially hard to make the service component a meaningful one, and it is included among the criteria for promotion, tenure, and discretionary salary increases. Of course, we have our cast of usual, service-oriented suspects at Fredonia. We try not to rely on them exclusively. When Ginny and I sat down to work out a joint appointment for a committee or task force, we strove to balance the membership. We worked to involve those members of the faculty and professional staff who had not yet had the chance to participate in campus-level governance.

Be efficient. The first reason a faculty member will avoid serving on a committee is the sense that time in committee meetings is time wasted. Agendas obviously help with organizing meetings, but in my first semester as senate chair, I discovered that without guidance, reports and discussion could easily take up an inordinate amount of time during meetings. For our third senate meeting of that first semester, I included a duration after each agenda item (e.g., President's Report [10 minutes]) and almost immediately we saw a marked improvement on the time management of the meetings. In addition, presentations and reports were much more streamlined and focused.

Set goals and work hard to achieve them. The second reason faculty may avoid service is the perception that nothing gets done. At the beginning of every year, our senate executive committee looks over the various initiatives and issues that the campus will be addressing, sets a tentative timeline, and assesses when they should be brought to the university senate. We determine both priorities and a sequence of actions.

Based on our experience, we have learned that when too many initiatives are concurrent, confusion can be created. Many pull back, due to a sense of "doing too much." Instead, we have found that it is possible to distribute items across the calendar to allow for adequate focus: when we do so, we are much more successful. Goals are announced publicly at the beginning of the fall semester, and updates go out regularly to the entire campus throughout the year.

Diversify the governance bodies. Fredonia's senate is a true "university senate," with representation from professional staff, students, and contingent faculty as well as full-time faculty. Standing committee representation is also spelled out in our bylaws. Subsequently, our past practice has encouraged a solid mix of disciplines and divisions, as well as a mix of new versus experienced faculty and staff on jointly appointed task forces and search committees.

In this age of heightened awareness, it should go without saying that it is also important to ensure diversity within governance groups in regard to sex, gender identity and expression, race, sexual orientation, religion, and so forth. However, care should be taken to avoid placing unreasonable service expectations on faculty members because they happen to be among the very few (or the only) members of a particular group. The overarching goal we attempt to meet is to ensure that as many viewpoints as possible are included: we do not to have diversity for the sake of optics.

Take leadership seriously. A recent SUNY Faculty Senate plenary provided two distinct mind-sets on governance that resonated with me. The first was a fellow campus governance leader who, after discussing a frustrating interaction with the campus president, stated, "What could I do? I'm just the chair of senate?" The second was a missive by New York State Senator Kenneth P. LaValle, one of New York's most powerful state legislators and chair of the Senate Higher Education Committee, when he told those in attendance that faculty governance leaders had a great amount of power at our disposal—if we only choose to use it.

Both statements, to my mind, speak to the need for intentionality of leadership. It is imperative for campus governance leaders and other governance members who have some type of leadership responsibility to avoid a passive, reactionary stance in their actions and rather accept the role of leadership with an active and investigative mind-set. This may create conflict with administrators or with one's constituents, but it is a much more responsible direction than inaction in the long run.

The dichotomy of being an elected representative, serving one's colleagues, while often being put in the position of weighing in on (or helping to make) decisions that will impact those colleagues is ever present. I have found that is important to understand and be comfortable with this seemingly dual identity.

Governance representatives and leaders are, in my opinion, not just caretakers or conduits for their constituencies. Instead, we need to see ourselves as individuals who can assess the situation at hand through our own filters and then compare the situation with our knowledge of the viewpoints of our colleagues.[3] Taking all this into account, we should then make an informed decision based on the aggregate.

Be judiciously unafraid to confront. It is inevitable that disagreements will occur within governance structures; one could not imagine any other result when so many thoughtful and critically minded individuals work in one place. The challenge is to create an environment that encourages vigorous discussion and disagreements—without risk of reprisal. At the same time, leaders must firmly but tactfully discourage badgering, stonewalling, or other forms of confrontation that serve only to inhibit the open flow of ideas.

The best solution is to create as many open channels of communication as possible. This can be done, in part, by anticipating potential points of conflict early. By addressing them in a constructive manner, the membership understands that differences of opinion are authentically welcomed.

Create the strongest possible bylaws, ensuring unambiguous policies and procedures. While nothing causes eyes to glaze over more than when the topic of bylaws arises, the importance of strong bylaws cannot be overstated. Effective shared governance is impossible to achieve without them.

For anyone—faculty or administrator—to trust the institution's governance system, the policies, procedures, and philosophies need to be written down, approved by the governance body, ratified by the campus, and approved by the president. We have found that because this extensive approval process is so inclusive, the content of the bylaws, or proposed amendments, is rarely questioned. The objective nature of our bylaws and the broad representation of the bodies that approve and ratify them provide unimpeachable credibility to all aspects of governance at Fredonia.

Rely on supporters; dialogue with naysayers. An easy trap to fall into when working in governance is to surround yourself entirely with like-minded people who eagerly support your ideas and initiatives. These supporters are important: you need to rely on them to help spread the word about governance ideas and initiatives. However, they should not be the only people with whom discussion takes place. There will always—*always*—be faculty members who will seek to find fault in whatever initiatives emerge from governance leaders or administrators.

Keep an open mind. Maintain an open, ongoing dialogue with naysayers. These conversations help to strengthen any proposals by making sure that issues raised by those with opposing, or critical, viewpoints are addressed as the proposals move forward. These discussions are not just for show: they ultimately strengthen the thinking about a proposal and its implementation. They also solidify the commitment to, and perception of, transparency and inclusivity that any shared governance endeavor should contain.

Encourage the silent majority to speak. In most debates, it has been my experience that there will be several advocates and opponents. However, their numbers are dwarfed by an even larger number of participants who observe the proceedings with little to no interaction or contribution to the conversation. Often these governance members have both questions and comments that would benefit the discussion, but for one reason or another they fail to participate.

Governance leadership should do whatever can be done—both in advance of and during meetings—to encourage those who rarely speak to participate in the conversation. Sometimes, a private conversation with a senator can lead to future involvement. It may be useful to clearly illustrate and ensure that any pressure (perceived or otherwise) from administrators or colleagues toward them to stay silent not be tolerated. One way that Fredonia ensures that this pressure is avoided is by using clickers in our senate voting procedures; by doing away with raised hands or voice votes, this technology has allowed our senators to vote their consciences, and subsequently the voting patterns have become much less one-sided.

Advisory means advisory. The relationship between a university or faculty senate and the president of a college or university is usually clearly defined within the bylaws and other policies. And yet, this relationship is still often misunderstood.

For example, the curriculum is certainly the responsibility of the faculty, working with the deans and provost. But the president is the final arbiter of the institution as a whole, which includes curricular matters. All curricular revisions, additions, and withdrawals require approval by the president to take effect.

As active and influential as a senate may be, all governance members (senators and committee members) must remember that the senate remains an advisory body to the president. That said, if a trusting and healthy collaboration can be fostered between governance and the president, the fact that the advisory relationship is in place rarely needs to be raised: both sides work to improve the institution with a shared sense of responsibility and ownership.

As I write this, four years have passed since Ginny and I formed those first committees. It seems long ago, and simultaneously, like it just took place. While our campus has experienced a healthy amount of change, the underlying foundation of shared governance and consultation upon which we have continued our work has endured.

If there is anything that truly concerns me as a campus governance leader, it is the stories I hear from my colleagues at other institutions, where the state of shared governance is not nearly where it could or should be. I am confident that our campus has created and implemented a model that other campuses could study because it will continue well beyond the individuals at the helm. I am hopeful that the efforts that my colleagues and I have made over the past decades can inspire others to improve shared governance at their universities and colleges as well.

Notes

1. A senate subcommittee to revise our General Education program, a task force to revise our mission statement, implementation teams for our recently approved strategic plan and baccalaureate goals, and search committees for a new provost, a new vice president of finance and administration, the first dean of a newly formed college of visual and performing arts, and a new position of chief diversity officer.
2. Charrettes are collaborations for problem-solving, often achieved in structured activities for small groups. Although frequently used by architects and designers, the model is useful for addressing many kinds of issues.
3. We need to take care not just to think about the people with whom we communicate frequently but also others from whom we can get different points of view.

3

A Governance Challenge Presents
a Governance Opportunity

Lessons from the State University of New York
Sexual Assault Prevention Working Group

Joseph Storch, Andrea I. Stagg, Peter L.K. Knuepfer,
Martha J. Asselin, and Lori Mould

The development of a uniform policy on sexual violence response and prevention for the State University of New York (SUNY) system followed a unique process of shared governance. Governor Andrew Cuomo held an unprecedented meeting with the SUNY Board of Trustees to urge passage of a resolution establishing a uniform policy across all SUNY institutions; previously, all SUNY colleges had such policies, but they were not identical. What followed was a combination of top-down administrative guidance, and bottom-up response, to address the resolution within a two-month deadline. SUNY's provost established a Working Group, led by members of the system counsel's office (bringing expertise in federal regulation around sexual violence response to the group); membership of the group included campus presidents, faculty governance leaders, campus and system student-affairs and Title IX practitioners, campus and system police leaders, students, and outside victim advocates, with additional input from faculty and staff experts—truly a shared governance body. The group converged rapidly on a policy that follows national best practices, but moves them forward in a new, coherent manner, and forwarded recommendations to the SUNY chancellor, Board of Trustees, and Governor Cuomo. The result also formed the basis for legislation creating a uniform sexual violence prevention policy for all New York colleges and universities. While large working groups and short deadlines often militate against successful outcomes, the combination of shared goals, thoughtful use of technology, collegiality among a diverse group of representatives, and a sense that there was no time to waste, led to success beyond initial expectations. This chapter ends with examples of how aspects of this process can be recreated on individual campuses to accomplish other tasks, particularly when challenges (such as tight time frames) conspire against conventional governance processes.

Introduction

On October 2, 2014, New York Governor Andrew Cuomo met with the State University of New York Board of Trustees, requesting that the board approve a resolution calling for a uniform, SUNY-wide policy regarding sexual assault prevention and student rights.[1] The meeting was historic: no one could remember another time that a sitting governor attended a meeting of the Board of Trustees. The governor, SUNY's board chairman, campus presidents, and other speakers recognized SUNY's work regarding sexual assault prevention. The board's message was that, while SUNY has five dozen very good policies, SUNY would be better served with a single cutting-edge policy that could serve as a model for state legislation and for colleges and universities across the country. The trustees passed a resolution calling for the chancellor and her designees to develop a set of uniform policies within sixty days.[2]

Within hours of the resolution's passage, SUNY personnel from the Office of General Counsel, University Life, University Police, and Provost's Office began to discuss how to move forward. With significant support from the Chancellor's Office, the group coalesced around the idea of putting together a temporary working group of some of the best thinkers in this area from within the SUNY system, while also reaching out to external experts who could bring additional perspectives to the table.

In late October 2014, the provost of the SUNY system appointed members to the group that were uniform only in their diversity and capabilities; he charged them with the development of uniform system-wide policies to prevent and address sexual and interpersonal violence on campus, in response to the resolution from the SUNY Board of Trustees. While the policies themselves were cutting-edge, something else came about in the process: a new method of truly *shared governance*. Members amazed themselves and others by being able to respond rapidly to short-term policy formulation. This chapter emerges from the actions leading to the specific goal achieved, and the subsequent belief that what occurred may have a secondary benefit—the process used may serve as a model for other initiatives at SUNY and other large institutions.

Background

SUNY is decentralized by design. A complex institution, the university has 29 state-operated colleges and 30 community colleges, as well as four statutory colleges at Cornell University and one statutory college at Alfred University. The SUNY Board of Trustees sets general policies and budgets at a high level, while administrators, faculty, and professional staff implement policies at the system and campus levels.[3]

SUNY as an institution is strongly committed to the principles of shared governance (e.g., Cramer, 2017), evident during the implementation of the Power of SUNY Strategic Plan developed under Chancellor Nancy Zimpher's direction. The faculty of the 34 state-operated and statutory campuses of the SUNY system are represented by a University Faculty Senate, comprised of senators from each campus, including an executive committee that can act on the body's behalf between its thrice-a-year plenary meetings.[4] The University Faculty Senate is empowered by the SUNY Board of Trustees "as the official agency through which the University Faculty engages in the governance of the University."[5] Similarly, faculty of the 30 SUNY community colleges are represented by a Faculty Council of Community Colleges, which meets as a body twice yearly and also has an executive committee that meets more often.[6] Students from across the 64-campus SUNY system are represented through the SUNY Student Assembly, which also meets twice a year and has an executive committee that normally meets once per month. The SUNY presidents typically convene monthly during the academic year to discuss emerging SUNY policy issues.

Historically, policy-making in student life and student affairs has been at the campus level, with high-level initiatives developed by the system and, on occasion, the board. Each campus maintains a Student Code of Conduct (or similarly titled document), which is developed and amended by campus professional staff with the advice of the university-wide Office of General Counsel and approved by a University or College Council (for state-operated campuses) or College Board of Trustees (for community colleges) that is local to the campus. Most members and the chair of the councils and boards are appointed by the governor and are joined by a student member at each campus. In general, these codes of conduct are locally derived rather than uniform across the SUNY system. None of the authors of this chapter, with a collective eight decades in SUNY/higher education are aware of any cases of detailed student affairs policies that all state-operated and community colleges have implemented uniformly.

SUNY has been a national leader in efforts to prevent and respond appropriately to violence, including sexual violence (e.g., Katz & DuBois, 2013; DeGue, 2014). The university uses the efficiency of system-wide offices that do the following:

- Analyze legislation and regulations.

- Routinely provide comprehensive and specialized trainings to keep at the forefront of policy development and program implementation.

- Maintain and share up-to-date awareness, in ways that are not possible at small public and private institutions that cannot devote the time and resources to this complicated topic.

- Gather together role-alike groups (representing chief student affairs officers, student conduct professionals, counselors, campus police and safety directors, student housing professionals, and others) regularly during the course of the year; these meetings allow campuses and system professionals to share best practices and models, while also allowing plenty of time for questions and discussions.

These strategies ensure that each campus has the appropriate information to meet the legal requirements and, just as often, go beyond those requirements. In so doing, services for students and employees can be designed to incorporate the most current best practices.

SUNY's Office of General Counsel conducts myriad trainings each year and operates a handful of listservs, including ones devoted to questions regarding the Clery Act and Title IX, federal laws about campus safety, and the prevention of violence and sex discrimination. SUNY attorneys draft guidance and analysis documents following statutory and regulatory changes and cull lessons learned from audits and program reviews at SUNY and externally. For example, after the Department of Education issued proposed regulations to implement the Violence Against Women Act (Department of Education, 2014), the Office of General Counsel conducted two trainings for more than 250 SUNY professionals in June and July and issued a 93-page guidance document in July 2014 (Office of General Counsel, 2015).[8] The guidance document was downloaded over 20,000 times by institutions within and outside New York over the next six months and more than 35,000 times over 18 months. In fact, the training has always operated under a model of sample documents and language that each institution could adopt or modify as meets the individual campus culture. Consequently, while campuses generally maintained compliant and innovative policy language, the actual policies themselves differed quite a bit.

The Challenge

The October 2, 2014, Board of Trustees resolution set a 60-day deadline for SUNY to

> adopt a comprehensive, uniform, system-wide sexual assault prevention and response plan to be implemented at all SUNY campuses that will include the following: (1) the uniform Sexual Assault Victims' Bill of Rights; (2) the uniform sexual assault student reporting amnesty policy; (3) the uniform freshman orientation training; (4) the uniform Confidentiality and Reporting Protocol; (5) the uniform campus climate assessment; and (6) the uniform definition of affirmative consent.[9]

This deadline imposed an aggressive timeline for completion of a difficult project, particularly given the desire of the governor and the SUNY Board to produce a set of policies that could serve as a state-wide and national model. It was also occurring in the context of a growing national conversation about sexual violence on college campuses (Storch & Stagg, 2016).

The short timeline also challenged the conventional shared governance structure within SUNY. Although each of the governance groups noted earlier has an executive committee or equivalent that can meet as necessary, as well as a process to appoint representatives to committees and task forces, the organizations are not constituted in such a way that they can nimbly respond to rapidly evolving policy initiatives. Given these constraints, engaging the governance groups was going to be challenging in the context of the tight time frame. Thus, it became evident that a nimbler governance model needed to be used, which led to the formation of the Working Group.

Part of a National Conversation

The Working Group's efforts did not occur in a vacuum. The issues of sexual and interpersonal violence on college campuses had become a part of the mainstream national conversation. It came up in legislation that made changes to the Clery Act via the Violence Against Women Act (VAWA) reauthorization of 2013,[10] in a White House Task Force report covering the issue and offering resources and model documents (White House Task Force to Protect Students from Sexual Assault, 2014), and in a number of high-profile news stories about assaults on college campuses that occurred both inside (Hobart and William Smith College, e.g., Bogdanich, 2014; Columbia University, e.g., Perez-Pena & Taylor, 2014) and outside (University of Virginia, e.g., Somaiya, 2015; Florida State, e.g., Macur, 2013) of New York. Informed by the White House Report, Title IX guidance, and VAWA, the Working Group sought to create documents that would be compliant with existing law and valuable (rather than confusing) to the students and employees reading them. While informed by what was happening nationally, the Working Group was independent of any legislative and other changes and intentionally sought to take the long view rather than react to any single story or proposal.

Context for the Work

In April 2011, the Office for Civil Rights (OCR), the office in the federal Department of Education that enforces Title IX, issued guidance on peer sexual violence in the form of a "Dear Colleague" letter (DCL); the letter outlined colleges' obligations to prevent sex discrimination, including sexual violence, and to respond promptly and appropriately when it occurs.[11] Since the publication of the letter, OCR has published a nearly 50-page question-and-answer document about the DCL[12] and a more recent package that contained a Title IX resource guide and two letters.[13]

The 2011 letter kick-started a national movement for colleges to update policies, hire new staff, and dedicate significant resources to training employees and students. In the policy updates, institutions of higher education had to ensure the following:

- At the outcome of an adjudicatory process or investigation, they would provide simultaneous notice of outcome to both parties—the accused/respondent and the victim.

- Colleges offering an appeal to an adjudication had to provide victims the opportunity to appeal as well, on the same bases as the accused individual.

- Importantly, the DCL mandated that every college use the same burden of proof or standard of evidence when considering complaints of sex discrimination: preponderance of the evidence.

  o A "preponderance of the evidence" standard requires the decision maker to ask whether it is more likely than not that the alleged discrimination occurred.

Many institutions have moved to hire additional staff since the DCLs (and subsequent guidance) were published. Schools either hired Title IX coordinators and investigators or designated existing employees to fill those roles. Before designating an existing employee, schools consider issues about workload, experience, and potential conflicts of interest. Importantly, the letter issued was not statute or regulation, but *guidance*. Some will take issue with the notion that the letter can "mandate" or "require" anything, yet it is by these standards that OCR is investigating and enforcing today.

The United States Congress has also reacted to the national concern about campus safety. In March 2013, Congress reauthorized the VAWA (originally passed in 1994), also amending the Clery Act.[14] The reauthorized VAWA added dating violence, domestic violence, and stalking to the list of Clery-reportable crimes to be counted and then disclosed in the institution's annual security report. But its focus is on *prevention* and *appropriate response* to those crimes as well as sexual assault.

Since its 2013 reauthorization, VAWA has required that every institution receiving federal funds do the following:

- Conduct primary prevention programs and annual awareness campaigns to educate students and employees about VAWA crimes, their prevention, and possible remedies and adjudication options.

- Thoroughly inform about accommodations and services offered by the institution.

These programs are not one-time, check-the-box events but rather are ongoing, diverse, creative efforts to reach the campus community and truly change the culture. VAWA also mandates that institutions provide certain information in writing to all victims of these crimes, and certain rights to parties in related institutional disciplinary proceedings. These rights include the victim's right to be accompanied by an advisor of his or her choice.

Importantly, VAWA amended a section of the Clery Act requiring that colleges have policies that offer students both the opportunity to notify on-campus officials or law enforcement of a crime and the right *not* to notify law enforcement. The new legislative language keeps the control of how far to proceed in a process where it should be, in the hands of the victim or survivor, and it was a tact that the Working Group used as well.

The Working Group at SUNY had to consider these recent changes in federal law and ensure that any new policies that were drafted would be complementary and not duplicative.

Developing the Working Group

So much had to happen in such a short time: there was no time to waste in moving ahead to develop policies. In thinking about meeting the requirements of the resolution, an expertly informed uniform policy within 60 calendar days, we understood that we would not be able to use a traditional governance model. This is not to say that we threw governance out the window (far from it), but that we would have to develop and adapt a new model on the fly if we were to meet this challenge.

The Working Group, formally titled the Chancellor's Temporary Working Group on Continual Improvement to Sexual Violence Prevention Policies (hereafter referred to as the Working Group), was charged by SUNY Provost Alexander Cartwright and coordinated by Joseph Storch and Andrea Stagg of the Office of General Counsel and Jessica Todtman of the SUNY Policy Office. The group was comprised of 34 members who represented SUNY constituencies ranging from campus presidents to faculty and students, to campus and system student affairs, Title IX, and police professionals, as well as outside experts.[15] Amazingly, the Working Group met only twice—once in late October 2014 to develop a draft set of policies, then again in mid-November to finalize the recommendations. Creative strategies were used to enable ongoing work to occur between meetings, guided by three principles that drove the development and work of the group:

1. The need for expertise as well as broad participation to provide legitimacy.

2. The importance of positive group dynamics.

3. The commonality of interest and commitment among the group members, both for the topics to be covered and for acceptance of the structure of the process.

These three principles are discussed further in the following sections of the chapter.

Expertise and Legitimacy

Key to every decision we made was an ethos of expertise and legitimacy. We (co-authors and Working Group conveners Storch and Stagg) recognized that we didn't possess the answers to every question within the walls of the SUNY System Administration Building. One of the authors, when thinking about the process to use, was reminded of the quote from former secretary of defense Donald Rumsfeld:

> Reports that say that something hasn't happened are always interesting to me, because as we know, there are known knowns; there are things we know we know. We also know there are known unknowns; that is to say we know there are some things we do not know. But there are also unknown unknowns—the ones we don't know we don't know. And if one looks throughout the history of our country and other free countries, it is the latter category that tend to be the difficult ones. (Rumsfeld, 2002)

There was significant expertise at our own SUNY campuses and within the higher education community. We reached out as broadly as we could, to bring these experts to the table. In the end, we asked about three dozen of the busiest people we could find to turn their calendars upside down for a month and engage in this process. Even with their busy schedules, not a single person refused the request. We were heartened by the active engagement of all those asked to serve.

True expertise applied in a transparent process can significantly increase the legitimacy of any policy. We sought participants who would meet the following test: Would others in their line of work, who wished themselves to be on the Working Group, look at the list of participants and say to themselves, "well, if I can't be on the group, at least __________ is a member of the group, and so our voice is being heard." That was the test and we applied that to every participant before we asked them to join.

Early on, we decided to solicit members and not ask for volunteers. We wanted the best thinkers on the topic, but we also sought out participants who had exceptional team-building, and positive group dynamic, skills. We were all very clear: we absolutely did not want meetings to devolve into the type of gatherings many in higher education (and large organizations of all types) have experienced: arguments about tiny rules of grammar, factions forming, insults hurled, and so on. We wanted participants who would roll up their sleeves and get to work in a collegial fashion. At the same time, we recognized the need to engage the leadership of the shared governance organizations to ensure legitimacy in the eyes of SUNY constituencies.

It was likewise important for us to hear voices outside the SUNY system. While SUNY has significant internal expertise stretched across our campuses, we believed we would not have a full knowledge base unless we gave a forum to outside voices. Outsiders also helped with the twin goal of legitimacy. We anticipated that opening ourselves up to the views of outsiders would allow others who were outside the process to know that we were not making recommendations solely to limit risk for SUNY; rather, we wanted to make significant headway on these important issues. As with the SUNY members we invited, it was crucial that each outside expert we considered have the complementary traits of true expertise and collegiality. We wanted people who would come to the table with good ideas based upon knowledge and experience, who also had willingness to work with others, teaching and learning in a collegial atmosphere. We were lucky to have four "all-stars" join us. As with our internal stakeholders, of the four people we asked, all four said yes.[16]

Thinking about Group Dynamics

If we were going to accomplish this task within the short time period, we believed strongly that we needed a cohesive group that worked well together and did not devolve into factions or castes. We took a few steps to ensure that all participants were treated the same, and all statements and ideas were accepted equally.

Economists bemoan the effects of *information cascades* and *reputation cascades* on individuals within groups (e.g., Easley & Kleinberg, 2010).

Information cascade occurs when individuals within a group subsume their own opinions on a matter based on what they hear from others who speak before them, assuming that the prior speakers have more information on the topic.

For example, if a group were questioned in order on a straightforward, easily provable question such as which ocean is bigger, Atlantic or Pacific, and the first three answer Atlantic (and perhaps show some confidence in their answer), the fourth answerer, who privately (and correctly) believes the Pacific to be larger may yet say Atlantic, assuming the others have more *information.*

Reputation cascades occur when individuals subsume their own opinions on a matter in deference to others who have a higher status or reputation in general or on a specific topic. They occur often in corporate and government settings wherein speakers are afraid to espouse opinions differing from their leaders' or those senior to them. Examples abound and have resulted in major errors and even wars where those with dissenting opinions hold their tongue for fear of disagreeing with leadership. We worked hard to avoid both cascades.

We took everything into consideration, including space, to make sure that we were conveying a consistent message. For example, prior to the first meeting, we looked at the boardroom initially assigned to us for the session. SUNY does not have many choices for conference rooms at the System Administration Building in Albany. The boardroom is a large room with a big center table flanked by rows of chairs. We went to meet with the special events team to request a different room. Our fear was that presidents and trustees would sit at the main table, vice presidents and deans would sit in the first row of chairs, and students and faculty would sit in the back. It was important to us that each attendee be at the same level.

Luckily, the special events staff were very interested in helping out. They switched several things around to move the meeting into a small courtroom, in a building adjacent to the SUNY headquarters. Although this meant that their staff had to turn that room over twice in a single day, they were very kind to voluntarily do so. We asked for round tables to discourage factions forming on different sides, or any question about who should sit at the "head" of the table. Coordinators sat at the same round tables as the members. We were thus able to achieve our goal, that no status would be conferred by physical position in the room.

We then set about planning the first meeting. The tent cards used to identify the participants had a very large font for the first name, very small font for the last name, and purposefully did not include titles. We didn't want an exchange to be "President Smith, what do you think about X?" "Well, Bill, I think Y." We strongly encouraged use of first names only. We also assigned initial seating so that every table had a mix of individuals, and we avoided seating together like-minded people or people with similar positions or backgrounds. We used a mix of "attendee choice" and "assigned sessions" when we broke out into groups to address different aspects of the policy; we used a purposeful design to ensure that very few people would be together in more than one breakout session. We wanted members who didn't know each other to meet, and interact, as equals.

At the beginning of the first meeting, we declared that the policies to emerge from the Working Group would be consensus documents. We would take no votes and make no executive decisions. We would not elect officers or elevate any Working Group member over any other. Each point and decision would be made by group consensus. Admittedly, this was a risk—disagreement from a single person could sink the entire process—but we decided to take that risk on this group. We were counting on what we knew about the membership, their expertise, and their collegiality. All opinions were listened to and put on the table, all suggestions were treated equally.

We were careful to make the environment resource-rich to avoid information cascades: we offered many accessible resources, including access to the web, documents, and resource experts in the room, available for consultation. We encouraged participants to bring laptops or tablets and provided charging stations. When a speaker made a statement that was not precisely accurate, other members were empowered (and given the resources) to respectfully disagree, and to offer evidence of why they disagreed. Maximizing information from multiple resources led to a more educated group, and better informed outcomes.

Moving people around, and having them meet other members with whom they would not otherwise come into contact, and leaving all discussions open to all members, helped us fight off reputation and information cascades. If hands were simultaneously raised by a more senior member and a more junior member, we called on the more junior member first. We encouraged respectful disagreement, and the members themselves encouraged respectful disagreement as well as encouragement. We found that some of our most senior members supportively said, "Good point" or "I agree," after a more junior member made a differing or disagreeing point. We also kept up the mantra that there are no single answers, and we would be reaching consensus as a group.

Commonality of Purpose

All the preparation in the world would have been for naught if the committee did not have commonality of purpose, and an overt commitment to collegiality. It helped that the initial resolution from the Board of Trustees set clear goals, and that accomplishing those goals would be a significant challenge. There was no time to waste, and the professionals and students at the table endeavored to work efficiently toward accomplishment of all goals. Admittedly, it is rare to have such unity of mission among a disparate group, but we were well served by the initial presence of both SUNY Chancellor Nancy Zimpher and Provost Alexander Cartwright. They gave a clear charge to the members and set a tone of collegiality and common intent. You cannot replace an active and positive "tone from the top," and those charges were taken to heart by each member of our dedicated group. The feeling generated at the outset of our work together continued through the process.

Feedback from Constituencies

It was very important to the process that the policies not be written in a vacuum. Even though the Working Group had been intentionally constituted with a diversity of membership, there were still bound to be additional voices and perspectives missing. Thus, once the Working Group had developed a set of draft policies, we sought additional feedback from the SUNY community, as well as outside groups. We realized that, depending on the topic and timeline, it may be best to share draft documents broadly to get the most unfiltered feedback rather than wait until the document was finalized.

Town Hall Meetings

We held two "Town Hall" meetings, using Webex™ webinar, for SUNY participants. The draft policies were uploaded to a SUNY web page and invitations to review the policies and participate in the webinar were sent to each state-operated and community college president and, via the presidents, to the campus communities. We also sent invitations over several listservs that the SUNY Office of General Counsel maintains to share information on Title IX, the Clery Act, and compliance in general.

The attendance at the Town Halls was impressive. Over the course of the sessions, approximately 180 sites signed on (many sites had more than one person, so we do not know the exact number of attendees). Coordinators briefly described highlights of each of the policies and then took feedback via phone and via chat. Many comments and suggestions came in; each contribution was incorporated into a master document that would be used to review each policy.

Concurrently, we placed a comment form on the Working Group web page. We received over 100 comments through that form and hundreds of additional comments and questions via email and telephone. This process worked very well for us, since items submitted via the form populated a database available to the coordinators, and all members of the Working Group. As with other comments received—either through the Town Halls or individual emails sent to the coordinators—all input was added to a comprehensive "comments and changes" document. This master document was subsequently used by the Working Group as it finalized the policy recommendations. The coordinators carefully went through the master document and redlined the policies, making use of all comments, realizing that each comment could be accepted, modified, or rejected. The coordinators worked jointly and deferred to each other's expertise. For comments that suggested changes to language or substance, the coordinators provided several language or policy options to the Working Group members based on the submitted comments, and the group evaluated whether and how to make changes based on the comment. Remaining comments or questions that could not be incorporated in the policies or were not appropriate for the policies were transformed into a guidance document provided to campuses after the policies became final. The guidance document included both background information and a catchall question-and-answer section.

Meetings with Advocacy Groups

In addition to meetings with SUNY stakeholders, the coordinators, with the assistance of the governor's office, held a number of meetings (in person and by video) with outside advocates and experts from around the state. Each expert reviewed the policies and provided feedback to, and asked questions of, the coordinators. The input from the outside advocates and experts was treated precisely the same as the suggestions from within the SUNY community. The outside experts offered many substantive comments, which ranged from small fixes in word choice or sentence order to large conceptual and resource suggestions. They were generous with their time, and the final policies were better for having had the interactions. As a bonus, SUNY was able to develop great contacts with advocates and experts. In the time since the completion of the policy process, many of these interactions have deepened into new partnerships; connections such as working together on grant ideas, sharing resources, attending conferences together, and cross-training constituents have all taken place as productive offshoots of the initial work.

Perspectives on the Governance Model

The process that was followed in convening the Working Group was outside of the normal governance procedures that SUNY usually employs when engaging in policy initiatives. For example, the policies for two recent major SUNY initiatives—seamless transfer and Open SUNY— were developed collaboratively by faculty and administrators working on committees that were jointly established and designated as "advisory" to the SUNY provost. As we have discussed, this particular initiative did not lend itself to the deliberative process that is characteristic of faculty-administrative committees typically formed.

But, in hindsight, we asked ourselves a question that we didn't have time to consider while the work was underway: was this an appropriate approach to *shared governance*? In this section, we consider three perspectives: that of a faculty leader, an interim college president, and a student leader, all of whom served on the Working Group. Relevant biographies of the three authors of this section are as follows:

Faculty: Co-author Knuepfer, at the time of the effort described in this chapter, was president of the SUNY University Faculty Senate, and in that capacity, he also served as a member of the SUNY Board of Trustees. He was asked to be a member of the Working Group to ensure representation from the faculty governance body of the state-operated campuses (then the president of the Faculty Council of Community Colleges, Tina Good, also was invited to serve on the Working Group and did so as representative of the community college faculty).

President: Co-author Asselin served for seventeen months as the acting president of Schenectady County Community College (SCCC). It was during this interim period as acting president that she was asked to serve as one of four SUNY college presidents on the Working Group. Her extensive prior experience working in student affairs within a community college setting added a unique and critical perspective to the Working Group. Co-author Asselin has returned to the position of vice president for student affairs at SCCC since the appointment of a new college president at Schenectady County Community College.

Student: Co-author Mould was serving as the president of the Student Assembly of the State University of New York (SUNY SA) during the

2014–2015 academic year. As such, she represented the interests of all 460,000-plus students enrolled at SUNY institutions, and she also served as a member of the SUNY Board of Trustees. With degrees from Genesee Community College and SUNY's Empire State College, she continued as a graduate student in higher education and student affairs at SUNY Empire State College after completing her work as a trustee.

Faculty Perspective: Peter L.K. Knuepfer

When the Board of Trustees convened an extraordinary meeting at the request of the governor, to consider establishing a uniform policy on sexual assault across SUNY, I had several reactions.

First, this is an important issue that should not be treated lightly, or in haste. Second, the way in which this was presented—with the governor speaking to the board and to the cameras a month before his reelection—gave me pause. Third, the timetable that was established by the board resolution appeared unrealistic, even though it was clear that we already had excellent policies in place at many if not most of our SUNY institutions.

Nonetheless, I grasped the reality—we had to move rapidly to develop policies. When I received the request to be a member of the Working Group, I felt it necessary to accept the fact that this was not the process to which I was accustomed. I also recognized, instead, that it would not be feasible to take the time to identify one or more SUNY faculty who have greater expertise on these issues that I had.

In accepting the invitation from the conveners, I made it clear that, during the process, I would seek advice from SUNY faculty who have conducted research on issues of sexual violence on college campuses. This proved to be a wise decision, as the additional expertise I received from SUNY faculty and staff members helped inform the Working Group in many ways. For example, they pointed us toward some of the most pertinent literature in the field. They also shared experiences that colleagues at other universities and colleges had had with affirmative consent approaches.

It was clear to me from the outset that the members of the Working Group were committed to the development of the best-possible policy, and they were more than willing to work together within the tight time frame (only a month by the time the first meeting was convened). It was also clear that the conveners of the Working Group had done a masterful job of preparing samples—possible policy wording, reflecting the best of SUNY campus policies and other policies. These samples allowed the Working Group members to consider and modify complex language. Indeed, it was the collegiality and shared purpose of the Working Group members, coupled with the level of preparation provided by the conveners, that made the process successful.

Administrative Perspective: Martha Asselin

When SUNY Chancellor Zimpher introduced her vision for "systemness" in 2012 during the State of the University Address, one could not fully comprehend the potential, strength, or magnitude of such a system-wide collective impact. Yet, just two years after first introducing the term, SUNY systemness was beautifully conveyed through the Working Group's collaboration to design and adopt a uniform SUNY sexual assault prevention and response policy.

I enthusiastically agreed to serve alongside the other 34 leaders on the Working Group. This was an innovative reform initiative designed to implement effective change for SUNY as a system and for each campus individually. The group was charged with the task of redefining sexual assault policies and positioning the SUNY system to set a national model for other institutions of higher education. What an honor it was to be called to this table.

Throughout my 30 years as a student affairs professional, I have long believed there is no duty more important than protecting our students, by fostering safe living and learning environments on our college campuses. I fully understood the impact a uniform sexual assault prevention policy would have and believed deeply in setting the example for others—inside and outside the system—to follow. Too often, campus judicial boards are challenged by the vagueness and ambiguity that comes with defining "consent" at the institutional level. The Working Group seized the opportunity to provide bold clarity with a uniform definition of "consent," while designing policies that reflect compassion for both survivors and those who might hold information regarding the complaint. The policies were written with respect for each member of the campus community and in full compliance with the federal law.

The Working Group collectively embraced the well-coordinated and thoughtful approach for engaging all 64 campuses within the system, while sharing a commitment to the purpose and common goal. Every member of the Working Group was fully committed to making the policy formation process fully transparent, open, and responsive to feedback collected from all stakeholders, as described earlier in this chapter. The

Working Group exemplified SUNY systemness throughout the inclusive process used to design a uniform SUNY sexual assault prevention and response policy, and, most importantly, through the final product of this collaborative work.

The SUNY Sexual Violence Prevention and Response Policy is cutting-edge, and outside advocates claim it to be the best in the nation. SUNY has taken a strong lead, and sets a high standard for other states and institutions of higher education to follow. The collective accomplishments of this Working Group will forever remain one of my proudest SUNY memories.

Student Trustee's Perspective: Lori Mould

As a trustee on the SUNY Board of Trustees, I was able to make important changes on the original resolution, which were meant to include all students within our diverse educational system, before it was presented to the board on October 2, 2014. I was impressed by the way in which my suggestions were handled and taken seriously. I believe that the resolution was a great starting point, as it served as the driving force behind the state's sexual assault prevention policies.

My role as president of SUNY SA and a member of the Working Group allowed me to bring the student perspective and insight into the meetings. The executive cabinet of SUNY SA and our advisor provided me with thought-provoking questions, information, observations, advisement, and clarity during this process. I reached out to students throughout the SUNY system (via email and social media). I needed to get a sense of what their perceptions were regarding how sexual assault/domestic violence was handled on their campuses, the process of reporting an incident, how the University Police/Campus Safety/Peace Officers dealt with the parties involved, and so on. I was able to sit down, face-to-face, with numerous students and have candid conversations regarding their ideas, issues, problems, and concerns about sexual assault/domestic violence. Together, we discussed how the students could and should have a voice in the new policy structure within the SUNY system. The students were very proactive in the conversations and offered valuable insights and stories of incidents—some of them had been involved with incidents, either first- or secondhand.

SUNY SA had numerous student leaders who spent time throughout the 2014–2015 academic school year talking to students and SUNY system administration about the importance of strong policies regarding sexual assault/domestic violence/student safety. We spent many hours on phone conversations with student leaders from across the country, representatives from the White House, the National Campus Leadership Council, and our student leaders within the SUNY system discussing this important issue.

We held Town Hall meetings across the state to discuss how we, as students, could bring valuable insight to these issues facing our fellow students. As students, we wanted to make sure that the student perspective was heard loud and clear. We had numerous students who spoke with faculty, staff, and administrators regarding any ideas, problems, or concerns they had at their various campuses.

The information we gathered in these various settings proved to be a valuable asset, regarding how and what our students wanted to see in these policies. I appreciate the candid conversations from all the groups that we were engaged with over the last year.

From the first day, I was struck by the diverse nature and makeup of the Working Group and the input from so many individuals across the system, communities, advocates, and our nation. Even though there were many of us, there was equal time for all parties represented to have a say about the who, what, where, when, why, and how of the content for the new policies. We broke up into various groups throughout the process so that we could give all the policies/procedures an adequate amount of time and discussion. I was impressed with the demeanor of the group when we worked through the vast amount of information that was discussed/presented. Our conversations and disagreements were handled in a cordial and respectful manner. The group was allowed the freedom for candid and frank discussions. I believe the means by which this process was handled is why we were able to put together such a comprehensive set of policies that has the potential to make all of our campuses throughout the state of New York safer for everyone.

I was privileged to have been asked to serve on the Working Group because I know that the strong policies that came from this group will serve as a safety net for our students and campuses. Together we are #SUNYStrong!

The Results

Key points from the SUNY Sexual Violence Prevention and Response Policy as passed by the SUNY Board of Trustees in December 2014 are:

A Uniform Definition of Consent to Sexual Activity[17]

Federal law and college policy prohibit sexual assault, which is briefly defined as sexual activity without consent. But what is consent? There is no federal definition, and the New York penal law definitions define consent more for what it is *not* than for what it is. For example, the New York penal law defines "lack of consent," which it says results from, among other things, "forcible compulsion" and incapacitation. Yet it does not define what consent *is*, such as the willing and voluntary engagement in an activity by an individual. For many years, SUNY colleges (and myriad institutions across the country) had used various definitions of affirmative or active consent. Such definitions put the onus on the person seeking sexual activity to obtain consent, rather than the traditional criminal law definitions that put the onus on victims to prove that they audibly and vigorously said no in a way that should have been understood.

But colleges are different from criminal courts, and have different aims. The criminal law and its courts exist to determine whether a person has committed an act that merits incarceration and removal from society. Colleges set rules of all types to create a community wherein students and other community members act in ways that encourage people to be respectful of each other. Often the standards on college campuses are higher than in society as a whole, and consent is no exception.

The Working Group looked at a compendium created by counsel's office of each college's definition; then, the group pulled the best parts from all to create a uniform definition. To avoid a patchwork-style paragraph, the group grabbed concepts rather than full sentences, so that the language of the policy had one voice.

The policy requires that anyone seeking sexual activity of *any type* with another person must do so with consent. The initial policy was silent as to how consent could be displayed, which would mean consent could be established through words or actions. The legislation passed (see following section) later made the display of consent more concrete.

Affirmative consent means that individuals are participating in sexual activity willingly, not against their will or while they are sleeping, or while they are so incapacitated from drugs or alcohol that they cannot make decisions about sexual activity.

The Working Group felt strongly that the policy needed to use *plain language*; we pilot tested our proposed language with students, to ensure that what they understood was what we meant. While the affirmative consent policies were similar to those already adopted by SUNY colleges individually, having a single definition would mean that a student who transferred between schools or went to a different campus for graduate school would not have to learn a different standard.

Notably, one of the advocates suggested that we include language making it clear that the policies protect students regardless of sexual orientation or gender identity, since some LGBTQ* students are not always aware that they are equally protected. All agreed, and the sentence stating that affirmative consent was the same regardless of sexual orientation, gender identity, or gender expression was incorporated and included in the resulting legislation, one of the first times in history that equal protections on these bases were enshrined in law.

Uniform Amnesty Policy to Encourage Reporting[18]

No SUNY college has ever responded to a report of a student sexually assaulted while they were using drugs or alcohol by charging that student under the student code of conduct for the drug or alcohol use. Yet, during the course of the process, when we reached out to students, they almost uniformly believed that the college would readily and eagerly charge the victim.

We initially thought that an amnesty policy would not be necessary, since we knew that colleges do not charge victims. However, learning that students consistently believed that such charges were possible—or even probable—led to the clear and firm amnesty statement.

Bystanders and victims who report sexual or interpersonal violence will not be charged under the code for a drug or alcohol use violation.

We knew it was important to note that this policy only applies to violations of the student code of conduct and does not keep an individual from being arrested by local police. The Working Group was extremely careful with the language, and the amnesty is only for individual drug and/or alcohol *use* violations—meaning that clubs or organizations cannot use the policy to get out of group violations and it only applies to *use*, not sale or drugging another person.

Bill of Rights[19]

The Working Group developed a Bill of Rights, which is intended to be a brief document informing victims and survivors of sexual and interpersonal violence of their rights. These rights include their option to report to local, campus, or state law enforcement and to access campus-specific resources, including obtaining a protection/no contact order and counseling, health, legal, and support services.

The Bill of Rights also contains firm statements about the type of respect victims and survivors should expect from college officials, including being believed, not being made to repeat the information unnecessarily to additional offices, and having their religion and civil rights respected. The Bill of Rights is accompanied by an Options in Brief statement, which provides readers with the "campus specific contact" options after an assault.

As with the consent definition and with amnesty, these rights are not new, but writing them down, hanging up copies of the rights in the residence halls, and sending them via email to every student, sends a consistent message to the campus community: all throughout SUNY should understand how to respond to these incidents.

Response Policy

The response policy was the heart of the changes brought about by the Working Group. This is one of the best examples of how our outside advocates brought an idea to the table that became a game changer. Working Group members were developing this policy using some samples we retrieved from SUNY's university centers. One of our outside advocates raised her hand and said that the order of the policies was all wrong. Victims and survivors don't need to first hear what the standard is when they are going through a student conduct hearing, or how to make changes in their academic or living situation. Colleges traditionally draft policies in manners that work well for colleges: we were challenged to redraft the policy, organizing it in such a way that it would work best for victims and survivors.

The Working Group took this to heart, tearing the documents apart before putting them back together in what we called a "Maslow's Hierarchy" ordering. First, victims need to know about who they can call immediately, 24 hours per day, to disclose events, and/or to get information. They need *immediate* information about crisis counseling and medical care. Once they have what they need, the equivalent of Maslow's basic needs, then we can provide information on accommodations, reporting to law enforcement and the campus, the student conduct process, and penalties for violations.

This was one of many examples of ideas brought to the table by outside experts, but it fundamentally changed the way we thought about the policy-making process. This encouraged us to develop policies that were consistently more student-centered.

The policy was developed to match and complement federal law on point, primarily the Clery Act as amended by the Violence Against Women Act and Title IX. In certain areas, the Working Group felt strongly that it wanted to build upon and strengthen the protections of these laws. The primary example is in the mandatory penalties for sexual assault. Federal regulations require that colleges list the sanctions available for, among other things, sexual assault, but it does not specify what those sanctions must be—each institution is free to decide for itself, but it must publish them clearly.

Some colleges made the national news by issuing inappropriate sanctions; for example, one institution imposed expulsions on students found responsible for sexual assault, but only after graduation. Another school was in the news for requiring students found responsible for multiple sexual assaults to complete an educational program in lieu of suspension or expulsion. SUNY colleges had long taken a different approach: Students who are found responsible (after a due process hearing) for committing sexual assaults should no longer be members of the college community. The Working Group unanimously adopted this as a uniform standard for the policy. The sanctions for students found responsible for sexual assault are limited by the policy to suspension, with additional requirements prior to reenrollment, and permanent dismissal. After heavy pressure by lobbyists, this element was one of the few that was not included in the legislation subsequently passed by the New York State Legislature.

Uniform Confidentiality and Reporting Protocol for All SUNY Campuses[20]

This document provides information about various methods to disclose and report sexual violence on and off campus. It begins with the most confidential resources and later describes how college officials (without privilege or confidentiality) may respond by conducting an investigation, or at least assessing whether they must conduct an investigation under the circumstances. This fill-in-the-blank tool ensures that students have consistent, timely, and accurate information about available confidential resources.

Uniform Campus Climate Assessments[21]

All SUNY campuses will conduct campus climate assessments to gauge the prevalence of sexual and interpersonal violence on campus, test students' attitudes and awareness of the issue, and provide colleges/universities with information to help them form solutions for addressing and preventing sexual assault on and off campus. A group of subject matter and methodology experts from around the system gathered virtually, and in person, over the course of the spring 2015 semester to draft the survey. When completed, and data are analyzed, this will be one of the largest surveys of its kind ever distributed. The hope is that the large sample size will allow for important lessons in addressing violence and educating students, especially after the biannual survey goes through several tests.

Student Onboarding and Ongoing Education Guide[22]

The Violence Against Women Act mandated an important shift in violence prevention education. Rather than requiring a single program or single orientation session (as longstanding New York law also required), the amendments to the Clery Act in VAWA require a "campaign" that includes several comprehensive elements. To help campuses accomplish this goal using best practices, the Working Group realigned the original board resolution requirement for a freshman orientation program to an onboarding process for new first year and transfer students at all levels, accompanied by training offered for all students and specific targeted populations.

We chose "onboarding," a human resources term, because it was evocative of a continuous process, rather than a single session. Orientations are already packed full of important information about a broad range of topics, and adding content likely would have diminishing returns. By shifting the focus to a process of onboarding, campuses would have the flexibility to educate students in the way that each campus could tailor to its own perspective regarding what would be most effective. Importantly, the program would not be limited to single sessions.

The Working Group assessed peer-reviewed research (including from the White House Task Force Report, 2014), as well as articles appearing in popular press. The group also drew on the experiences of members (and outsiders) who, jointly, have decades of experience training students. All collaborated to find ways to focus the policy on the most important concepts that must be covered in the onboarding, and the most effective ways to educate students. The resulting guide includes the basic concepts that must be covered and suggests over a dozen methods to convey that information, including online training, social media outreach, faculty teach-ins, and peer education programs. Each campus has the flexibility to determine how and when to use a particular training method. Flexibility in delivery is vital for a campus system that has "traditional" four-year residential institutions with students 18 to 24 years old, two-year community colleges that are largely nonresidential, and a nontraditional college that holds most classes online or at various locations throughout the state. Campuses are expected to use various training delivery methods and assess their effectiveness through attendance, participation, and even climate survey results.

Federal law requires that the aforementioned campaign includes programs offered to everyone, and the SUNY policy adopts that requirement. The Working Group went beyond the federal minimum in two important ways.

- The policy requires that institutions offer *tailored programs to specialized groups*, chosen by each campus, who could benefit from that additional information.

- Additionally, while programming would be *offered* to everyone, the SUNY policy (and the resulting New York law) requires that athletes *complete* training prior to competing in intercollegiate athletics and that club and organization leaders and officers *complete* training prior to their club or organization being registered or recognized. The reason for the final point is that benefit can come from focusing on our student campus leaders. Realistically, a college cannot comprehensively train every single student, but by training leaders who could model pro-social behavior, a campus can improve its culture for all students.

As with other trainings, the method and content is left up to each campus to design, in consideration of its campus culture.

Implementation

The strong initial buy-in by SUNY campuses to the policy language continued throughout the implementation process. The Offices of University Police, University Life, and General Counsel organized trainings, developed guidance, and hosted conferences to allow SUNY campuses to share best practices with each other. While there were a lot of policy and technical questions, the anticipated cries of top-down unfunded mandates never came. The decentralized SUNY system, used to accomplishing tasks campus-by-campus, had come together to develop the policies, and campuses worked to implement them with very positive attitudes.

Information Sharing

The Working Group's legitimacy and expertise were not only crucial to policy development, but also to implementation. Of course, policymakers were comfortable implementing the policies that they had written with their peers at the table. Still, not every institution had a stakeholder from that college or university at the Working Group table, yet somehow SUNY needed buy-in from all 64 campuses.

At the end of the second working group meeting, the members all agreed to send the policies to their colleagues across the SUNY system, along with a message in their own words. For example, a director of a health center sent out an email about the policies to the listserv of health center directors. Two community college presidents sent a joint message to their fellow community college presidents. Rather than the policies coming top-down from lawyers, the information came from colleagues who had represented their peers' interests and expertise at the drafting table. They not only felt like they were in the loop, they *were*—they were informed, they were asked for feedback, and they were able to meaningfully contribute to the process, even though they did not sit at the table. Having these experts send the content directly to their colleagues continued the process of expertise and legitimacy working hand in hand.

Use of Technology

Building on the online comment form used for feedback on the policies, group members found that it was important to use technology throughout the process. Technology allowed members to save time—policy creators as well as those who would be implementing/using the policies. The coordinators worked to make the implementation as efficient as possible.

To maximize ease of use, SUNY developed fill-in-the-blank templates and hosted several face-to-face/online conversations among campuses. Part of the original resolution required each SUNY college to report back to the chancellor by March 31, 2015, on its progress toward implementation of the policies.

Traditionally, this would have required professionals at each institution to spend hours creating a document that described its work in prose and submitting it to someone at System Administration. That individual would have to read all the submissions, summarize content, organize the levels of response, and get back to campuses that were not in compliance. All told, this would have required thousands of hours across the university.

We decided that we would rather have these professionals spend their time working with students. We eschewed the traditional report and instead took it to its basics.

- Each campus needed to notify the chancellor about its progress toward adopting and implementing the policies.

- We developed a one-page electronic form to accomplish this notification with brief biographic information about the person responding, yes/no reply to having implemented each policy, as well as date, if yes, or on what date anticipated, if no.

Campus members saved time; instead of completing a narrative report, someone filled out the online form, which automatically populated a spreadsheet. We were able to report implementation level to leadership in real time, without having to wade through hundreds of pages of extraneous text. Campuses responded positively to this reduction of bureaucracy—and saving time.

Coda: The Policies Form the Basis of Legislation

Following the chancellor's issuance of the university-wide policies, the governor's office reached out to SUNY to turn the policies into legislation, to be applied to all of the colleges and universities in New York, not just the SUNY schools. The Office of the General Counsel (co-authors Storch and Stagg) drafted the legislation and represented SUNY in discussions with lawmakers to negotiate state-wide legislation.

Since Article 129-A of the New York State Education Law was already so filled with various policies and mandates developed over many different legislative sessions, SUNY's initial draft started with a clean slate: a new Article 129-B. The governor's office submitted the policies as part of his budget legislation in January 2015.[23]

One of the most useful pieces of feedback received concerned the applicability or inapplicability of certain provisions to private colleges. We didn't disagree. The original policies were drafted specifically for SUNY colleges, colleges that already had certain provisions in place, spoke a common language using certain terms, and were bound by the constitution in areas like due process. Our private college colleagues used different standards and had different experiences and training. We benefited significantly from the feedback of higher education attorneys representing private colleges, who are themselves experts in these laws. As was the case with SUNY, the intent of these attorneys was not to diminish or weaken the law, but to make changes that made more sense for the system used by private colleges without harming the system used by SUNY and CUNY.

What became known as the "Enough Is Enough" legislation was omitted from the Enacted 2015–2016 New York State budget. But the leaders of the assembly and senate higher education committees sponsored separate legislation to make a uniform sexual violence policy for colleges and universities a part of state law. The longer time period between the failure of the bill to pass as part of the budget (at the beginning of April) and its eventual passage at the end of the legislative session in June also allowed for very careful consideration of every single word and the meaning that some may ascribe to it.

In many cases, we were surprised by misinterpretations of standard terms well known to everyone in the SUNY professional community. Many out there, perhaps with less experience and exposure to violence prevention on college campuses than those in the Working Group, misunderstood what certain terms meant. Rather than try to push back and demand the original language, we regularly worked with representatives of the governor's office and legislative staff to find common ground. The results included new terms and phrases that accomplished the same goals, but used plainer, clearer language. For example, while the SUNY policies used the term "victim/survivor" to refer to someone who had experienced sexual or interpersonal violence, the legislation uses the phrase "reporting individual." Like any other document written by insiders with some level of knowledge about the topic, we were well served by exposure to the public, and other stakeholders, who pushed us repeatedly to simplify the language used.

Alongside the positive changes, however, many proposed changes would have been harmful, in our opinion. The legislative process is quite different from the policy-making process we had used with the Working Group. Not all stakeholders came seeking a cutting-edge bill that would aid and educate students, while maintaining fairness toward reporting students and accused students. Some wanted to kill the bill outright. Others saw opportunities to advance alternative agendas, while still others saw dollar signs and tried to amend the bill to require that colleges hire them or their colleagues. The process was very different than the working group process, but it must be said that the attorneys in the governor's office who worked on the legislation and stewarded it through the legislative process did not settle for expedience or quick victory. Instead, despite difficulties, they held the line in many important areas. The bill *is* a better one because of this review process. The bill was also well served by several legislative staff members of good faith. They came to the table with fresh ideas, a willingness to compromise and maintain the integrity of the legislation, while accomplishing the goals of their legislative leaders.

The policies were passed unanimously by the state senate on June 17, 2015, as bill S5965-2015, and passed the next day by the assembly with all but four voting in favor. The bill was signed into law by Governor Cuomo on July 7, 2015. The legislation gave 90 days for all colleges in New York State to come into compliance (with the exception of two sections on climate surveys and reporting to the State Department of Education, which are effective after one year).

Enactment of the legislation could have presented a new implementation challenge for SUNY colleges. With the support of university leaders, shortly after the bill passed, the Counsel's Office developed a redline document to show the differences between the original policies and the legislative changes. We were pleased to see that there was very little "red" in the redline. Most sections of the policy were all but intact with tiny technical changes, while others had a few substantive changes and reordering of sentences. SUNY lawyers provided campuses with a redline edit of the 2014 Working Group policies to specify the differences between the policies and the new legislation; luckily, there were very few changes. This guidance was provided to make it as easy as possible for campuses to comply. These changes came just as campuses were completing the summer revisions to their codes and preparing to have the codes printed. In fact, several SUNY campuses reported back that they had made all the legislative changes in the redline and sent their code to print even before the governor officially signed the legislation.

Final Thoughts: A One-Trick Pony or a New Model of Governance?

A natural question that arises is whether the process that led SUNY to a rapid result is repeatable or whether this issue, at this time, with this group, uniquely led to the results that it did. Was the result only a "one-trick pony" and not a sustainable model for governance? The authors of this chapter have given this considerable thought. Our response centers on two aspects of this experience.

First, when faced with an extremely aggressive timeline, traditional shared governance structures are not likely to be nimble enough to respond. This risks the development of policy by administrative fiat. Second, the development of a rapid policy response requires a group of willing and able participants who share a commonality of purpose and accept the need to bypass conventional processes. Such an approach is unlikely to replace conventional models of deliberative governance; many issues of policy are best served by careful, albeit not excessive, discussion and consideration.

However, for those situations in which timeliness is most essential (as might be the case, for example, after a natural disaster), a hybrid model of administratively driven shared governance that includes key stakeholders and experts can successfully respond, while still adhering to the basic principles of shared governance.

If an organization does wish to use this model to accomplish a discrete task, attention paid to *expertise*, *legitimacy*, *openness*, and the *use of technology* will be time well spent. It is clear that without any one of these pillars, this process would not have succeeded. Each of the pillars complemented the others.

To use this model well, group leaders must commit to *transparency*. Their process can be enhanced if they use technology to keep group members informed, for data collection (during the pilot stages as well as to measure success) and to push the boundaries towards the cutting-edge.

But even more importantly, to use this model well, group leaders *must acknowledge that they don't know everything about the topic* and must give real respect to the group members and to their constituencies. *Respect* given to the members engenders respect for the process and a better product. A product built with expertise and thorough opportunities for input from the community is a legitimate product. Products seen as legitimate are adopted constructively, not with opposition and anger. We could not be prouder of the results of this Working Group, but at the same time, we are deeply proud of the members, and of the process that got us here.

Notes

1. http://www.suny.edu/about/leadership/board-of-trustees/meetings/webcast-docs/Agenda%20-%20October%202%202014.pdf.
2. The Board of Trustees Resolution is found at http://www.suny.edu/about/leadership/board-of-trustees/meetings/webcastdocs/Sexual%20Assault%20Response%20and%20Prevention%20REVISED-Merged.pdf.

3. Fifteen of the 18 trustees are appointed by the governor to set terms, with the advice and consent of the senate. Additionally, the presidents of the Student Assembly, University Faculty Senate, and the Faculty Council of Community Colleges serve as trustees. See bylaws of the Board of Trustees, State University of New York, available at https://www.suny.edu/media/suny/content-assets/documents/boardoftrustees/BY-LAWS.pdf.

4. http://system.suny.edu/facultysenate/.

5. Policies of the Board of Trustees 2014, State University of New York, Article VII, Title A, §2, http://www.suny.edu/media/suny/content-assets/documents/boardoftrustees/SUNY-BOT-Policies-June2014.pdf.

6. http://www.fccc.suny.edu/.

7. http://www.sunysa.org/

8. http://system.suny.edu/media/suny/content-assets/documents/generalcounsel/SUNY-VAWA-Guidance-2014.pdf.

9. Board of Trustees Resolution, http://www.suny.edu/about/leadership/board-of-trustees/meetings/webcastdocs/Sexual%20Assault%20Response%20and%20Prevention%20REVISED-Merged.pdf.

10. http://www.nacua.org/documents/VAWA2013.pdf.

11. http://www2.ed.gov/about/offices/list/ocr/letters/colleague-201104.pdf.

12. http://www2.ed.gov/about/offices/list/ocr/docs/qa-201404-title-ix.pdf.

13. http://www2.ed.gov/about/offices/list/ocr/letters/colleague-201504-title-ix-coordinators.pdf; https://www2.ed.gov/about/offices/list/ocr/docs/dcl-title-ix-coordinators-guide-201504.pdf.

14. Violence Against Women Act, http://www.gpo.gov/fdsys/pkg/BILLS-113s47enr/pdf/BILLS-113s47enr.pdf.

15. The full list of members, with links to their biographies, is found at http://system.suny.edu/sexual-violence-prevention-workgroup/bios/.

16. The four outside experts were Robin B. Braunstein (http://system.suny.edu/sexual-violence-prevention-workgroup/bios/robin-braunstein/); Laura Dunn (http://system.suny.edu/sexual-violence-prevention-workgroup/bios/laura-dunn/); Libby Post (http://system.suny.edu/sexual-violence-prevention-workgroup/bios/libby-post/); and Gwen Wright (http://system.suny.edu/sexual-violence-prevention-workgroup/bios/gwen-wright/).

17. http://system.suny.edu/sexual-violence-prevention-workgroup/policies/affirmative-consent/.

18. http://system.suny.edu/sexual-violence-prevention-workgroup/policies/drugs-amnesty/.

19. http://system.suny.edu/sexual-violence-prevention-workgroup/policies/bill-of-rights/.

20. http://system.suny.edu/sexual-violence-prevention-workgroup/policies/disclosure/.

21. http://system.suny.edu/sexual-violence-prevention-workgroup/policies/campus-climate/.

22. http://system.suny.edu/sexual-violence-prevention-workgroup/policies/student-guide/.

23.   2015 New York State Proposed Budget, available at http://open.nysenate.gov/legislation/bill/S2006-2015.

References

Bogdanich, W. (2014, July 12). Reporting rape, and wishing she hadn't; how one campus handled a sexual assault complaint. *New York Times*. Retrieved from http://www.nytimes.com/2014/07/13/us/how-one-college-handled-a-sexual-assault-complaint.html (accessed August 15, 2015).

Cramer, S. F., Editor. (2017). *Shared Governance in Higher Education, Vol. 1: Demands, Transitions and Transformations*. Albany: SUNY Press.

DeGue, S. (2014). Preventing sexual violence on college campuses: Lessons from research and practice; part one: Evidence-based strategies for the primary prevention of sexual violence perpetration. *Prepared for the White House Task Force to Protect Students from Sexual Assault*, 36 pp. Retrieved from http://responsesystemspanel.whs.mil/Public/docs/meetings/20140505/EvidenceBased-Strategies_Prevention_SV_Perpetration.pdf

Department of Education. (2014). Proposed regulations to implement the Violence Against Women Act, 79 FR 35417. Retrieved from https://www.federalregister.gov/articles/2014/06/20/2014-14384/violence-against-women-act

Easley, D., and Kleinberg, J. (2010). *Networks, crowds and markets: Reasoning about a highly connected world*. New York: Cambridge University Press.

Katz, J., & DuBois, M. (2013). The sexual assault Teach In program: Building constructive campus-wide discussions to inspire change. *Journal of college student development, 54*(6), 654–557.

Macur, J. (2013, December 13). In Florida State case, a tangle of questions. *New York Times*. Retrieved from http://www.nytimes.com/2013/12/14/sports/ncaafootball/no-one-wins-in-florida-state-case.html (accessed August 15, 2015).

National Public Radio Staff. (2014, April 6). Rape on Campus: Painful Stories Cast Blame on Colleges. Retrieved from http://www.npr.org/2014/04/06/299521814/students-stories-of-sexual-assault-puts-schools-to-blame-too

Office of General Counsel, State University of New York. (2015). *Policy and programming changes pursuant to the campus SaVE provisions of the Violence Against Women Act*. Retrieved from http://system.suny.edu/media/suny/content-assets/documents/generalcounsel/SUNY-VAWA-Guidance-2014.pdf (July 2014, updated January 2015).

Perez-Pena, R., & Taylor, K. (2014, May 3). Fight against sexual assaults holds colleges to account. *New York Times*. Retrieved from http://www.nytimes.com/2014/05/04/us/fight-against-sex-crimes-holds-colleges-to-account.html (accessed August 15, 2015).

Rumsfeld, D. (2002, February 12). News transcript: DoD news briefing—Secretary Rumsfeld and General Myers, Department of Defense. Retrieved from http://

archive.defense.gov/Transcripts/Transcript.aspx?TranscriptID=2636 (accessed March 13, 2017).

Somaiya, R. (2015, April 6). Rolling Stone article on rape at University of Virginia failed all basics, report says. *New York Times*. Retrieved from http://www. nytimes.com/2015/04/06/business/media/rolling-stone-retracts-article-on-rape-at-university-of-virginia.html (accessed August 15, 2015).

Storch, J., & Stagg, A. (2016). Missoula: Jon Krakauer's story of college sexual violence that is both complex and entirely common. *Journal of College and University Law, 42,* 451–478.

White House Task Force to Protect Students from Sexual Assault. (2014). *Not alone.* Retrieved from http://changingourcampus.org/publications/

4

The Development of Shared Governance for the Budget Allocation Process at Stony Brook University

A Positive, yet Cautionary Tale

Debra Sabatini Dwyer, Norman Goodman, and Mark Maciulaitis

This chapter serves as a case study of how shared governance can work efficiently to produce better policies and procedures. The process by which Stony Brook University developed a new budget allocation model benefited from the inclusion of diverse perspectives of administration and faculty through shared governance. We describe the evolution of a finance and budget committee that was originally composed predominantly of administrators and administratively appointed faculty to one that was more balanced between the administration and faculty with the addition of elected faculty representatives. We also describe how these diverse perspectives led to a budget model that is uniquely appropriate for Stony Brook University, and one that is considered a significant improvement by all parties given the inclusiveness of the process by which it was developed. An indicator of success was the achievement of transparency of budget allocation decisions that is a key component of this proposed new process. We conclude with some cautionary advisement over how to successfully incorporate shared governance into university decision-making.

What Was the Campus Budget Allocation Process— And Why Did It Need To Be Changed?

In 2011, after an especially challenging period in Stony Brook's history of funding and resource allocation, including three years in a row of significant budget reductions, President Samuel Stanley directed the appointment of a committee of administrators and faculty to research models for institutional budgeting The goals of the committee were to develop a budgeting process that was rational, transparent, and predictable, while encouraging excellence as well as fiscal accountability throughout the university.

What Process Was Established to Consider Necessary Changes to the Current Campus Budget Allocation Process?

The committee established by the president, called the Finance and Budget Committee (F & B Committee), was composed of 17 members, 15 of whom were administrators and only two who were full-time faculty members, and the faculty were selected by a steering committee consisting of senior campus administrators, deans, and the president of the university senate. The committee was charged to review the current budget allocation model, to identify problems, and to consider transforming it into more of a Responsibility Centered Management (RCM)–based model. After completing its work, the committee was to present a recommendation for a new budget allocation model to the Budget Working Group (BWG), which consisted of the president and his senior vice presidents.

At Stony Brook University, each of the standing committees of the university senate includes a "cognate administrator," the senior administrator in the area of the committee's responsibility. One of the senate's standing committees is the Committee on Academic Planning and Resource Allocation (CAPRA), and the provost serves as its cognate administrator. In addition, it has been past practice to include the associate vice president for budget as a consultant to the committee because of the key role this office plays in the resource allocation process. These administrators typically meet with the committee at least once a year to go over the campus budget and they also join the committee whenever an issue is being considered where their knowledge and experience would be helpful.

The president of the University Senate informed the chair of CAPRA, Norman Goodman, of the establishment, charge, and membership of the F & B Committee. As a result, Professor Goodman asked Provost Dennis Assanis and Associate Vice President for Budget Mark Maciulaitis to attend the next meeting of CAPRA to discuss the establishment of the F & B Committee. At that time, they would also discuss the process by means of which a new budget allocation model for the campus should be developed. At that meeting, the members of CAPRA made clear their considerable unhappiness with the events that led to the establishment of the F & B Committee, specifically:

- Their lack of knowledge of the establishment of the F & B Committee until its activities were well underway.

- The composition of the F & B Committee; the ratio of administrators to faculty (15 to 2).

- How its faculty members were selected.

Without questioning the integrity of the two faculty members on the F & B Committee, the members of CAPRA expressed their distress that these faculty members were selected to represent the faculty's expertise and knowledge by the administration and not through a process of shared governance. Such a process would have allowed the faculty, through its authorized governance body, the University Senate, a role in selecting its representatives to a committee whose work would have a significant effect on the functioning of the campus.

Moreover, the budget allocation process being considered did not include a formal consultative role for the University Senate. In general, governance consultation on budgetary matters are generally allocated by the University Senate to CAPRA.

In preparation for the meeting with Provost Assanis and Associate Vice President Maciulaitis, the members of CAPRA had done research on the RCM model and how it has worked at other universities. As a result of this research, the members of CAPRA believed that the tentatively proposed RCM model that the F & B Committee was considering had significant potential problems for the Stony Brook situation.

As a consequence of both the substantive and process concerns expressed at this meeting, a series of consultations (taking place over several months) was arranged between Associate Vice President for Budget Mark Maciulaitis, who was the chair of the F & B Committee; and the chair of CAPRA, Norman Goodman; and Debra Dwyer, then chair of CAPRA's relevant subcommittee and subsequently co-chair of CAPRA. During these consultations, Dwyer and Goodman pressed the point that the F & B Committee needed a much more balanced ratio of administrators and faculty for several reasons. A more balanced ratio would benefit the process not only for the sake of shared governance, but also because of what the faculty would bring to it. Faculty have considerable expertise, knowledge, and experience that are valuable to establishing an effective budget model that advances the academic goals of the campus. Equally important, they pointed out that faculty on relevant standing committees of the University Senate had a perspective, useful knowledge, and experience that would be valuable to establishing an effective budget allocation model: Such individuals should be included on the F & B Committee. Specifically, Dwyer and Goodman recommended that the additional faculty to be selected to rebalance the administrative to faculty ratio of the F & B Committee should come from the following University Senate committees: CAPRA, the Undergraduate Council, the Graduate Council, and the Senate Research Committee, areas of academic functioning for which academic budget allocations are crucial.

Early during these consultations, there was agreement to add faculty members from the first three senate committees; there was already a key researcher on the F & B Committee who could ensure consideration of the research component of the campus's mission in any budget allocation process. Not only were additional faculty members included, but upon reconsideration by the administration, a number of administrative offices were deemed less relevant to the charge of the F & B Committee and their representatives were dropped from the committee. The result of this reconstitution of the committee was that it now consisted of seven full-time faculty members, nine administrators, and two members who were regular members of the faculty who were currently serving in administrative positions.

This reconstitution of the composition of the F & B Committee dramatically changed the dynamic of its functioning.

What Were Substantive Changes Produced by Adding Additional Governance-Recommended Faculty to the F & B Committee?

Given the greater diversity of perspectives that more fully represented the various campus constituencies, the new makeup of the committee allowed for very thoughtful and thorough discussions. Of specific note:

- The committee members examined the goals that underlie the task before it as well as different models for achieving the goals. Specifically, its members took into account many tradeoffs and constraints necessary to accomplish the goals.

- Given the number of tradeoffs and challenges, it was critical to include multiple perspectives. These necessitated extended discussions, which likely cost the F & B Committee something in terms of the time to develop a recommendation for a new budget model. However, in the long run, these discussions likely benefited the process given how well the resultant outcome was received.

- The committee had started off with the RCM framework but began to chisel away at it until it became a hybrid incentive-based system that would work well for an institution like Stony Brook University. Faculty and administrators on the committee worked together toward producing pieces of a draft of this process that became a "white paper."

- Not only was careful thought put into the development of each component of the budget model, but considerable time and effort was put into how to best communicate the plan to the general campus community.

- The length of the document and its level of detail were given serious consideration. The members of the F & B Committee agreed that there should be a balance between length (providing enough information to avoid unnecessary ambiguities) and brevity (short enough that it would not become a burdensome task to read).

- Language that crossed disciplines was continuously revised. Assuring that all budget allocations would be transparent (i.e., available down to the level of academic departments) was one of the key goals of the faculty representatives, and it was accomplished.

- While in the end the "white paper" represented a common voice (in that any one of the committee members could explain its content), it was the result of an iterative and interdisciplinary endeavor that went through many drafts. Once the "white paper" was approved by the F & B Committee, it was sent to the BWG. In the end, it was approved by the BWG and then presented to the deans for comment. The deans strongly endorsed it with some relatively minor modifications.

How Were the Substantive Changes in the Proposed Budget Allocation Process Resulting from the Inclusion of Additional Faculty in the F & B Committee Viewed by the Administration?

The university administration clearly appreciated the additional perspectives provided by the inclusion of more faculty in the F & B Committee. There was a general feeling among the administrative members of the committee that, as a result of adding more faculty members, the variety of perspectives of important budgetary issues were better able to be considered prior to the final recommendations that were ultimately developed.

While it may have delayed the completion of the final product, the thoughtful consideration of those different perspectives resulted in the model becoming a better fit for the campus than earlier versions. Ultimately, the final product was recognized as one that would stand a much better chance of being supported by the various campus constituencies. Because of its involvement in this process, going forward, CAPRA can legitimately be a supportive ally in helping to explain and to support the implementation of the new final budgetary allocation process when it is ultimately approved by the BWG.

What Was the Consultative Role of University Senate in the Budget Allocation Process?

Despite the prevalence of a constitution for the campus governance body that sets out the terms of consultation in shared governance, the campus president has a significant role in determining the actual level of consultation to take place. Over the years at Stony Brook (as we suspect, in most universities), the level of consultation has varied according to who was campus president. During previous administrations at Stony Brook, the president of the University Senate or the chair of CAPRA participated in the meeting in which the various vice presidents made their budget requests to the campus president. More recently, however, governance involvement in the campus budget allocation process was limited to having the provost and the associate vice president for budget meet with CAPRA to go over the proposed budget allocations. Though the members of CAPRA could comment on these allocations, the committee did not necessarily or routinely have any significant effect on the allocation process. CAPRA did not at any time meet directly with the president during the negotiations previously spelled out.

Given the desire of the administration to establish a new budget allocation process, CAPRA believed that it was an auspicious time to seek a more direct and active role as the representative of the University Senate in budgetary matters. To that end, its co-chairs, Debra Dwyer and Norman Goodman, continued a series of discussions with the associate vice president for budget (the chair of the F & B Committee) about the proper role that CAPRA would play in the budget allocation process. Dwyer and Goodman proposed two places in the budget allocation process in which CAPRA should be formally consulted:

- Goal 1. CAPRA would receive copies of the budget requests of all the vice presidents that were submitted to the Budget Working Group for final decision and would send its comments on these requests to the BWG.

- Goal 2. CAPRA would be able to comment on the subsequent decisions of the BWG before they are made final.

After discussions with representatives of the administration (the provost, the vice president for finance, and the associate vice president for budget), it became clear that the BWG would likely accept the proposed insertion of CAPRA in this budget allocation process outlined in Goal 1, but that the decisions of the BWG was final, thus obviating any role for CAPRA after those decisions were made. This was clearly a compromise between the current lack of any serious consultative role for CAPRA in the budget allocation process and what it had proposed as being more appropriate to shared governance.

At a subsequent meeting of CAPRA, Dwyer and Goodman discussed this compromise with the members of CAPRA, and the members agreed that accomplishing Goal 1 was a significant and important step forward in shared governance. The accomplishment of Goal 1 gave CAPRA an important consultative role in the budget allocation process. Dwyer and Goodman worked with the administration to insert appropriate language that confirmed the agreed-upon role for CAPRA in the proposed new budget allocation process.

Final Comments

This chapter describes a process that had a positive result for the principle and practice of shared governance. From an initial point in time when the campus's University Senate, through its most relevant standing committee (CAPRA), had little to no significant input to the process of budgetary allocations, this chapter outlines a process through which governance will have a significant consultative role in this critically important area of campus functioning once implemented. It has outlined a process that required patience, persistence, mutual respect, and ultimately, compromise to achieve a significant and salutary outcome both for the campus and for shared governance. As those of us in higher education understand, the budget is everything. It is the crucial mechanism that is necessary to accomplish a campus's goals that are often outlined in a strategic plan. Consequently, the faculty, through its organized representative body, must have a substantial and timely role in these budgetary decisions. That is what the process outlined here accomplished for Stony Brook University.

But why include the phrase "a cautionary tale" in the subtitle? We do so as a reminder that shared governance is not an automatic feature of institutions of higher education. Shared governance, like a successful marriage, requires vigilance, sensitivity to the "other," cooperation, thoughtfulness, and hard work. Through the process described, we were reminded of the importance of some of the key elements necessary to effective shared governance; these include:

- Identifying situations and activities that require shared governance. For example, the hiring of administrators with "line" responsibilities should involve a consultative role for campus governance. Hiring those with "staff" responsibilities (i.e., those who play a supportive but not policy-making role for an administrative office) may not require governance participation.

- Being persistent in pressing for shared governance in relevant situations and activities.

- Identifying and working with cooperative, flexible, and collegial negotiating partners to accomplish shared governance goals.

- Understanding the perspective of your negotiating partners and how shared governance may impact their abilities to successfully do their jobs.

- Being flexible enough to accept reasonable compromises that not only accomplish much of what you initially wanted but also keep your lines of communication open for continued work with your negotiating partners.

- Demonstrating the value of shared governance to the final product.

- Reminding ourselves of Voltaire's recommendation not to let the desire for the perfect be the enemy of accepting the good.

Part II

Critical Analysis of Shared Governance and Associated Issues

5

From Shared Governance to Shared Accountability

Steven C. Bahls

Shared governance often fails because faculty members, board members, and administrators have conflicting views of what shared governance should be. The traditional views of shared governance are not sufficient to align priorities of faculty, boards, and administrations in a way to meet complex and changing needs within higher education.

The three traditional views of shared governance are (1) equal rights to governance, (2) the obligation to consult, and (3) rules to divide responsibilities and engage when responsibilities overlap. This chapter offers a fourth and newer definition of shared governance as a system of aligning priorities. The fourth definition states that shared governance is a system where faculty, trustees, and administrators, as integral leaders, actively engage to move past the fragmentation of traditional governance to shared responsibility for identifying and pursing an aligned set of sustainable priorities and outcomes, for which each constituency is accountable.

For shared governance to operate effectively to align priorities, four components are necessary. Faculty members, trustees, and administrators must (1) work deliberately to build and sustain a culture of trust, transparency, and open and respectful three-way communication; (2) jointly commit to consider difficult issues associated with change and jointly develop strategic directions; (3) develop a shared set of metrics to measure success, identifying who is responsible for achieving these metrics; and (4) develop a set of effective checks and balances to ensure that the institution remains mission focused.

Introduction

Faculty members, board members, and administrators invariably espouse a commitment to shared governance.[1] But each view shared governance

83

very differently. Board members view shared governance as a vehicle to build consensus, most importantly to move universities and colleges forward during times of disruptive change (AGB, 2014). College presidents view shared governance as critical to their success in maintaining the credibility and authenticity necessary for effective leadership (Bornstein, 2003). And faculty members view shared governance as an indispensable element of maintaining time-honored traditions within higher education (AAUP, 2015). Each is focused on their own rights and territories.

At many colleges and universities, widespread agreement about the importance of shared governance is accompanied by concurrent widespread agreement that shared governance is not effective (Gaff, 2009). Board members too often view faculty pleas to share governance as potentially interfering with the board's fiduciary duty to supervise almost all aspects of its institution. Faculty members often believe that boards and administrators give lip service to shared governance but aren't committed to timely and respectful sharing of governance. And administrators frequently find themselves caught in the middle, frustrated that shared governance is a messy and inefficient way to make timely decisions.

Throughout higher education, the treasured concept of shared governance is too often used as a sword or an "I gotcha" (Zemsky, 2013). Too often, when administrations stumble by not providing sufficient timely information (or failing to start the process of shared governance early enough), faculty leaders accuse administrators of abandoning shared governance. In some cases, faculty members use these administrative errors as the rationale for walking away from the hard and messy work of truly sharing governance. At the same time, administrators too often become frustrated with faculty leaders who slow down a decision-making process to give their views of shared governance time to work, accusing them of putting their own provincial interests before the long-term interests of the institution.

I have had the opportunity to conduct workshops for boards, faculty, and administrators about how to make shared governance work effectively. In addition, I've had the opportunity to serve on accreditation teams at various colleges and universities, with the opportunity to observe how effectively governance is shared. I always ask those representing various constituencies to define shared governance and their responsibilities within systems of shared governance. Here is what I have found.

Board members tend to view shared governance as an obligation to consult with faculty before major decisions go forward—particularly those touching the academic program. They talk about needing "sign off" or "buy-in" from the faculty. Sometimes they talk about "sign off" in a way that might lead faculty members to believe they are expected to rubberstamp board decisions.

Other board members are more advanced in their views of shared governance. They recognize that meaningful consultation with faculty helps improve the decision-making process, while still retaining the board's fiduciary responsibility. But in most cases, they focus on their right to retain ultimate control more than on their obligation to share governance in the most meaningful way.

Faculty members tend to view shared governance very differently. Most faculty members agree that the starting points for effective shared governance are the rules promulgated by the American Association of University Professors (AAUP). As a general matter, these rules create primary areas of responsibility, give guidance when authority is overlapping, and provide for rules of engagement when constituencies disagree (AAUP, 2015). Faculty members object to the notion that their authority amounts to little more than the right to be consulted. And they are quick to assert their right to have almost exclusive control over decisions traditionally within the faculty domain.

When faculties see undue intrusion into their traditional domains, they are quick to use their "negative authority" to block administrative and board initiatives touching on the academic program. "Negative authority" includes not approving new academic programs or initiatives that are part of the strategic plan. It also includes more subtle powers, such as withdrawing from meaningful engagement, failing to promote programs or initiatives to students, or speaking out against them to the press and social media.

How *college presidents* (and other administrators) view shared governance is harder to characterize. Most are seeking some middle ground between the board's understanding of its own absolute authority and the rules-based system espoused by the faculty. Increasingly, presidents feel caught in the middle between faculty expectations and board demands (Bataille, Asfew, & Jackson, 2013).

Administrators know that their legitimacy and legacy is dependent on their ability to lead. And in many institutions, where trustees and faculty perceive that the administration does not engage in effective shared governance, members of both these groups lose confidence in the president. Taking shared governance seriously—in actions as well as words—builds credibility with the faculty (Bornstein, 2003). And when the president takes shared governance seriously, it is much more likely the faculty will, in turn, support presidential and board initiatives.

Shared governance cannot be fully effective until there is a common definition of effective shared governance that moves from primarily a rights-based and constituency-based system to a system of accountability. This chapter will examine the elements indispensable for effective shared governance, then show how the most common definitions of shared governance address, or fail to address, the system of accountability needed in higher education. This chapter proposes a new definition of shared governance—one that faculty, administrators, and board members will likely agree advances shared governance. As an illustration of how this definition can be applied, this chapter will examine how accountability-based definitions of shared governance might aid in strategic planning.

Shared Governance Develops Better Approaches to the Challenges Facing Higher Education

Clayton Christensen, the Robert and Jane Cizik Professor of Business Administration at the Harvard Business School, observes that higher education is experiencing a seismic shift involving both its spiraling cost and the rise of new economic models (Christiansen, Horn, Caldera, & Soares, 2011). Christensen contends that higher education is on the brink of a deep crevasse and that most in higher education do not realize it. He further argues that there is doubt about whether traditional institutions in American higher education can adapt fast enough to address the new set of external circumstances.

Christensen argues that faculty traditionally focus on preserving support for their own historical activities (Christiansen & Eyring, 2011), yet this is not the only reason for making them an essential part of higher education. Faculty creativity is necessary for institutions to remain strong. Analogizing an institution to a bus, he calls faculty both the bus's engine and its brakes. For an institution to thrive, faculty must help develop the roadmap to sustainability. To do so, Christiansen writes, the institution must assure faculty members that their jobs will continue and they will have a meaningful voice (Christiansen & Eyring, 2011).

Robert Zemsky, professor of education at the University of Pennsylvania and chair of the Learning Alliance for Higher Education, asserts that higher education is stuck in an Ecclesiastes Moment—the world is changing all around and those leading our institutions are oblivious. There are calls for change, but as the teacher of Ecclesiastes says, "what has been done is what will be done," and "there is nothing new under the sun" (Zemsky, 2013, p. 15). Zemsky observes that higher education may be encamped "just north of Armageddon" (Zemsky, 2013, p. 20). He decries today's higher education leaders, who look "over the ridge and see the destruction that would await them" but do little to pursue change. He argues that the notion that "change comes slowly in higher education" is overly charitable, as he views colleges and universities as stuck where they were in the 1980s (Zemsky, 2013, p. 16).

Zemsky agrees with Christensen about the role of faculty, but again puts it more bluntly. Zemsky argues that many faculties have largely abandoned their role in governance. He argues that faculties must strengthen their ability to take collective action as a prerequisite to meaningful participation in overall governance. Part of doing so is to tone down rhetorical excess against perceived opponents (the administration or trustees) and find ways to engage in idea-centered discussions (Zemsky, 2013). Uncivil rhetoric can drive many to the sidelines, making widespread collaboration impossible.

In their book, *Locus of Authority: The Evolution of Faculty Roles in the Governance of Higher Education*, William Bowen and Eugene Tobin note that the challenges and changes impacting higher education require revisiting the role of faculty in governance (Bowen & Tobin, 2015). They ask whether institutions of higher education can make the changes necessary to educate a changing student body. Can faculty make effective decisions that transform departmental structures? What is the impact of greater loyalty to discipline than loyalty to the institution as a whole? They argue for a stronger centralized voice of faculty and contend that this centralization transcends more parochial interests.

One way of achieving Bowen and Tobin's call for a more effective faculty voice is to depart from the view of shared governance focused on rights and territories and move toward a view that ensures joint accountability for the institution as a whole. I will provide my ideas about how to make that shift later in this chapter.

Today's Disruptive Changes Require a Reexamination of Shared Governance

Disruptive change in higher education has clearly caught the attention of boards, faculty leaders, and presidents. They know that they need to respond, preferably within systems of shared governance, but too few are ready, or have developed strategies, to respond. Board members are typically out front in urging aggressive strategies, as they have experienced similar unsettling changes in their businesses or within other organizations. Faculty members wonder how this will impact them, fearing that disruptive change will impact the values they hold dear. Presidents are deeply concerned but grapple with how to develop the capacities to respond, which is requisite to creating alignment between all constituencies. In most institutions, what is missing is a strong system of governance to address this change in a timely and effective way that holds responsible parties accountable. And what are missing are strong leaders within the board, faculty, and administration to do the hard work of strengthening governance. If institutions sink into the abyss of not adapting to change, it will be due to the failure of leadership and governance.

Though most agree that shared governance is increasingly important, some take a more cautious approach. The America Council of Trustees and Alumni (ACTA, 2014), which tends to adopt a politically conservative and combative approach to higher education, argues that disruptive change requires new strategies, including a closer and more critical look at shared governance (ACTA, 2014). ACTA's publication, *Governance for a New Era*, states, "Shared governance—which demands an inclusive decision-making process—cannot and must not be an excuse for board inaction at a time when America's preeminent role in higher education is threatened" (ACTA, 2014, p. 2). *Governance for a New Era* is too dismissive of the role of faculty and administration, stating, for instance, "faculty is often focused on their disciplines and administrators on the growth and prestige of their institutions" (ACTA, 2014, p. 2). Instead, it relies on boards, suggesting that boards are at the center of protecting student interests. This assertion flies in the face of what nearly every president knows: student growth is at or near the heart of faculty raison d'être.

I agree with ACTA that shared governance should be reevaluated in light of disruptive change. But for the reasons I state in this chapter, to effectively address new realities, the role of faculty in shared governance should be elevated, not diminished as ACTA suggests. The combative approach that ACTA recommends boards take toward the faculty and administration will be far less effective in bringing about effective alignment than the more conciliatory approach of the Association of Governing Boards (AGB). The AGB recognizes that successful and consequential boards embrace effective shared governance (AGB, 2014).

Shared Governance Is Necessary to Empower Boards, Faculties, and Presidents to Accountability Within Their Realms of Influence

Because shared governance is difficult (and sometimes frustrating) work, those championing shared governance must make clear and cogent arguments for the importance of shared governance to recruit and retain active members across all constituencies. In my book on this subject, I've offered five primary reasons for assessing effective shared governance (Bahls, 2014b). Effective shared governance:

- Leads to higher quality decisions.

- Moves institutions' management of yesterday's realities to an entrepreneurial approach to tomorrow's challenges.

- Helps institutions move from each constituency protecting its own turf to developing cooperative plans to move in sustainable directions.

- Helps institutions implement decisions more completely and in a timelier basis.

- Creates shared responsibility for student learning outcomes.

The most compelling reason for shared governance is the first—*shared governance leads to higher quality decisions*. It does so by creating a marketplace of ideas among faculty, board members, and administrators. And the marketplace of ideas is even stronger when students and staff members also share their voices.

United States Supreme Court Justice Oliver Wendell Holmes aptly noted in the 1919 decision of *Abrams v. United States*, "The best test of truth is the power of the thought to get accepted in the competition of the market." Faculty members, board members, and administrators each view higher education from differing vantage points. When shared governance produces open and robust discussion, each brings unique expertise to the debate, shaping the debate and the outcomes in ways that ideally avoid unintended consequences.

In his study of institutions needing to make hard decisions (such as discontinuing academic programs), Peter Eckel, senior fellow and director of leadership programs at the University of Pennsylvania, describes how the marketplace of ideas adds value (Eckel, 2000). These decisions pose a particular challenge to shared governance because, in hopes of strengthening the institution and thereby strengthening remaining programs, faculty members are asked to decide whether to discontinue another faculty member's program.

Eckel found that involving shared governance throughout the decision-making process strengthens the process in several ways (Eckel, 2000). First, when institutions rely on an effective system of shared governance, they gain a forum within which it is possible to present to the campus the urgency of the challenges to higher education, after which it is more likely many will be persuaded regarding the need for a timely strategy to address these challenges. As such, shared governance creates a predictable space for the marketplace of ideas—in contrast to a gathering precipitated by a crisis. Second, he noted, effective shared governance brings the stakeholders together in legitimate ways to discuss high-stakes issues. Shared governance generates a sufficient number of participants to create a market for ideas. And finally, he concludes, shared governance creates a mechanism to prevent errors. Bringing everyone's expertise together minimizes half-baked solutions with unintended consequences.

To be effective, a system of shared governance must already be in place in advance of the needs generated during crises. Shared governance participation can help each group have an effective role:

- Boards can invest their efforts in ways that have the greatest positive consequences.

- Faculty are empowered to provide the best outcomes for their students and the mission of their institution.

- Administrations enjoy the credibility to help align the efforts of boards and faculty to best advance their mission.

Consequential Boards

For effective shared governance, boards must invest their time in what is most consequential: aligning resources and processes for the very best outcomes to advance the institution's mission (AGB, 2014). An indispensable part of doing so is empowering faculty to shape effective faculty governance of academic programs and empowering administrators to build legitimacy by aligning the priorities of faculty, administrations, and boards. Doing so will strengthen the institution, for the benefit of students.

A report released by the National Commission of College and University Board Governance in late 2014 forcefully argued that boards need to refocus their efforts on what is of the most consequence: strengthening their institution (AGB, 2014, p. 11). It observed that many boards insert themselves into roles that are not properly theirs, thereby losing focus on their broader fiduciary duties to the institution.

According to the commission, in order for a board to be most effective, it must reinvigorate faculty in shared governance. The commission asked all boards to review their "institution's policies and practices of shared governance with faculty in order to ensure that such policies are appropriate to the realities of the current workforce, reinforce the delegated authority of faculty for academic policies, and ensure that processes for consultation are clear and are routinely followed by all responsible parties" (AGB, 2014, p. 18).

Empowered Faculty Governance

Faculties that are dysfunctional in their own operation will have a difficult time sharing governance. Effective faculty governance of the academic program includes some centralization, such that trustees wanting to work with faculty can identify those who have a legitimate claim as faculty leaders.

This is not always easily done. In fact, more than a few faculty members are less than satisfied with how institution-wide faculty governing bodies operate. In a national survey by Center for Higher Education Policy Analysis, 53 percent reported "a low level of interest in Senate activities," 43 percent stated that "involvement in the Senate was not highly valued," and 31 percent agreed that the "goals of the Senate were not clearly defined" (Center for Higher Education Policy Analysis, 2003, p. 13).

Faculties that do not have a meaningful level of effective, centralized governance have a difficult time participating in shared governance. If the faculty can't govern itself, it is almost impossible to work collaboratively with the administration and the board. Often when the faculty senate is weak, academic departments are strong. And when the locus of faculty decision-making is at the individual department level, overall institutional academic planning is difficult, particularly when academic departments have differing views on college-wide issues. By definition, some departments are highly resource dependent, which can skew their involvement with institution-wide decision-making.

Accordingly, boards and administrations that work to encourage and foster strong and more centralized systems of faculty governance are more likely to enjoy effective governance. Board members should make it a priority to do all they can to encourage their institutions to foster an effective faculty senate and other organs of faculty and support the faculty leaders who make them effective.

Building Credibility for Administrations

Rollins College president emerita Rita Bornstein (Bornstein, 2003) argues that, to be effective, presidents must earn "legitimacy" among their most important constituencies: faculty, boards, and other administrators. She argues that there are five types of legitimacy: individual, institutional, environmental, technical, and moral. Without legitimacy, presidents are incapable of gaining acceptance of their leadership and risk a failed presidency. Shared governance helps the president earn "technical" or managerial legitimacy by employing decision-making processes that are inclusive and demonstrate trust, thereby building the social capital necessary to be effective (Bornstein, 2003). Likewise, I submit, a president who shares governance demonstrates the humility necessary to earn the respect of his or her colleagues as a moral leader.

Presidents who effectively partner with the shared governance leaders and members on their campus can become more "legitimate" leaders. Jim Collins, in his monograph *Why Business Thinking Is Not the Answer: Good to Great and the Social Sector*, notes that the most advanced level of leadership within the social sector, which, of course, includes higher education, is the ability to get things done within a diffuse power structure (Collins 2005). Institutions of higher education, to be sure, usually have diffuse power structures. A president who succeeds in this environment needs to help faculty centralize decision-making, while still respecting a degree of faculty and departmental authority. Those successfully doing so would count as high-level leaders.

Collins observes a difference between many business organizations and social sector organizations. In business organizations, he argues, executive leadership has concentrated power, which enables the leader to have access to all the necessary information and resources to ensure the right decision and make sure it is carried out. In the social sector, with power being more diffuse, leaders do not have enough structural power to have access to all the necessary information to make the decision themselves, or be in the position to mandate implementation. Instead, to be effective, the leader must rely on persuasion, political capital, and shared interests.

Effective shared governance helps administrators and governance leaders in higher education align priorities into shared interests, helping all to be effective leaders.

Unfortunately, not all presidents are high-level leaders. Trachtenberg, Kauvar, and Bogue have studied over 50 failed presidencies. In many cases, presidents failed to earn the respect of their faculty and board (Trachtenberg, Kauvar, & Bogue, 2013). Because they did not develop a pool of goodwill with important constituencies, those groups were not there to help catch these presidents when they stumbled. Effective shared governance, among other things, demonstrates respect for the opinions of others and, over time, builds a pool of goodwill. All presidents stumble occasionally and can rely on individuals within that pool of goodwill to help them recover, reestablish themselves, and remain effective.

When presidents have legitimacy, in part earned through effective shared governance, they are able to move their institutions from management of territorial disputes to entrepreneurial and accountable approaches to tomorrow's realities.

Four Views of Shared Governance

I agree with Zemsky, Bowen, and Tobin that shared governance needs to be reexamined in light of the changes confronting higher education. But I disagree with Bowen and Tobin when they argue that shared governance is too amorphous to settle questions about the role of faculty (Bowen & Tobin, 2015). If faculties, boards, and administrations can agree that systems of shared governance should (a) be defined to clarify relations of faculty, boards, and administrations in decision-making; (b) encourage faculty, boards, and administrators to work together to align institutional priorities; and (c) hold each other accountable, then shared governance moves from an amorphous concept to a fundamental framework for addressing the challenges ahead.

Trustees and college presidents over the past 30 years seem to have different definitions of shared governance. These definitions could be summarized as follows (Bahls, 2014b):

1. *Shared governance as equal rights to governance*: Shared governance ensures that faculty, staff, and administration have equal say in all governance matters, including budgets, academic directions of the institution, and strategic planning. No decisions are made until full consensus is reached.

2. *Shared governance as consultation*: Shared governance requires nothing more than for the party responsible for making decisions to consult with others. No attempt is required to ensure that consultation continues up to, and including, identification of solutions.

3. *Shared governance as rules of engagement*: Shared governance is a set of rules about the various roles and authority of the board, faculty, and administration in such things as academic decisions, budget decisions, selection of the president, and other decisions. Shared governance also describes rules of engagement when faculty, board members, and administrators disagree. Whether consensus is to be reached is defined within the set of rules.

Note that all these views focus on the territories of constituencies and their right to participate in governance. Because none of the three traditional views sufficiently focuses on accountability, I've proposed a fourth one (Bahls, 2014b):

4. *Shared governance as a system for aligning priorities*: Shared governance is a system where faculty, trustees, and administrators, as integral leaders, actively engage to move past the fragmentation of traditional governance to share responsibility for identifying and pursing an aligned set of sustainable priorities and outcomes, for which each constituency is accountable.

The first three traditional views of shared governance do not adequately address the institution's ability to make the best decisions during this time of disruptive change. Because the fourth definition aligns faculty, administrators, and trustees in a common direction, decisions will tend to be higher quality and more effectively implemented. And because this process of alignment is forward-focused, decisions do not dwell on yesterday's issues. Instead, this process creates shared responsibilities for institutional sustainability and excellence.

Any of the first three definitions, particularly when strictly viewed, do not allow institutions to make the strategic, directional decisions demanded by the disruption in higher education. To be effective in higher education, institutions must plan strategically for changing demographics, new learning styles, and new methods of teaching using technology. For many institutions, the issue is how to maintain mission, yet strategically meet new realities. This chapter will consider in depth each of the traditional definitions of shared governance and demonstrate how traditional definitions stand in the way of making difficult decisions about such things as extending existing programs to new demographics and new markets, as well as developing new programs and using new technologies for traditional markets. Traditional structures also stand in the way of making difficult decisions about program reorientation, retrenchment, or closure.

Perspective One: Shared Governance as Equal Rights to Governance

Shared governance as "equal rights to governance" involves the most literal interpretation of the word "shared" in "shared governance." Essentially, it means "share and share alike." As such, those holding this view believe that all important decisions at a college should be made jointly. This view of shared governance effectively gives the faculty a veto over board decisions and, when taken to its full extent, gives the board a veto over faculty decisions.

Many trustees and administrators believe that faculty members in their institutions hold this view of shared governance. When faculty members do hold this view, most would not want to give boards and presidents equal rights and authority with respect to decisions traditionally within the faculty domain: decisions on hiring, tenure, curriculum, and graduation requirements.

Shared governance as equal rights to governance, while attractive in theory, is problematic in practice. Because it effectively gives the faculty veto power over decisions within the board's primary fiduciary responsibility and gives boards veto power over matters commonly recognized as primarily within faculty responsibility, it is a formula guaranteed to result in indecision and deadlock. For some faculty members, deadlock over decisions central to the college is not all bad—it preserves the decentralization and independence they value. This, of course, is unacceptable for trustees in discharging their fiduciary responsibilities over the affairs of their college or university. Mutual trust (described later, as essential for the successful functioning within an institution) is likely to be undermined within this perspective.

Assume that an institution is facing eroding enrollment such that its continued health is in jeopardy. Most institutions might consider changing the mix of academic programs and invest to reach out to new markets (e.g., more executive programs, nondegree programs). A few faculty members might object to this expansion, fearing (perhaps legitimately) the next step as reallocating resources from their departments. For those institutions whose faculty governance does not approve a proposal unless nearly all faculty consent, proposals for needed change are held hostage to just a few, who might seek costly concessions from the institution for their support.

Viewing shared governance as equal rights, while involving all constituencies, does not lead to higher-quality decisions, because, to achieve agreement, constituencies will be tempted to develop compromise solutions that appeal to the least common denominator. Likewise, shared governance viewed as equal rights to make decisions does not speed the process of making decisions because no constituency can set an aggressive timetable for decision-making. Under this model, decisions are not made when they need to be made, but when the last party agrees. Grumblers can exercise a "grumblers' veto" with the effect of delaying or sidetracking decisions that most agree are needed.

Better views and definitions of shared governance have evolved and should be explored.

Perspective Two: Shared Governance as Consultation

Trustees often view shared governance as merely one step in the decision-making sequence: they agree to an obligation to consult with the faculty before major decisions are made. Trustees and presidents understand that consultation with faculty aids in better decision-making, because faculty are closer to the issues than many board members. Trustees assume that if faculty views are considered and if faculty members sometimes "see their own fingerprints" on decisions, they are more apt to "buy into" the decision and work with the board in implementing them.

While it is a necessary condition of shared governance for boards and administrators to ask faculty members for their input, it is not a sufficient condition. In addition to inviting faculty to express their opinions, boards and administrators must engage faculty in a meaningful dialogue throughout the process, designed to create the full marketplace of ideas necessary to sustain the institution. But boards and administrators too often dismiss the input of faculty as uninformed or even naïve. It does little to sharpen quality decision-making to consult with faculty without providing them with all the meaningful, understandable, and actionable information needed for effective deliberation. Too often, when information is provided to faculty, it is too little (leading faculty to believe it has been sanitized), or too much (so voluminous that faculty feel like they are being asked to drink from a fire hose), or too late (faculty realize that the outcome has already been envisioned, and seeking their input is only a pro forma request). For faculty to share governance effectively, administrators must provide them with sufficient, usable information that help them identify and address issues in a timely and cogent way.

Assuming that faculty members will "buy into" decisions simply because they have been consulted is something most faculty members see as demeaning. It is viewed as "window dressing" that insults their intelligence, and it is dismissive of true shared governance. And when faculty feel their views are not respected, they are likely to withdraw from other, more meaningful, efforts to share governance.

When the institution needs high-quality decision-making in times of disruptive change, shared governance viewed as mere consultation falls short. Mere consultation, when substituted for the hard work of building trust and common understandings, does not lead to sustainable and shared priorities. If faculty members feel the consultation is simply pro forma, they will not have sufficient ownership of the directions determined through the decision-making process. Without faculty ownership, priorities are much more difficult to implement effectively. This view of shared governance encourages faculty to be reactive, not proactive, in creating the meaningful dialogue necessary to make strategic and difficult decisions.

Consider again the institution with precipitously declining enrollment. Boards, often dominated by those whose careers are not in higher education, might mandate a solution after pro forma consultation with faculty. The problem with doing so is that there has not been an engaged and full discussion with the faculty of the proposed solution, a discussion of options, and the opportunity for the faculty to influence the decision in a way they are able to effectively implement. If mere consultation, without collaboration, is the way shared governance is viewed, decisions made by the board are more likely to have unintended consequences, as well as be difficult to implement because of faculty opposition.

Perspective Three: Shared Governance as a Defined Set of Rules of Engagement

Some see inescapable tension between faculty, board, and administrative cultures. In their view, this tension needs to be managed through establishing boundaries, with rules of engagement when boundaries overlap.

There is an inherent tension between state law, which holds boards responsible for all aspects of their institutions, and academic tradition, which yields major responsibility for the academic program to the faculty. Many feel this tension can best be resolved through boundaries and rules of engagement.

Those viewing shared governance as a set of boundaries often cite the Association of Governing Boards' *Statement on Governance of Colleges and Universities* (developed by three organizations, published by AAUP), which was adopted in 1967. Despite its age, it continues to be seen by many faculty members as the most important statement of how faculties, boards, and administrations share governance.

At the heart of the AAUP *Statement* is the acknowledgment that the complexity of higher education means "an inescapable interdependence among governing board, administration, faculty, students and others" (AAUP, 2015). In response to this interdependence, the AAUP calls for "adequate communication" between faculty, staff, and administration. But the AAUP *Statement* calls for the creation of boundaries between the voices of various constituencies.

The AAUP *Statement* also provides for rules of engagement when the constituencies disagree. These rules include who makes the initial decision, how constituencies should communicate with each other, and the standard of review when one constituency approves the decision of the other. For example, on matters of faculty status, including faculty appointments, tenure, and promotion, the AAUP determines that these decisions are in the primary realm of faculty. If the board and president disagree with faculty personnel decisions, the AAUP seeks to narrow the authority of them both: "The governing board and president should, on questions of faculty status, as in other matters where the faculty has primary responsibility, concur with the faculty judgment except in rare instances and for compelling reasons which should be stated in detail" (AAUP, 2015, p. 121).

The recent spate of faculty no-confidence votes in their president (Trachtenberg, Kauvar, & Bogue, 2013), and sometimes in their board, illustrates the limitations of the AAUP's approach of setting boundaries and rules of engagement. Most no-confidence votes are coincident with deterioration, followed by a predictable meltdown, which is almost always accompanied by a failure of governance. Though these votes are often attributed to a perceived lack of communication and transparency from the president's office, as well as a perception of an imperial attitude, a closer examination of many of these votes reveals deeper underlying causes.

Often what underlies these votes is disagreement about who decides what at the institution, accompanied by deep distrust and deep disagreement about important strategies. At institutions with deep disagreement, the AAUP's approach of defining rules of engagement among constituencies has not been sufficient to prevent governance meltdowns. This is because the AAUP's rules do not do enough to create alignment between the board, the faculty, and the president to develop shared responsibility for the direction of the institution.

Rules of engagement are most helpful when constituencies disagree on everyday matters, but are less helpful when an institution needs to address planning and institutional direction. In fact, rigid rules of engagement interfere with the process of open communication, which is often informal and outside the boundaries of rigid notions of governance. Traditional rules that create boundaries do not facilitate consistencies working to create a robust marketplace of ideas, where the best ideas are used to align priorities for the institution's future.

Viewing shared governance in terms of boundaries and rules of engagement can be helpful in determining how day-to-day decisions are made, but it does not serve to align faculty, boards, and administrators toward shared solutions. With its emphasis on boundaries, this perspective tends to perpetuate fragmentation. Though it creates pathways for making important decisions, it does not lead to the necessary give and take between faculty, administration, and board that build high-quality, timely decisions. Boundaries create territories where people tend to focus on the past, and they do not encourage the cross-fertilization necessary for bold and entrepreneurial approaches. Most importantly, boundaries and rules of engagement do not create shared and joint responsibility to move the institution forward.

Consider one more time the institution facing enrollment declines. The president, consistent with AAUP guidelines, might assert his or her role as chief strategist. The president might appoint those sympathetic to his or her views as a "strategic planning task force," an expedient vehicle to develop a plan. Consistent with AAUP guidelines, the board may provide the budget for the plan. And consistent with AAUP guidelines, the faculty could refuse to develop new curricula envisioned by the plan or hire and tenure the type of faculty members necessarily to implement the plan. Each claims their territory, but the result is a stand-off.

Though viewing shared governance as a set of rules of engagement helps identify responsibilities in daily decision-making, it is insufficient to provide the shared vision that colleges and universities need to thrive.

A New Perspective: Shared Governance as a System of Aligning Priorities, Sharing Accountability, and Creating Checks and Balances (The "Systems" View)

The definition of shared governance that I have proposed (Bahls, 2014b) views it as a system where faculty, trustees, and administrators (1) identify and pursue an aligned set of sustainable priorities and outcomes; (2) share accountability, at times individually and at times collectively; and (3) develop a system of checks and balances for addressing more routine, nondirectional decisions.

The first component is a system for *aligning strategic priorities* of the board, the administration, and the faculty by developing common understandings of the challenges the institution faces. Common understandings facilitate alignment. And alignment, when systems are properly structured, moves beyond fragmentation to lead to a shared vision of sustainable strategic directions. Shared governance as a system for aligning priorities can ensure that timely, high-quality decisions are made that can be implemented in a timely and effective way. Most importantly, a strong shared governance system creates the shared responsibility, as a result of mutual trust, which is essential for sustainable solutions to today's challenges.

The second component is *sharing accountability for outcomes*. As explained later, there are two levels of accountability for outcomes. The first level assigns separate types of accountability. Faculty must remain accountable for areas within their traditional responsibilities, particularly academic outcomes. Boards must be accountable for their duty to ensure the financial, human, and other resources of the institution's best advance mission. And administrators must remain accountable for their work, as they make the many tactical and day-to-day decisions for the institution. The second level of accountability develops a sustainable strategic direction for the institution that addresses the disruptive change facing higher education. Faculties, administrations, and boards share this responsibility.

The third component, the *system of checks and balances*, for nondirectional, day-to-day decisions, is often guided by those provisions of the AAUP *Statement* or faculty handbooks addressing such issues as tenure and promotion or budget decisions.

The systems view, which I advocate, sees shared governance as a system for aligning priorities for directional decisions, with checks and balances for nondirectional decisions. There are four important elements to building this system (Bahls, 2014b):

- Build and maintain a culture of transparency and three-way open communication.

- Foster a shared commitment and a higher level of trust to jointly consider difficult issues associated with disruptive change, and then jointly develop strategic directions.

- Develop a shared commitment to forwarding-looking measures of success.

- Implement a system of effective checks and balances to ensure that the institution remains mission-focused.

Hospitals learned long ago that if the goals of the physicians, the board, and the hospital administration can be aligned, they will better be able to achieve the triple goals of quality patient outcomes, affordability, and financial sustainability. In the same vein, institutions of higher education must seek alignment on the triple goals of quality student learning outcomes, affordability, and financial sustainability. Many hospitals strive to be physician-led and professionally managed. The same goal, faculty-led academic programs with professional management and oversight, is a worthy goal in higher education. Hospitals have an easier time achieving physician alignment because they have the financial resources to create economic incentives for alignment. To develop such alignment, institutions of higher education need to develop a commitment to reject divided perspectives and commit to sharing governance effectively. That commitment is best built with transparency, mutual respect, and a joint commitment to best serve students and the mission of the institution.

This approach does not necessarily require that each and every faculty member, administrator, or board member agree to the specific strategic directions. Nor does it require a widespread consensus. But it does require sufficient acceptance, even if a bit grudging, of the strategic direction by the president and a sufficient majority of faculty leaders and board members. Sufficient acceptance is a level of acceptance where a sufficient number of individuals from each constituency will put aside individual interests to implement shared directions. Exactly what percentage of faculty leaders and board members must accept the direction cannot be stated with mathematical precision. The necessary level of agreement will vary from institution to institution, depending in part on the willingness and ability of faculty leaders, board leaders, and the president to move forward in the face of some dissent.

While consensus is not required with shared governance, effective systems of shared governance often yield a level of agreement approaching consensus. Sharing governance encourages exploration of "win-win" decisions. Sharing governance effectively entails a commitment to identify shared goals, shared vision, and shared strategy in a context of trust and transparency. And effective shared governance makes it clear to all the timetables and procedures for decisions to be made, as well as who has ultimate responsibilities for making and implementing decisions. When shared governance is at its best, levels of trust are sufficient for individuals to put their parochial interests behind the collective interest of the institution.

Four Conditions for the Success of Shared Governance as a System of Aligning Priorities and Ensuring Accountability

Shared governance as a system of aligning priorities and ensuring accountability requires four commitments from faculty, administrations, and boards to be successful.

1. *A culture of trust, transparency, and open and respectful communication.* Shared governance cannot be effective without trust. Adrianna Kesar, higher education professor at the University of Southern California (Kesar, 2004), observes that the structures of shared governance are far less predictive of success than whether the relationships between the governing boards, faculties, and administrations are relationships of trust. When parties trust each other, shared governance is much easier to execute and is, in the end, more effective.

Without trust, faculty members will not fully participate in shared governance. Myron Pope, of the University of Central Oklahoma, describes the research concerning the elements of trust necessary for faculty participation (Pope, 2004). Trust is multidimensional, he observes, and includes openness, reliability, benevolence, and competence. Transparency advances all these attributes. Indeed, transparency is the most tangible evidence of openness. Similarly, whether one is reliable is, in part, measured by consistency and openness of communication. Sharing the right information with faculty shows trust and benevolence. And administrators perceived to be transparent are more likely to be regarded as competent.

Unfortunately, trust is far from a given at most colleges and universities. As previously described, faculty members have a variety of reasons for placing a high value on independence and autonomy. This, combined with a perception, often correct, that institutions are becoming more "corporate" means that administrators must earn trust.

Administrators earn trust by extraordinary transparency. Transparency in communication must be "early and often." Critical elements of effective transparency involve eight elements:

- Committing to early communication allowing sufficient time to formulate a response.

- Communicating with digestible amounts of information.

- Refraining from communicating primarily with "chosen faculty members," who are more likely to agree with their opinions.

- Deliberately and regularly communicating with elected faculty leaders and not primarily with those whose terms have expired.

- Listening carefully to the response to the information provided.

- Responding to requests for additional information.

- Clearly communicating about how decisions are made.

- Communicating in a timely way when decisions are made.

One part of transparency often overlooked is communication about the process by which decisions are made. Too often, faculty participate in good faith in discussion of policies or budgets, only to be surprised to learn, at the end of the process, that their role was much more limited than they thought, or were lead to believe. Some institutions help ease this confusion with a shared governance grid (Bahls, 2014b). On one axis of the grid are the types of decisions the institution makes using shared governance (e.g., hiring a president, developing the institutional budget, program closures). Across the other axis are the constituencies of the institution that participate in shared governance (e.g., the board, the president, the faculty, the faculty senate). Within each cell, the institution identifies the role of each constituency (e.g., offers recommendation, is consulted, makes decision, approves decision, and hears appeal of decision). Grids like these should be developed in a transparent way and with the opportunity for faculty to comment.

Effective transparency also includes a commitment to providing digestible amounts of information. Too little information does not enable faculty or boards to effectively and meaningfully participate in decision-making. But the opposite is true. Reams of information that do not identify the heart of the issue can obscure what is most important. To expect faculty and board members, for example, to meaningfully participate in decisions to help formulate budgets by giving them stacks of audits, sheaves of budget reports, and endless budget worksheets is simply naïve. True transparency is not found in the detail of the information provided, but in the usefulness of the information. Useful information identifies the issues, provides information about the alternatives, and enables the user to add value to the discussion of the alternative conclusions that might be drawn from the information. Often it is helpful for administrations to take the same presentations and information that they share with boards and board committees and share them with faculty leadership and faculty committees.

Effective communication provides an opportunity for dialogue. When faculty leaders take their responsibilities seriously, they are likely to ask for additional information. Ideally, a time frame should be agreed upon in advance, so that such requests can be made in a timely way. While requests for additional information might annoy some administrators, these requests should best be viewed as evidence of faculty engagement in the process. High levels of faculty engagement create the marketplace of ideas from which the best plans emerge.

Too often, presidents and boards view "communicating information to faculty" as a box to check before finalizing decisions. Effective communication involves a dialogue, not simply a one-time transmission of information. Effective communication with faculty entails communicating information when issues are first emerging, prior to responses being formulated. Effective transparency means providing information about alternative responses to an issue, and the administration's views of the pros and cons of each. And importantly, effective transparency gives faculty members the opportunity to comment on important preliminary drafts of policy statements.

It is important to understand that transparency and communication are best viewed as three-way, and not simply as adequate communication between administrators and faculty. Presidents are well advised to provide the same information about major issues to the board and to the faculty. Too often, presidents engage in a type of divide-and-conquer approach: provide one set of information to the board and another set to the faculty. The problems with this approach are compounded when the administration assures the board that it is protecting the board from an "ivory tower" faculty, while assuring the faculty that it is protecting them from a "drive-by" corporate board. Sharing the same information with all constituencies builds trust and fosters the marketplace of ideas.

How a decision is communicated can be as important as the decision itself. Too often the final decision is simply announced, without a description of how and why the decision was made. Communicating a complex or unpopular decision requires a high degree of skill from presidents, faculty leaders, and board leaders. Above all, it is important to respect dissent and reinforce that "reasonable minds can differ." In these cases, it is desirable, when possible, to communicate difficult decisions jointly with faculty and board members. Often, however, that is not possible. Board members and faculty members may desire to stay out of the front line of the fray, seeing that it is the administration's responsibility for difficult communication. Part of respecting dissent entails setting the decision clearly, together with the process by which the decision was made and the rationale for the decision. Particularly for decisions where there is not widespread support, it is important to acknowledge the arguments against the decision and explain why those arguments were not persuasive in the end. Doing so acknowledges the input of others and helps those disappointed by the decision to better understand it.

Often the best clarity for complex decisions is made by communicating the decisions in writing, sometimes with written questions and answers that anticipate questions raised. Though many administrators will resist, it is often helpful to follow up with an open forum or community meeting to discuss the issue. Doing so creates opportunities to address misperceptions and to demonstrate that difficult decisions are not made lightly. Those opposing the decision and wanting to "demonize" decision-makers will have a more difficult time doing so when the decision makers are accessible and open to questions.

But faculty also must communicate with their presidents and boards. The AGB encourages boards to "oversee" academic quality—not by micromanaging the academic program, but by understanding an institution's academic program (AGB, 2012). For the board, the point of understanding the academic program is to ensure that the financial resources are adequate to support the program. The AGB charges boards with the responsibility of understanding student learning outcomes and seeking evidence those students are achieving those outcomes. When faculty members and administrators are transparent with boards, boards are more likely to make strategic and budget decisions that best support the academic program.

2. A commitment to jointly consider difficult issues associated with disruptive change and jointly develop strategic directions. I advise my students to ask the "who and why questions" before asking the "what questions." Students should ask who they are and why they are that way before they ask what they want to be. Our institutions of higher education should take the same approach. Ask who they want to be and why, before developing the tactics to get there. Similarly, those participating in shared governance should ask the deeper strategic questions before developing the tactics to implement those decisions. If a system of shared governance foregoes the step of asking who the institution is, as defined by mission, the discussion of what the institution should do will be a rudderless exercise.

The approach of first asking the "who and why questions" is consistent with the advice of Richard Chait in exhorting nonprofit institutions to focus their attention on generative issues (Chait, Ryan, & Taylor, 2005). Chait identifies the core of a board's responsibility as generative thinking. It is, he writes, acting creatively in discerning problems and engaging in "sense making." By the nature of their training, faculty members are particularly adept at engaging in high-level discussion in this way. And trustees, most of whom are appointed to the board because of their ability to engage in "sense making" within their businesses, professions, or communities, are also well positioned to engage in this level of inquiry.

According to Chait and his colleagues, generative thinking considers upstream issues: the issues at the headwaters. Generative thinking in colleges and universities focuses on the more philosophical issues. It focuses on strategic, directional issues, not on tactics. Who are we? Why do we do what we do? How did we get to where we are, and how does that inform where we are going? Where do we want to be in five years? Ten years? An organization can't develop effective strategies to advance mission and move forward in a changing world until these who, why, how, and where questions are asked. In effective organizations, these questions are asked before the "what" questions: What are our tactics? What will the budget look like? What do we do first?

Chait aptly notes that generative thinking involves questions of culture, assumptions, and values. If administrators and board members discuss values and culture with faculty members, they can develop a baseline trust. All groups can then go forward and pursue, together, the difficult, higher-order questions.

In times of transformative change, faculty, boards, and presidents must together look over the horizon. What do we think tomorrow's realities will be? How do we know? How certain are we? Where do we need to be to seize tomorrow's realities? How do we get from where we are to where we need to be? How do we build capacity to do so?

Administrative leaders, faculty leaders and board leaders all need to publicly commit, early and often, to considering these issues as among the most important ones facing their institutions. And these leaders should take extraordinary care to ensure that their individual responsibilities (e.g., for the faculty, tenure and promotion, and, for the administration, annual budgets) do not preclude a meaningful focus on each of the issues identified earlier.

Institutions cannot hope to convince faculty members to invest time in asking these complex questions unless faculty members are actively engaged in their institutions. Sadly, faculty engagement is not very high in most higher education institutions. According to a recent study by Gallup and *Inside Higher Ed*, only 34 percent of faculty members are engaged, as defined by the Gallup Employee Engagement Index (Jaschik & Lederman, 2015). Engagement varies by type of institution, from a low of 29 percent at public baccalaureate institutions to a high of 39 percent at private baccalaureate institutions. One element of employee engagement in the Gallup Index is whether faculty members believe their opinions count. Effective shared governance involves all opinions being heard and considered, increasing the likelihood that faculty members will feel that their views count. Another element of engagement is whether faculty members believe that administrators at their institution care about them as individuals. Involving faculty members in a meaningful way in governance is an excellent way for administrators to demonstrate to faculty members that they care about their views and that they understand the importance of faculty in creating strategic visions for their institutions—and that they care for them as individuals.

While effective shared governance requires a high level of faculty engagement, it also serves to build that engagement. Engaged faculty members are much more likely to jointly consider difficult issues associated with disruptive change and jointly develop strategic directions.

3. A shared set of metrics to measure success, identifying who is responsible for achieving these metrics. Although self-evident, it is worth stating: Institutions that identify where they want to be have a much easier time determining how to get there. One way of creating alignment between faculty, administration, and boards is to discuss core measures of institutional effectiveness. Those participating in shared governance should explore four questions:

1. What are the core measures of institutional effectiveness?

2. What strategies does our institution have to assure that the core measures of institutional effectiveness are achieved?

3. How will our institution assess its progress in achieving core measures?

4. How can the gap be narrowed between current performance and desired performance?

But identifying core performance measures and assessing them is not enough. Institutions should also address who is responsible for achieving them.

When I wrote the book *Shared Governance in Times of Change: A Practical Guide for Universities and Colleges*, I thought about changing the first two words of the title from "Shared Governance" to "Shared Responsibility." The idea came from my conversations with Bob Zemsky when he told me he would banish the term "shared governance" from the lexicon, because it focuses too much on the right to govern instead of the responsibility of governing. By focusing too much on the rights of faculty, boards, and administrators, we reinforce a balkanized view of shared governance at the expense of a more holistic view.

But "shared responsibility" does not quite capture what higher education needs. To imply, by use of the words "shared responsibility," that each holds equal responsibility does not advance the discussion.

Since I wrote the book, I've concluded that a better term than shared responsibility might be "shared accountability." Faculty, boards, and administrations must be accountable in their *individual* spheres of influence and must also be *collectively* accountable.

But though faculty, boards, and presidents are accountable for their primary spheres of influence, they are *together* accountable for their institutions in three ways.

- First, faculty, trustees, and senior administrators should jointly undertake, and be accountable for, asking deeper, probing questions about whether the resources of the institution are best used to advance its mission.

- Second, each is responsible for developing plans to ensure that the resources of the institution, within their control, are best used to advance the institution's mission.

- Finally, all constituencies are responsible for asking whether the institution is a high-functioning organization where the majority of faculty, staff, and administrators are deeply engaged in the success of the institution.

4. A set of effective checks and balances to ensure that the institution remains mission-focused. Though the most important part of effective shared governance aligns the priorities of faculty, boards, and administration to setting a strong course for the institution, the fact remains that a significant part of shared governance is more quotidian and routine: hiring faculty, promotion and tenure, curricula, annual budgets, and such. Often, areas of responsibility overlap. For example, the faculty initially determines tenure and promotion cases, subject to review by the board. Similarly, the president is primarily responsible for strategic planning but must seek the faculty's support for the plan. This overlap provides for the checks and balances to help ensure responsible decision-making. This overlap also aids in maintaining a mission focus of the institution.

The best set of checks and balances is found in the time-tested AAUP. *Statement on Governance of Colleges and Universities.* As discussed, the *Statement* was jointly formulated by the AAUP, AGB, and the American Council on Education. Though the AGB has approached the *Statement* in different ways over the years, the fact remains that each of the three associations has endorsed most of its principles.

Agreeing that the AAUP *Statement on Governance of Colleges and Universities* is the primary vehicle for checks and balances enhances trust, such that the larger issues of institutional direction and outcomes can be effectively addressed. Most faculty members expect the AAUP principles to be honored in spirit, if not in letter. Honoring those principles builds the goodwill necessary to sustain effective shared governance when more challenging decisions must be made.

Alignment of Formal and Informal Governance

The fourth definition of shared governance should serve not only to align board members, faculty leaders, and administrators on a more common vision of the direction of the institution. When done well, it should more closely align the formal and informal systems of governance found in institutions of higher education.

Robert Birnbaum is correct when he observes that there are two types of governance within America's colleges and universities (Birnbaum, 2004). The first type, which he calls "hard governance," can also be called "formal governance." Formal governance is established by law and by the institution's governing documents, as well as academic traditions codified in such places as the AAUP *Statement on Government of Colleges and Universities*. These governance vehicles that formally allocate decision-making authority often have the force of law or the force of a contract.

Birnbaum points out that "soft governance," which can also be called "informal governance," is rooted in organizational culture. Informal governance, in fact, determines what gets done. Faculty highly prize their independence and autonomy and their centrality in soft governance. At the faculty level, members usually teach what they want to teach, and outside mandates are typically viewed as advisory. At the departmental level, curricular changes often don't advance without the support of senior faculty. Sometimes initiatives are not implemented if "grumbling" about the initiative rises to a certain level. In many cultures, there's a degree of "civil disobedience" for policies adopted through formal governance, under the guise of faculty or departmental autonomy or respect for colleagues. In the words of Birnbaum, "soft governance rules" (Birnbaum, 2004, p. 11).

Using an effective shared governance system to align priorities of faculty, administration, and trustees can also help to align formal and informal governance. When faculty members, board members, and trustees can agree on outcomes and metrics for evaluating outcomes, it is more likely that faculty members will not engage in the "civil disobedience" that sometimes stands in the way of effective formal governance.

Richard Morrill, former president of the University of Richmond, is correct when he observes that faculty define themselves as autonomous professionals who have the right, and in the eyes of many, the obligation to work independently. He observes the natural tension between faculty who value autonomy and boards and presidents who value order and dependability (Morrill, 2002). Administrators seek to make order out of chaos, while faculty members see administrative efforts to increase order as efforts to corporatize higher education. Faculty often view change through the lens of loss, while administrators view change through the lens of organizational development. These conflicts, at times, erupt such that all want to walk away from the hard work of shared governance.

It helps—and advances shared governance—to focus on forward-looking outcomes, not backward-looking territorial disputes.

Whatever the definition of shared governance that prevails at an institution, how it is really operationalized and structured varies significantly. There are major differences between how faculty govern themselves on single-campus institutions or within system-wide institutions. Faculties at small institutions may govern as a faculty of the whole. Others may have small faculty councils or larger faculty senates. Likewise, administrative structures vary widely, depending upon whether the institution is public or private. Even within public and private institutions, how boards and faculty are organized varies widely. Simply put, there are many ways colleges and universities divide authority.

Do the specific ways that institutions divide authority have much impact on the effectiveness of shared governance? Professor Gabriel Kaplan of the University of Colorado argues that specific structures allocating authority may not matter that much (Kaplan, 2004). He argues that the "implicit understandings shared by parties in governance animate and give life to the structures of decision making." And he accurately observes that "where faculty, boards, and administrators all shared the same values, institutions are likely to pursue the same policies regardless of who wields the greatest power" (Kaplan, 2004, p. 32).

If Kaplan is correct, as I believe he is, viewing shared governance as a system of aligned priorities can be effective at almost all institutions, notwithstanding specific governance structures. It is the willingness of faculty, administrators, and boards to find common ground that is as important as the details of how authority within an institution is allocated. Indeed, it's considerably more important.

Peter Eckel also concluded that when faculty, boards, and administrations engage in meaningful dialogue about difficult issues (in the case of his study, program terminations), the structure of governance (informal decisions versus more formal passing of recommendations back and forth for approval) is not as important as whether hard decisions can be made effectively (Eckel, 2003). What is important is the quality of the dialogue and the way the effective shared governance could bring about "supportive coalitions." When making difficult decisions, Eckel noted, shared governance facilitates better decision-making because different groups have access to different information. This type of three-way transparency (between faculty, boards, and administrators) provides the information needed to avoid errors through a system of checks and balances.

A Blueprint for Alignment and Accountability: Effective Strategic Planning Processes

The greatest opportunity for building effective shared governance that aligns priorities and ensure accountability is to involve faculty deeply and meaningfully in strategic planning. While most—including the AAUP—agree that the president of the college is its "chief planning officer" (AAUP, 2015), an institutional strategic plan can't be effective without the engagement of the faculty. Using shared governance effectively in strategic planning processes establishes the goodwill necessary to sustain shared governance in more routine, and more controversial, decisions.

When strategic plans are considered by faculty to be "top-down," whether primarily created by the administration or the board of trustees, they are difficult to implement because, without faculty input, they often lack faculty investment and support. On the other hand, plans that are developed primarily by faculty are sometimes seen by boards as "developed by committee," with something for everybody. Boards tend to view these plans as focusing unduly on tactics for maintaining existing silos, instead of strategically advancing the college. Effective shared governance, and involvement of all constituencies in the strategic planning process, avoids both problems.

Strategies for engaging boards, administrations, and faculty in effective strategic planning processes must be intentional and thoughtful. Here are five strategies that will help ensure that a strategic planning process fully engages faculty, staff, administration, and trustees in a way that is likely to create a sense of shared responsibility for making the plans successful (Bahls, 2014b):

1. Properly structure a process that encourages wide involvement of faculty early in the process.

2. Carefully develop ground rules for strategic planning that maximize the probability of creating alignment.

3. Engage in deliberate discussions assessing the institution's competitive position as the landscape of higher education shifts.

4. Intentionally focus the initial discussions on strategies rather than tactics.

5. When developing and implementing tactics, respect the role of traditional vehicles of governance.

1. Structure a process that encourages wide involvement of faculty. Wide involvement of faculty is a critical component of a quality strategic plan, but fostering wide involvement of faculty requires deliberate and careful planning.

Faculty members are not likely to be deeply involved in planning unless they believe that the invitation to help plan is meaningful—more than window dressing. Faculty, like other groups invited into the process, will ask whether their input is likely to help shape the plan. To answer that question, the institution must be clear about whose plan it is. In most cases, strategic plans are formally approved by the board, so in that sense the board owns the plan. But it is equally common for the plan to be developed internally or jointly with trustees, administrators, faculty members, and other stakeholders. Those who participate in developing the plan internally or jointly (and present it for board approval) also own the plan. It is important to state clearly at the outset that the plan, although finally approved by the board, is developed organically by the larger community for the board's consideration. In that way, the plan becomes collectively owned and is not simply the board's or the president's plan. It also is, therefore, likely to outlast departures of individuals central to the plan's development.

The more shared interaction, deliberation, and discussion of strategies and objectives, the more legitimacy the plan will have. The most common way of involving faculty in the planning process is through membership in a planning committee and various subcommittees. But for plans to generate a sense of shared ownership from the larger faculty community, much more faculty involvement is needed. Here are some ways to engage faculty in the strategic planning process:

- Devote a faculty retreat to strategic planning, and, with the permission of faculty leadership, invite board leaders to parts of the faculty retreat.

- Devote a board retreat to strategic planning, inviting a substantial number of faculty to the retreat. Because of the symbolism, institutions should consider inviting an equal number of trustees and faculty members.

- Create strategic planning roundtables, where an equal number of board members, faculty members, administrators, students, and other community stakeholders engage in a focused discussion of strategic issues. These can be held over a meal, perhaps on the day of an on-campus board meeting in lieu of the traditional board dinner.

- With faculty permission, invite the chair of the board to talk about the process with key faculty bodies, including the full faculty, faculty senate, and other faculty policy committees.

- Create opportunities for board members, faculty members, and administrators to visit other colleges where strategic planning has been successful.

- Develop joint faculty and board panels to make a presentation to the board, during regular or special meetings, about strategic and generative issues.

A visible commitment to faculty involvement in the process speaks volumes and is likely to generate a host of good ideas and speed the implementation of the adopted plan.

2. *Develop ground rules for strategic planning that maximize the probability of creating alignment.* For successful strategic planning, faculty, administrators, and boards should take the time to develop clear and realistic ground rules for the strategic planning process at the outset. The process should respect the investment of time each brings to the table.

Time spent together in the shared governance process should be treated as a valuable resource of the college. Trustees, administrators, and faculty members are extremely busy people, so time spent developing the strategic plan is above and beyond their other duties. Institutions with the most effective systems of shared governance resolve to use each constituency's time well.

It is easy to waste time while constructing a strategic plan. A time-wasting strategic planning process is one that focuses unduly on the past rather than the future, on inputs rather than outputs, on tactics rather than strategies, and wants rather than needs. To help focus a strategic planning discussion so it best uses everyone's time, urge everyone involved to consider these parameters:

- Focus on the institution's core strengths and mission. Ask what makes the institution distinctive and what can be done to make it more so.

- Focus on the needs of students, and not on wants and desires that aren't linked to student achievement.

- Focus more on outcomes than inputs.

- Focus on building capacity to meet new realities, not merely on better marketing what the institution has now.

- Ask how to move the institution from autonomous departments toward distinctive departments aligned in a common mission.

- Recognize that resources are scarce, and that scarce resources must be invested in a fairly limited number of creative strategies.

- Create a timetable for the process with specified dates to report progress and a target date for the board to consider and approve the plan.

- Encourage a focus on a workable number of directions (perhaps three to five) upon which to focus the limited resources of the institution.

Strategic plans are most effective when they assess an institution's strategic position, and its readiness to sustain its mission within the changing landscape of higher education. Doing so focuses the discussion away from the wants and needs of various siloed interests to a more data-driven and analysis-driven view of the institution and its challenges. Analysis of the institution's competitive position is advanced by shared discussion, because faculty members, trustees, and administrators tend to view these issues very differently.

3. Intentionally focus the initial discussions on strategies rather than tactics. Strategic planning discussions, within the context of shared governance, are most effective when discussions between board members focus on strategies rather than tactics. A system of shared governance is best at developing strategies. Other governance mechanisms (e.g., the administrative cabinet, the faculty senate, and the board finance committee) are best at developing tactics. Seeking out, and using, a facilitator experienced in strategic planning can maximize the use of time for all.

Strategies ask about major directions that advance the goals of the institution. Strategies identify, within the context of *who* we are, *what* we are trying to accomplish. Competitive strategies are strategies that make the institution distinctive. Tactics are *how* the institution will achieve its strategic directions. So, for example, a strategy might be achieving excellent job placement rates and graduate school placement rates. Tactics to achieve that strategy might include better advising and making more internships available to students. Another strategy might be to remain affordable to mid-income students. Tactics to achieve those strategies might include increasing the endowment and reducing costs.

Participants in the strategic planning process typically jump into a discussion of tactics before strategies. Trustees, for instance, might consider doubling the endowment as critical to the strategic plan. Administrators might consider better funding of various administrative functions as the most important part of the plan. Faculty might consider better morale and better student to faculty ratio to be central to the plan. But that is putting the cart before the horse. Better morale to what end? Bigger endowment to what end? Each of these tactics may be important, but these are not strategic issues. Better morale, for example, may be critical to building an entrepreneurial, engaged faculty to better use new teaching modalities for better student learning outcomes. So the strategic issue, from which that tactic might flow, would be "better student learning outcomes."

Too much emphasis on tactics at the expense of strategies will lead to a disjointed, uninspired strategic plan. Tactics, without strategies, focus on fixing past problems (e.g., poor morale, inadequate program funding), not seizing future opportunities. They also tend to focus on inputs (e.g., improve entering credentials of students), not on learning outcomes.

Too much time spent developing tactics during the strategic planning process also threatens to tread on other governance mechanisms that are working well, such as the faculty senate, the president's cabinet, and the board's finance committee. Precious strategic planning time together is better spent on strategic issues that will benefit from board, faculty, and staff alignment. Then tactics, which are developed later, will be easier to delegate, identify, and implement.

This is not to say that board members, administrators, and faculty should not share the effort of developing tactics. New strategies will never be well implemented if they are not supported by workable and realistic tactics. But the discussion of tactics can only happen after strategies have been developed.

4. *When developing and implementing tactics, respect the role of traditional vehicles of governance.* Making the most of shared governance to develop strategic directions paves the way for developing tactics. After strategic directions are developed, each constituency should be asked to develop tactics to implement certain strategies. Faculty will have a more central role in developing tactics for implementing academic strategies. Administrators will have the central role in developing and organizing the resources to support the plan. The role of a strategic planning committee is to evaluate these tactics, prioritize, and coordinate them.

Suppose that through the shared strategic planning process an institution decides that a strategic direction is to increase the percentage of graduates getting jobs requiring a college degree within six months of graduation. Once this strategy is chosen, the institution's regular systems should be able to develop and implement tactics. The faculty senate might decide that more certificate programs within majors would support the strategic direction. The administration might decide that strengthening and reorganizing a career services office is a critical tactic. And the board might determine that one thrust of the next fundraising campaign will be to support or endow student internships.

Implementation of tactics is usually best left to existing vehicles of governance to implement (e.g., the faculty senate, the president's cabinet, and various board committees). The faculty, through its normal channels, is responsible for the final vetting, approval, and implementation of academic tactics. The board finance committee is responsible for creating and allocating budgets. And the president's office is responsible for refining an administrative structure to support the initiatives.

Conclusion

One question that might linger in the minds of readers is whether it's realistic to think that trustees, faculty, and staff would be willing to agree on the new, fourth definition of shared governance as a system for aligning priorities, ensuring accountability, and establishing systems of checks and balances. My experience from conducting workshops at institutions that range from seminaries to medical schools, from small liberal arts colleges to large community colleges and multi-institution public institutions is this: most (if not all) constituencies will agree that a new definition of shared governance is necessary and will coalesce around the fourth definition of shared governance as aligning priorities.

Board members increasingly recognize that faculty participation is indispensable to moving their institutions forward, particularly in times of disruptive change. Many faculty members recognize that it is in their interests to have more meaningful participation in aligning priorities through strategic planning, and that priorities cannot be aligned in silos. Faculty members who support the new fourth definition often condition their support on meaningful checks and balances through honoring established academic traditions codified by the AAUP *Statement on Governance of College and Universities*. Presidents and other senior administrators are usually eager to advocate for the new fourth definition, because they are charged with leading strategic planning for their colleges. The fourth definition creates a way for all to align priorities. Likewise, senior administrators often feel primarily responsible for institutional outcomes. Usually these administrators are eager to help faculty leadership assume joint accountability for outcomes.

With a common understanding of what shared governance means, a college or university has a way to move beyond the territoriality and rivalries of the past. Instead, its members can develop the engagement and trust to work together and move toward being the kind of unified, mission-driven institution needed to thrive in these times. Universities and colleges that achieve this common understanding will be able to move beyond traditional territory and constituency-based views of shared governance, which tend to protect the status quo, to systems of shared accountability necessary to keep institutions of higher education sustainable.

Note

1. This chapter builds on my previous publications about shared governance cited in the references. The chapter develops more fully the case for sharing governance in times of disruptive change, refines my description of the four most common views of shared governance, and advances four conditions for the success of shared governance as a system of aligning priorities and ensuring accountability. It proposes a new "blueprint for alignment and accountability," through effective strategic planning processes.

References

American Association of University Professors (AAUP). (2015). *Statement on governance of colleges and universities* (1967). In *Policy documents and reports*, 11th ed. (pp. 117–122). Washington, DC: American Association of University Professors.

American Council of Trustees and Alumni (ACTA). (2014). *Governance for a new era*. Washington, DC: American Council of Trustees and Alumni.

Association of Governing Boards (AGB). (2014), *Consequential boards, adding value where it matters most: Report of the National Commission on College and University Board Governance*. Washington, DC: Association of Governing Boards.

Association of Governing Boards. (2011). *Board responsibility for the oversight of education quality*. Washington, DC: Association of Governing Boards.

Bahls, S.C. (2010, January 10). Administrators must dispel the derogatory myths about faculty. *The Chronicle of Higher Education*. Retrieved from https://chronicle.com

Bahls, S.C. (2011, November 15). Faculty myths about trustees. *Inside Higher Ed*. Retrieved from https://www.insidehighered.com

Bahls, S.C. (2014a). How to make shared governance work: Some best practices. *Trusteeship*, 22(2), 27–31.

Bahls, S.C. (2014b). *Shared governance in times of change: A practical guide for universities and colleges*. Washington, DC: AGB Press.

Bataille, G., Asfew, A., & Jackson, B.A. (2013). *Presidents: Caught in the middle*. Washington, DC: American Council on Education.

Birnbaum, R. (2004). The end of shared governance: Looking ahead or looking back. In W.G. Tierney & V.M. Lechuga (Eds.), *Restructuring shared governance in higher education* (pp. 5–34). San Francisco: Jossey-Bass.

Bornstein, R. (2003). *Legitimacy in the academic presidency: From entrance to exit*. Westport, CT: Praeger.

Bowen, W.G., & Tobin, E.M. (2015). *Locus of authority: The evolution of faculty roles in the governance of higher education*. Princeton, NJ: Princeton University Press.

Center for Higher Education Policy Analysis. (2003). *Challenges for governance: A national report*. Los Angeles: Author.

Chait, R.P., Ryan, W.P., & Taylor, B.E. (2005). *Governance as leadership: Reframing the work of nonprofit boards*. Hoboken, NJ: John Wiley and Sons.

Christensen, C.M., Horn, M.B., Caldera, L., & Soares, L. (2011). *Disrupting college: How disruptive innovation can deliver quality and affordability to postsecondary education*. Washington, DC: Center for American Progress.

Christensen, C.M., & Eyring, H.J. (2011). *The innovative university: Changing the DNA of higher education from the inside out*. San Francisco, CA: Jossey-Bass.

Collins, J. (2005). *Why business thinking is not the answer: Good to great and the social sectors*. Boulder, CO: Jim Collins.

Eckel, P.D. (2000). The role of shared governance in institutional hard decisions: Enabler or antagonist? *The Review of Higher Education* 24, 15–39.

Eckel, P.D. (2003). *Changing course: Making the hard decisions to eliminate academic programs*. Lanham, MD: Rowman & Littlefield.

Gaff, G.G. (2009). Academic freedom, peer review, and shared governance in the face of new realities. In H.W. Hamilton & J.G. Gaff (Eds.), *The future of the professoriate: Academic freedom, peer review and shared governance* (pp. 19–39). Washington, DC: Association of American Colleges and Universities.

Jaschik, S., and Lederman, D. (2015). *The 2015 Inside Higher Ed survey of college and university faculty workplace engagement: A study by Gallup© and Insider Higher Ed*. Washington, DC: Inside Higher Ed.

Kaplan, G.E. (2004). Do governance structures matter? In W.G. Tierney & V.M. Lechuga (Eds.), *Restructuring shared governance in higher education* (pp. 23–34). San Francisco: Jossey-Bass.

Kesar, A. (2004). What is more important to effective governance: Relationships, trust, and leadership, or structures and formal process? In W.G. Tierney & V.M. Lechuga (Eds.), *Restructuring shared governance in higher education* (pp. 35–46). San Francisco: Jossey-Bass, 2004.

Morrill, R.L. (2002). *Strategic leadership in academic affairs: Clarify the board's responsibilities.* Washington, DC: Association of Governing Boards.

Pope, M.L. (2004). A conceptual framework of faculty trust and participation in governance. In W.G. Tierney & V.M. Lechuga (Eds.), *Restructuring shared governance in higher education* (pp. 75–84). San Francisco: Jossey-Bass, 2004.

Schmidt, B.C. (2014). *Governance for a new era: A blueprint for higher education trustees.* Washington, DC: American Council of Trustees and Alumni.

Trachtenberg, S.J., Kauvar, G.B., & Bogue, E.G. (2103). *Presidencies derailed: Why university leaders fail and how to prevent it.* Baltimore, MD: Johns Hopkins University Press.

Zemsky, R. (2013). *Checklist for change: Making American higher education a sustainable enterprise.* New Brunswick, NJ: Rutgers University Press.

6

Better Budgeting Is Good Governance

Applying a Best Practices Framework to Public Universities' Budgetary Processes

Chelsea Reome and Thomas A.P. Sinclair

State and local governments as institutions have, for some time, been expected to adhere to a set of budgeting best practices as a way to remain transparent and accountable to the public. Organizations such as the National Advisory Council on State and Local Budgeting (NACSLB) and Government Finance Officers Association (GFOA) have long-established best practice guidelines of this kind. However, state university systems, complex government entities themselves, are not subjected to the same set of budgeting expectations as state and local governments.

While both the academic literature and municipal best budgeting practices recommend wide stakeholder involvement, shared goals, clear expectations of purpose and timeline, and measurable goals and objectives, these practices are infrequently reflected in public university budgeting practice. After comparing 67 public universities' budget processes to municipal best budgeting practices, we found most of the colleges and universities sampled within state university systems lacked transparency and best practice principles. There was a deficit of information regarding the budget process and stakeholder involvement, as well as minimal budget transparency made publicly available on the universities' websites. This held true for public universities both within and across systems. We also found that, regardless of structural or institutional arrangement, there was wide variation in budgeting practices between and within state university systems. State university systems are centralized government entities, no more complex than state and local governments. Therefore, a transition to utilizing the same budgeting best practices proscribed to the rest of the public sector should be considered.

Budgeting, the allocation and distribution of financial resources, is a core administrative function of any organization. For public institutions in particular, transparency and accountability in this process are of utmost importance. To highlight the importance, and encourage consideration, of these two principles, the National Advisory Council on State and Local Budgeting (NACSLB) created a set of best practices for budget processes for use by state and local governments. That framework was endorsed by the Government Finance Officers Association (GFOA), which uses the same principles to present the Distinguished Budget Presentation Awards Program for municipal governments. Since state universities and state university systems are public institutions, the extent to which they maintain transparency and accountability in creating and disseminating their budgets is important to their stakeholders. The purpose of this study is to evaluate the extent to which public universities' budget systems and processes are transparent, and how well they adhere to the best practices.

The first section of this chapter discusses the importance of a transparent budgeting process for governmental entities. We will discuss how stakeholders within a university (especially faculty and students through their mechanisms of shared governance) can contribute to budgetary decision-making. Following this examination of context is a review of the current budgeting practices of a sample of 67 state universities across the United States. These practices are then compared to budgeting best practices for governmental entities. The chapter concludes with a discussion of how universities can strengthen their budgeting practices.

Importance of Transparency in Budgeting for Government Entities

Public budgeting scholars and practitioners have long recognized that budgetary review and decision-making processes that are open to public scrutiny and debate are valuable tools in effective and accountable democratic government. Nearly 20 years ago, the National Advisory Council on State and Local Budgeting (NACSLB) was convened to provide guidance for implementing budgetary practices that supported these core values. The council's product, *Recommended Budget Best Practices: A Framework for Improved State and Local Government Budgeting* (1998), was groundbreaking in that it created a comprehensive and consolidated set of guidelines for effective budgeting. According to the NACSLB, a budget should not simply provide a reader with an allocation plan for an organization's resources. Instead, "The budget process consists of activities that encompass the development, implementation, and evaluation of a plan for the provision of services and capital assets" (NACSLB, 1998, p. 3). Given this definition, an annual budget should be a powerful tool that incorporates long-range planning, accounts for changes in finances over a period of years, and provides a detailed record of how governmental resources are being utilized (NACSLB, 1998).

Among local and state governments, publication of annual all-funds budgets detailing their revenues and expenses has become a common practice. Often, governmental executives accompany the budget with a report highlighting changes reflected in the budget since the previous year(s), or new program initiatives being funded in the upcoming year, as a way of communicating with taxpayers. Budgets are used to convey trends in both revenues and expenditures. They can illustrate what costs drive expenditure increases, as well as how economic conditions or mandated program requirements impact an organization's finances. Budget documents are important tools to dispel public misconceptions about the relative costs of programs. They can highlight organizational accomplishments and challenges. In short, the regular, systematic release of financial information is a critical feature of all levels of democratic government.

Although public colleges and universities are not governments of general jurisdiction, there are at least two reasons to advocate for the transparency of their budget practices. First, state universities, as public institutions, are often among the largest employers in their communities, play active roles in economic development, and engage influential stakeholders. Since they are supported by both tax revenues and tuition paid by state residents, one could argue that universities have an obligation to report how they use those resources and to explain their priorities to citizens. Second, one could more positively argue that budgetary transparency can help colleges and universities garner support for their activities and allows members of the public to make their own evaluations about the efficiency and efficacy of university programs and services. Thus, transparency can make all kinds of public institutions more accountable and better, including colleges and universities.

Budgetary Documents

An all-funds *operating budget* provides "a summary of major revenues and expenditures, as well as other financing sources and uses, to provide an overview of the total resources budgeted by the organization" (GFOA, n.d., p. 5). The release of a published operating budget is a good first step in evaluating transparency because of the basic insight it provides into an organization's spending priorities and revenue sources. Usually reported as line-item budgets, operating budgets can provide a detailed picture of an organization's planned expenditures, or they can be aggregated by type of expense (such as salaries and equipment) or department. Operating budgets give stakeholders information about an organization's inputs, but not outputs or outcomes of that spending.

In contrast to an operating budget, a *performance budget* focuses on results, rather than where money is spent. Performance budgets provide rationales for budget allocations and set measurable objectives for budget allocations to projects, programs, and departments (National Conference of State Legislatures, 2015). As public higher education increasingly adopts performance measures via accrediting organizations or trustee requirements, it would seem to be a logical objective to connect them to financial resources. Theoretically, such a focus could redirect resources to high-priority, or high-impact, activities and alter how a university functions.

Performance measurement and performance budgeting are not without their challenges, though. For many organizations, performance budgeting is difficult to implement, because it is challenging to agree upon (and measure) desired outcomes. What's more, performance measurement could also promote competition and debate over scarce resources between stakeholders. For this process to remain fair, transparency and stakeholder engagement are key. When designing and implementing any kind of performance measurement system, representatives from units that are directly and indirectly affected by performance measurement should be at the table for every stage, from conception to review.

One crucial aspect of budgeting best practices for NACSLB and GFOA is *creating short- and long-term goals with objectives for measurable progress toward realizing them*. While strategic planning, per se, is often independently initiated and/or carried out separate from budgetary processes, linking strategic plans to funding priorities ensures that resources are allocated and used in accordance with university goals (NACSLB, 1998; GFOA, n.d.). A strategic plan without accompanying financial resources is a weak attempt at addressing organizational priorities and challenges.

NACSLB explains that documenting a budget timeline, and indicating where budgetary stakeholders fit into it, are crucial steps in the budget process; these clear guidelines allow all stakeholders to plan and participate (NACSLB, 1998). The GFOA's criteria for the Distinguished Budget Presentation Awards Program calls for the following:

- An explanation of where various stakeholders fit into the budget process.

- A timeline of responsibility for production and amendment of the budget.

- A description of the activities, goals, and objectives of individual units. (GFOA, n.d.)

For stakeholders, the ability to influence budgetary decision-making begins with understanding where they have a legitimate opportunity to contribute to budgetary discussions and decisions. Within university systems, the budget process should clearly delineate the roles for shared governance structures, thereby defining the level of involvement and oversight allocated to each group. Such clarification of roles should indicate who is involved at each stage—budget formulation, implementation, and evaluation.

Budgetary Stakeholders

The NACSLB recommends that all potential stakeholders be involved in the budget process; this includes "elected officials, governmental administrators, employees and their representatives, citizen groups, and business leaders" (NACSLB, 1998, p. 2). Including all institutional stakeholders will create a budget that better represents the combined interests, goals and needs of the institution. If this is not done by seeking deliberate input, issues of concern to some stakeholders may be overlooked.

Within University

Within the university, transparency and stakeholder involvement in the budget creation process allows for shared interests held by administrators, faculty, and staff to come to light in ways that they cannot when budgeting remains a function held solely by administrators. Transparency in process, and a process of participative stakeholder involvement, promotes the possibility that these interests may become shared goals (Harris,

2007). Because faculty and staff know their departments' administrative, academic, and research needs so intimately, their input may be seen as especially valuable to the budget process (Jarzabkowski, 2002). Their expertise makes them valuable stakeholders.

Furthermore, purposefully valuing faculty and staff expertise in the budgetary decision-making process can yield higher levels of trust in the institution among participating individuals (Simmons, 2012). Therefore, the expertise and trust that incorporating stakeholders provides to the budget process can create a more accurate assessment of departmental needs, a stronger vision of university priorities, and greater intra-university cohesion. In the absence of broad stakeholder involvement, budgetary decisions made by administration may seem arbitrary or baseless. Including more stakeholders in the process does not eliminate tensions that resource allocation causes; there are always winners and losers, but transparency about how those decisions are made contributes to everyone's understanding about how and why decisions were made. For example, if an increased share of budgetary resources is shifted to units with growing enrollments, those with flat or declining enrollments know why cuts might be made and perhaps what they might do to gain more resources down the road.

Faculty participants in shared governance can make several significant contributions to the evolution of budgeting best practices both on campuses and at the system level. Of particular significance, they can advocate for budgeting practices adopted by university administrators and policymakers that conform to established governmental norms rather than tradition and history on their campuses. Established governance procedures provide faculty with access and voice in university decision-making, which is vitally important. However, with access and voice comes a concomitant responsibility to be knowledgeable advocates. The faculty objective should not be limited to protecting its prerogatives, but to ensuring that financial decisions that have an impact on public educational institutions are thoroughly vetted, deliberately enacted, and carefully evaluated.

Students are the principal beneficiaries of higher education services, and their input should be considered valid and valuable in all decision-making processes, including resource allocation and budgeting. Student involvement in budgetary decision-making matters can take several forms. Students might have their own committee that weighs in on the university-wide budget process, which reports to a faculty or administrative committee. Students might also have seats on faculty or administrative budget committees. Regardless of the arrangement, the biggest consideration for student oversight is the education required for them to make meaningful contributions to conversations and decisions on budgetary matters. Such education for student participants would need to be frequent to accommodate student turnover, but it could take any number of forms—a faculty advisor, for example. The level of involvement that students specifically should contribute is unspecified in the literature. However, because student tuition and fees provide a substantial portion of any college or university's revenue base, their participation is vital on equity grounds alone. Their participation also ensures that their multiple interests and needs are duly considered in a budget process.

Opaque budgetary processes that are exclusionary often serve the interests of stakeholders who are "in-the-know," especially administrative staff with budgetary functions. As stakeholders, administrators often occupy privileged positions to strongly influence, if not control, budgetary outcomes. The risk is that other stakeholders (e.g., faculty) are seen as "interest groups" when they are invited to the table. Typically, non-administrators are only granted a few seats on the university's budgetary committee (Facione, 2002, p. 45). Facione goes on to say that the treatment of faculty committee members as interest groups, advocating solely for their department's needs, can halt collaboration and fuel distrust between faculty and administrators (Facione, 2002). Nonetheless, primary responsibility for using financial resources to implement policy and carry out the functions of a university resides with university administrators. Facione argues that a budget process that is open, and truly values all members' contributions, will be more likely to advance strategic, institution-wide goals for using those financial resources (Facione, 2002).

State university systems are governed by system-wide elected or appointed boards. Such governing bodies make policies that apply to the system and its constituent campuses. A state-level mandate on budgetary policy, such as one requiring meaningful involvement of shared governance structures in evidence-based resource allocation decisions, will drive system-wide budgetary reform on individual campuses. As policy decisions often impose significant financial costs, governing boards should evaluate the financial implications of their decisions as an important factor in their deliberations. Consequently, governing boards should be consulted during the budget process (Chabotar, 1995).

To conclude this discussion of internal stakeholders, budgeting has long been recognized as an area of internal operations where joint governance among policymakers, boards, administrative leaders, and faculty is appropriate (AAUP, 1966). We argue here that—with the inclusion of students—these stakeholder groups perform essential functions that support effective and accountable financial planning and decision-making by universities. But while budget processes that engage internal stakeholders in decision-making are arguably preferable to those managed only by administrative personnel, they still lack transparency and accountability to other important stakeholders. Those who are external to the university, whose support is vital to the continued fiscal health of a university, must be brought into the process.

Outside University

In many places, state university campuses have budgets that are larger than the municipal governments within which they are located. They are often among the largest employers, and increasingly expected to actively support economic growth and community development. Because they are such important (and tax-exempt) entities, community stakeholders (such as local government officials, community leaders, and residents) have legitimate interests in what campuses are doing, and how they are managing their resources. In many cases, community members are employed by the university and benefit from outreach programs from the university. When students live in neighborhoods, community members can be both landlords and neighbors. And if the university builds residence halls within neighborhoods, it is responsible for becoming a good neighbor.

The feedback that community members and the press provide in speaking out about or reporting on university activities is known as *latent oversight* (Lane, 2007). By virtue of their public status, state university systems receive oversight from the state government and receive funds generated by taxes. The oversight maintained by state officials and agencies is called *manifest oversight*. It is more direct and includes meetings with state and federal legislators and executive branch officials, wherein various levels of oversight take place (e.g., reporting requirements, accreditation, etc.). For stakeholders at each of these input levels to be up-to-date with regard to the institution, they must be regularly informed about university policies and procedures, including the budget.

Variation can exist in both type and ease of access (i.e., the level of transparency given) to information available to stakeholders outside of a university. When these stakeholders lack reliable budgetary information, it is difficult for them to provide meaningful contributions, feedback, or oversight. It should be understood that some stakeholders outside the university receive more information about the inner workings of university expenditures than do others. Shakespeare (2008), in studying the stakeholder alignment in New York State's policy decisions surrounding the Tuition Assistance Program (TAP), found that the informational access granted to different groups varies by virtue of their status. Multiple public and political stakeholders (including the governor and his cabinet, legislature, and public interest groups) were stridently advocating either for or against the program. Shakespeare reports that groups of the same type (e.g., public interest groups working on the same issue) generally accessed the same sources of information, and the same content. However, groups with qualitatively different functions (e.g., state legislators vs. public interest groups) accessed information from different sources, with those sources privileging some stakeholders and intentionally withholding information from others (Shakespeare, 2008). This speaks to the overall transparency and access to information that some organizations have over others, in the realm of state university politics. It is indeed difficult for communities and the press to exercise latent oversight over public institutions of any kind, if the information they have access to is limited. In turn, members of the public are better able to inform political officials of their concerns when they themselves are informed. When there is a lack of transparency, the accountability that this manifest-latent oversight "cycle" provides fails to function properly. Without the opportunity for the public to critique the policy that directly affects them, public institutions lose their ability to effectively serve the public.

Gaps in Literature

Several gaps exist in the literature on university budgeting research. These gaps are primarily in the areas of *best practice* and the *implications of transparency and accountability for performance*. The importance of the presence of faculty, staff, and student stakeholders at the table, when budgets are discussed, is well established; the benefits of their inclusion are also well documented (Simmons, 2012). However, this chapter presents a point that has not appeared in the literature, examining whether, and how, the best practices developed for public institutions can be applied to universities.

There is little evidence that public universities uniformly address concerns of maintaining transparency and accountability via budgetary process and reporting. Absence of best practices in this area has led to use of an eclectic variety of models to allocate university funds, with little consistency across institutions (Jarzabkowski, 2002). None of the models used propose a clear recommendation of best practice. Models of best fit can be considered models of allocation that adhere to a university's needs and culture as opposed to those that adhere to uniform best practices. Some research suggests that models of best fit for budget allocation are most appropriate for universities, as each institution has its own goals and priorities (Jarzabkowski, 2002). It is also suggested that, especially for state universities, unpredictable political and economic forces state-wide can unexpectedly influence decisions at the system- and university-wide levels, placing schools in the dangerous positions of receiving their resources "at the whim" of state allocations and mandates (McLendon, Deaton, & Hearn, 2007).

Little research exists that describes the best way to release information regarding university budget systems and processes to the public. Due to state university systems' status as public institutions, this is a crucial function of public universities, but it often remains unmet. Also absent from the literature are recommendations about the level of detail that should be included in budgets that are available to the public. Discussion of budget dissemination to the public inevitably turns to questions of how much detail is appropriate, and whether there are legitimate proprietary restrictions on some budgetary details. In the absence of best practice, different institutions have addressed these issues in their own ways, leading to a great deal of variance between them in terms of publicly reported content. Some argue that, due to the fundamental difference between universities and other public institutions, a certain degree of nontransparency to some stakeholders is permissible (Jarzabkowski, 2002).

A final gap in the current literature is the absence of information about how performance measurement links up with budgeting issues in higher education. The present discussion comes at a time of increased emphasis on performance measurement in higher education, and heightened emphasis on performance budgeting in municipal budgeting (National Conference of State Legislatures, 2015). For public university systems, the administrative system (and the actions it takes) should support the academic mission of the system as a whole, as well as its individual institutions; any process of transparency needs to continue to support that core mission. Using performance measurement to maintain transparency, and, ultimately, uphold institutional and system-wide accountability, can be further studied and improved.

Arguments against Uniform Best Practices

In contrast to adopting the same set of standards, those also used by state and local government, to guide and assess the budget process, there are arguments in favor of other decision-making models for universities. Jarzabkowski argues that *resource allocations models* should be applied based on best fit, instead of the *best practice* approach presented here. She contends that the budget process and reporting should be tailored to university goals. She gives the example of the London School of Economics and Political Science, whose professors are granted a good deal of autonomy in conducting their research. The allocation model used at the London School of Economics and Political Science places a good deal of responsibility on the faculty and their departments to create the institution's budget. Alternatively, Warwick University's allocation model showed a high degree of administrative oversight and relatively little faculty involvement; the university's centralization was longstanding (Jarzabkowski, 2002). Notably, Jarzabkowski's study sampled British universities, all of which were state funded, in some capacity. Of course, private universities are a different beast than state-funded universities. But the argument that universities are unique institutions, with needs so unique as to entirely differentiate themselves from that of other public institutions, remains for some. However, this perception does not absolve state universities, as public entities, from engaging in accountable practices that uphold the values associated with governmental institutions.

Institutional needs may not be the only reason for public universities to not reform their budgeting processes. McLendon, Deaton, and Hearn caution that, while transparency is necessary, education reform leading to changes in performance budgeting may not work for all states at all times. The degree to which a university can (or chooses to be) transparent is contingent on the political, social, and economic landscape of the state government (McLendon, Deaton, & Hearn, 2007). As public institutions, state universities are not divorced from the reality of state politics and economic distress, when such circumstances arise. Earlier, McLendon (2003) explained that the process of higher education reform does not follow a step-by-step, predetermined process, with an exact route. Rather, educators and politicians often fall into the "perfect storm" for reform; when the right people come along at the right time, change is successfully implemented. He cautioned that uniform, mandated change, such as that proscribed by an inflexible set of guidelines or rules, does not always work

(McLendon, 2003). Therefore, dictating a new set of criteria to be used by *all* public universities at the time of budget reform ignores the situational circumstance of the schools and the state, and the leadership of both.

Conversely, though, a set of best practices could halt some of the politically opportunistic use of public universities by state politicians. Instead of being driven by circumstances, best practices would insulate state universities from inappropriate meddling or unwanted changes encouraged by outside forces, because of the checks provided in maintaining transparency. In this way, reform across the board to incorporate best practice for public universities' budgetary processes and reporting provides more accountability.

The National Association of College and University Budget Officers (NACUBO) is an organization for budget staff at colleges and universities. NACUBO's *College & University Budgeting: An Introduction for Faculty and Academic Administrators*, published in conjunction with the American Association of University Professors (AAUP) in 1984, was written to serve as "a handbook for faculty members elected to budget committees and in other ways involved in the budget process" (Meisinger & Dubeck, 1984, p. vii). While the aim of the authors of this book was first to be a guide for faculty, and second a guide for academic administrators, it does not advocate strongly for the inclusion of shared governance in the decision-making process. Instead, NACUBO assumes that faculty committees will *review* decisions, rather than *contribute* to the decision-making process. Furthermore, the authors call for openness within universities so long as such openness is congruent with institutional culture and the expectations of university departments, which would allow schools that employ exclusively administrative involvement in budget preparation to avoid a more transparent process. There is heavy emphasis on navigating the budget review process by the university system and the state, with expertise housed among staff and not shared among, or with, faculty (Meisinger & Dubeck, 1984). Ultimately, this is more similar to Jarzabkowski's proposition of a "model of best fit" than a proposition to incorporate shared governance as an accepted best practice into the budgetary decision-making process. Further, despite its focus on college and university budgets, NACUBO as an organization offers no clearly defined budget best practices in its literature or on its publicly accessible website (www.nacubo.org).

Conversely, some could argue that budgetary transparency under such political and economic environments increase universities' vulnerability to political interference. It is not hard to imagine advocates targeting particular unpopular line items for reduction or elimination. But, in truth, such debates occur anyway. Opponents operating in an environment where information is scarce are free to advance their positions unrebutted.

Research Question and Design

State universities have significant status as public institutions; however, current literature indicates that there is a dearth of established best practices for higher education budgeting processes. This is problematic because, in the absence of such practices, budgeting processes can become susceptible to a lack of transparency and accountability. As public institutions, state universities, in particular, should strive for all of their processes and actions to be transparent and accountable, particularly those concerning resource allocation. The research question guiding this study is: *To what extent do universities employ budgeting best practices for public institutions and communicate with and engage important internal and external stakeholders?*

The following section is a content review of state university websites. The NACSLB guidelines served as the basis for a set of criteria used to evaluate how well each university engaged in budgeting best practices, based on their websites' content. The content surveyed was only that which is publicly available. The amount of publicly available information regarding the budgeting process on a university's website indicates its level of transparency in disseminating budgetary practices. Information obtained via intranet connections or interviews with faculty and staff are not publicly available, and therefore were not obtained for this study.

Methods

School Selection

For the purposes of this study, we define a state university system as one that has a network of campuses that function as independent institutions rather than satellites of a single large institution, that are all united under a shared system name, that share funding between institutions based on state appropriations, and are jointly governed by one policy-making board. In reality, universities and university systems employ a broad range of governance structures. Our sample included eight state university systems that meet this definition, two other university systems with alternate structures (Commonwealth System of Higher Education and University of Michigan), and three other public universities (Eastern Michigan University, Michigan State University, and Western Michigan University).

The study sampled 67 public universities in total. Of those 67 universities, 57 belong to a formal state university system with some degree of centralized oversight of member campuses; the member campuses possessed varying degrees of autonomy. The remaining 10 are different in governance structure. The four schools associated with the Commonwealth System of Higher Education in Pennsylvania (Lincoln University, Penn State University, Temple University, and University of Pittsburgh) are public-private hybrid institutions. Each university is granted a high degree of autonomy and is controlled by a different, school-specific governing body.

The remaining six schools in the sample hail from Michigan. The University of Michigan encompasses three campuses: Ann Arbor, Dearborn, and Flint. Ann Arbor is the flagship campus, while Dearborn and Flint are satellite campuses of the same institution. In this way, it is not a traditional system but rather a satellite system. Eastern Michigan University, Michigan State University, and Western Michigan University are all public universities in the state of Michigan, but they are each controlled by a different, school-specific governing body. The role of governing boards in Michigan public higher education is unique and worth discussion here. Michigan's Constitution grants public universities constitutional autonomy, meaning that (1) each school has its own governing board, and (2) each school works directly with the state legislature to determine state appropriations (Ferris State University & Public Sector Consultants, Inc., 2003). Michigan, therefore, stands in contrast to the rest of the universities in the sample (and most across the United States), where a centralized authority with its own governing board creates policies that are handed down to individual campuses.

The systems in this sample were selected based on geographical region. Foremost, this was an attempt to capture differences in university governance centralization/decentralization that may be present, since there are differences in state politics and governance centralization/decentralization from state to state. Additionally, the foundations of higher education vary across states, leading to variance in the overall landscape of higher education in a given state. For example, beginning in the colonial era, the historical legacy of formation of Massachusetts universities has led to a different structure and a denser landscape of higher education as public mingle with private institutions. This pattern is different than in western states, with generally newer public and private institutions. Many public universities in western states, though not all, were established early on in statehood through land grants (Tandberg & Anderson, 2012).

The schools within the systems of this sample were selected in a way that would maximize variation among schools within a given system. Three to four campuses were selected per institution. If a flagship campus existed, it was included in the sample; otherwise, the largest school (determined by operating budget or enrollment) was chosen; typically, the flagship campus was the largest constituent school. Schools within the system that were the smallest (or close to the smallest, as determined by operating budget or enrollment) were also chosen. The exception to these rules is the SUNY system. The SUNY system's population in this study contains all 34 of its four-year campuses. The increased representation of the SUNY system in this sample allows for an explanation of variance seen both across systems and within them. By looking at such a large number of campuses within the same system, it is possible to look at the variance that occurs between campuses within a system that adheres to one overarching regulatory system. The observable trends that occur when drilling down *within* a system are just as valuable to understanding shared governance in the budgeting process as when we look *between* systems.

Criteria Selection

The selected criteria are meant to evaluate how well state university systems utilize best practices in creating and disseminating their budgets. They are based on the guidelines set forth by NACSLB and GFOA. The criteria selected were originally proposed to create a best practices framework for state and local government budgeting processes (NACSLB, 1998; GFOA, n.d.). Although the subjects of the present study are state universities rather than municipalities, these criteria were chosen because of the standard of accountability and transparency to which they hold public institutions. Because public universities receive allocations from the state, which are garnered from taxes, and because they exist to serve the public, it would be prudent for these institutions to use the same budgeting guidelines to which state and local government entities adhere.

Six criteria, one with two components, emerged through examining NACSLB guidelines as critical to budgeting for state university systems as public institutions. Broadly, the criteria evaluated transparency of information regarding stakeholder involvement and short- and long-range planning as it relates to the annual budgeting process. For the purposes of this study, the level of transparency displayed by universities was determined by how many of the eight criteria were available to the public on the school's web page.

Operating budget. The first criterion for determining budget transparency was the answer to a yes/no question: Is an operating budget available on the school's website? This criterion was considered "present" based on three factors: (1) there was an operating budget on the website; (2) the budget was in the form of a line-item budget or a performance budget; and (3) that the public budget document was recent (2011 or later).

Budget process. Whether the budget process was outlined was the second criterion used in this study. To determine if the process was outlined, two conditions had to be present: (1) a budget timeline was shown, and (2) clearly delineated stakeholder involvement in the budget process was described. If only one of the two conditions were present and the other was missing, the budget process was not considered outlined. A qualifying budget timeline was characterized by the following: clearly specified major start, end, and due dates for the budget process; and specification of institutional requirements for completion of the budget from actors such as the state, university system, campus, academic department, among others. Stakeholder identification and involvement can be defined as a clear indication as to when and where various stakeholders fit into the budget formulation process, and a description of their role in the decision-making process.

Faculty role. Because of the importance imparted to stakeholder involvement under NACSLB recommendations for the budget process and recommendations seen in higher education literature, the role of two non-administrative stakeholders were examined at length in this research. To determine whether there was a faculty role, evidence of faculty involvement on an institution-wide committee addressing budgetary decisions was required. That committee could be formed by the faculty senate or similar governing body of faculty, or it could be appointed by administration or another institutional body of the campus.

Student role. Students are important stakeholders in the budget process. Students were considered to have a role in the budget process if evidence of student involvement on an institution-wide committee addressing budgetary decisions was present. Committee membership could be in the form of a reserved student seat or seats on a faculty senate or similar governing body of faculty, a reserved student seat on a committee appointed by administration or another institutional body, or a student-only group appointed by administration or another student body.

Strategic plan. In this research, a strategic plan was considered "present" if (1) the strategic plan document was found on the website; (2) that the plan be current (i.e., that it includes the 2014–2015 school year); and (3) that it have specific objectives, goals, and/or strategies that define how the university will achieve the vision laid out in the plan. For universities, it is important for this information to be made public so that the institution is accountable to those it serves, or those who contribute to its funds via taxes.

Performance budget. The last criterion is a good indicator in transparency in higher education budgeting: a *performance budget.* Such a budget document indicates that the institution in question has a set of specific goals and the means to achieve them, allocating a specific dollar amount to accomplish them. Furthermore, this kind of budget should include both inputs (the resources dedicated to accomplishing a goal) and outputs (what is being done with those resources); when possible, desired outcomes (the impact) should also be stated (GFOA, n.d.). These criteria connect performance measures to the financial resources needed to achieve them.

Procedure

After the institutions were selected and conceptual criteria developed, researchers searched through the website of each university and coded the presence or absence of each criterion. Both members of the research team reviewed coding decisions to ensure inter-coder reliability.

Results

In the entire sample, there were 67 schools (appendix 6.1). Thirty-three (49.3%) presented an operating budget online. Eleven (16.4%) laid out their budget processes, with 16 (23.9%) including a budget timeline and 14 (20.9%) identifying budget process stakeholders. Speaking further on stakeholders (table 6.1) in the total sample of 67 schools, 56 (83.6%) described a faculty role and 27 (40.3%) described a student role in the budget process. Forty-four (65.7%) schools had strategic plans posted on their websites. Altogether, three schools in the sample had performance budgets publicly available online (4.5%) (table 6.1). These figures provide a snapshot of how state university systems across the country conform to best budgeting practices, but there is more to be seen by looking deeper within systems.

There were 34 SUNY schools in this sample. Seven (20.6%) of these schools had an operating budget publicly available on the school website.

Table 6.1. Number of Schools in Systems Meeting Criteria

University System	Number of Schools Surveyed	Operating Budget on Website	Budget Process Outlined		Faculty Role	Student Role	Strategic Plan	Performance Based
			Budget Timeline	*Stakeholders Identified*				
CSHE(PA)	4	3	2	3	3	1	3	0
CUNY	4	1	1	1	4	3	4	0
TAMU	3	3	2	0	3	1	3	0
UC	4	3	2	2	4	2	1	1
CSU	3	3	1	2	3	3	2	0
SUSF	3	3	0	0	3	1	3	0
U of M	3	3	0	0	3	2	1	0
n/a Michigan*	3	3	1	1	3	1	2	0
UNC	3	1	1	1	3	1	1	0
UTenn	3	3	1	1	3	1	1	0
SUNY	34	7	5	3	24	11	23	2
Total	67	33	16	14	56	27	44	3

*n/a Michigan refers to the 3 Michigan public universities in this sample that are unaffiliated with a university system

Each individual university was surveyed for its best-practice compliance, as recommended by NACSLB and GFOA. The data were then compiled for each state university system to measure the system's compliance, as represented by the population of its schools within our sample. Reome & Sinclair, 2015.

Three (8.8%) schools were found to have their budget processes outlined, with five (14.7%) identifying a budget timeline and three (8.8%) providing a description of stakeholder involvement. A faculty role was defined by 24 (70.6%) of the campuses and a student role was defined by 13 (38.2%). Twenty-three (67.6%) of these universities had a current strategic plan available online, and finally, two (5.9%) SUNY schools had a performance budget on their websites.

Looking at the SUNY schools on their own provides an example of variation *within* a system, but comparing SUNY schools to non-SUNY schools allows for a view of variation *between* systems. Of the 33 non-SUNY schools in our sample, 26 (78.8%) made an operating budget publicly available on their website. Eight (24.2%) outlined their budget processes (with 11 [33.3%] providing a budget timeline and 11 [33.3%] identifying stakeholders involved in the budget process). Thirty-two (97%) described a faculty role and 14 (42.4%) described a student role in budget decision-making processes. Twenty-one (63.6%) schools had a current strategic plan that was accessible from the website. Finally, one (3.0%) school out of 33 in the non-SUNY sample had a performance budget online (figure 6.1).

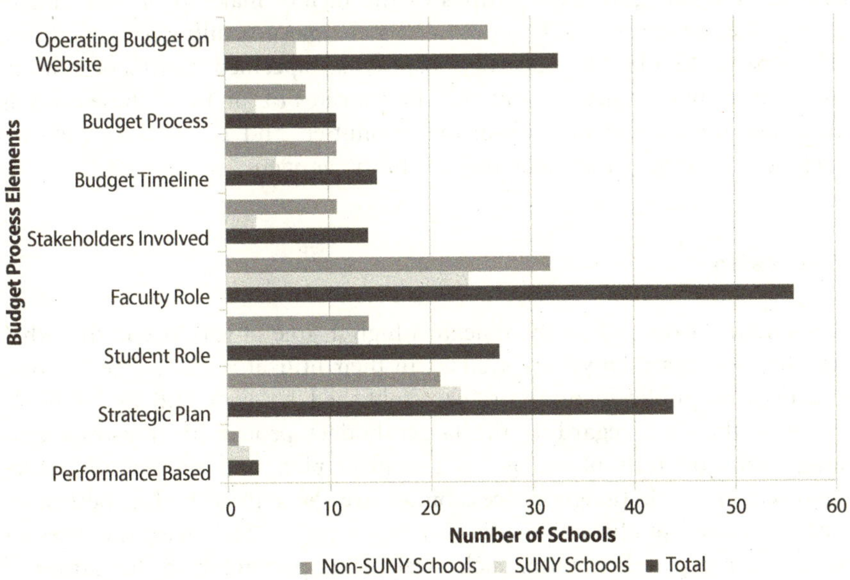

The total universities in the sample that met the budget best practice criteria, drawn from NACSLB and GFOA literature. This depiction represents the total number of universities in the sample, as well as the SUNY population and non-SUNY population data separately. Reome & Sinclair, 2015.

Figure 6.1. Budget Process Information on School Website

Nonadministrative stakeholder involvement, being crucial in shared governance budgeting arrangements, was further examined. The committees offering faculty and student involvement in the budget process were studied via a content analysis of data available on university websites for all universities in the sample (appendix 6.2). All but one (97%) of the non-SUNY schools specified a faculty role on a budget committee on the institutional websites, and 30 (90.9%) provided a description of the faculty makeup of budget committee membership. Thirty-one (93.9%) offered a charge of faculty responsibilities for that committee. Fourteen (42.4%) non-SUNY schools indicated on the website that designated student involvement on budget committees exists on a budget committee at their institutions. Five (35.7%) of these were independent from the faculty budget committee and were student-only or student appointments to other budgetary committees. All 14 (42.4%) of these schools described the student makeup of committee membership, and 13 (39.4%) described the charge of student responsibilities for that committee.

Twenty-four (70.6%) SUNY schools indicated, via statements on the institutional websites, that there were faculty roles on a budget committee, and 22 (64.7%) gave explanations of the faculty makeup of that budget committee. Nineteen (55.9%) provided a charge of faculty responsibilities. There were 13 (38.2%) school websites that specified a student role on an institutional budget committee. The websites of all 13 of these schools described the student makeup of the committee, and 12 (34.3%) websites included a charge of student responsibility, as well.

Discussion

The findings from this study indicate a high degree of variance both within and between state university systems in their utilization of budgetary best practices as public institutions, as established by NACSLB and GFOA. Broadly, the data regarding the larger budget process demonstrate that long- and short-term planning (via a strategic plan) and mention of faculty involvement in the budget process online are elements of budget best practice that most public universities already employ. However, less present were other expected criteria, such as elements pertaining to the nature of the faculty and other stakeholder roles, and linking funding descriptions to performance measures. The principle of shared governance with faculty is widely practiced, at least in the presence of institutional structures that provide faculty with formal input in budgetary decision-making. However, without detailed descriptions of committee charges, it is less clear whether faculty actually have input and offer advice in decision-making, or if their role is more limited (e.g., to receiving budgetary information after decisions had been made).

Most universities in the sample specified a faculty role in the budget process and had a current strategic plan on their websites. However, closer examination reveals that while SUNY campuses and non-SUNY schools published current strategic plans at almost the same rate, SUNY campuses indicated the presence of faculty stakeholder involvement at three-quarters the rate of non-SUNY schools. Non-SUNY schools also offered operating budgets online more consistently than did SUNY campuses; the number of SUNY schools with an operating budget was approximately half that of non-SUNY schools. When looking at the entire sample, public information about student stakeholder involvement is clearly absent across the board.

The budget process was not clearly outlined for the sample as a whole. While non-SUNY schools did outline the budget process more than SUNY campuses, only a sixth (16.4%) of the total sample described how their budget process was conducted on their campuses. In many cases, a university produced a timeline without specified stakeholder involvement, or vice versa. Both elements are crucial, as NACSLB points out, because they give all stakeholders an idea of what they should be doing, and when (NACSLB, 1998).

Finally, despite an increased interest in metrics and performance measurement in higher education, performance budgeting is not widely practiced in this study's sample. Within the SUNY system, Potsdam (http://www.potsdam.edu/offices/businessaffairs/reports.cfm) and Fredonia (http://www.fredonia.edu/admin/budget/) are good examples of performance budgets, as they describe university activities across departments and schools, provide specific dollar amounts for goals and/or projects, explain departmental and school-wide goals and achievements to date, and demonstrate effectiveness of current programs (National Conference of State Legislatures, 2015). Some notable GFOA and NACSLB recommendations found in the budget document for each of these two schools are (1) descriptions of the population being served, (2) explanations of the impact of changes in funding, and (3) discussion of where stakeholder committees fit into the budgetary decision-making process. The budget published by UC Riverside (http://rpb.ucr.edu/budgetvista.html) utilizes elements of a performance budget that differs from the two SUNY schools. It also incorporates many principles from NACSLB and GFOA. For example, it (1) includes an overview of budgetary trends, including increases and decreases in funding; (2) long and short term goals; (3) revenue streams; (4) budget calendar; and (5) an overview of stakeholders. However, it does not mention measurable goals with specific dollar amounts tied to them, excluding the important element of performance measurement from the document.

Importance of Budgeting Best Practices for Public Universities

Because this study was focused on transparency as it relates to *publicly available* information, whether universities actually embody any of our criteria *without* putting it on their websites is unknown and irrelevant. It is possible that the university systems in the sample meet all our criteria but that they are not published online, or are only available to campus members, via an intranet. If either is the case, a change to having that information that details the budget process available publicly, online for anyone in the world to access, would be an easy way to increase transparency.

It is also possible that these universities do not utilize these practices internally. In that case, adopting NACSLB and GFOA guidelines in first creating and then disseminating budget processes and reports would exemplify transparent budgetary practices, as well. Transparent budget practices like those developed for state and local governments by NACSLB and GFOA are important for public universities to employ, because transparency itself helps to develop accountability. By openly discussing the budget process, goals, and allocations, universities essentially provide an open invitation to the public to review institutional activity. This generates accountability, in that it contributes to an open system wherein the public can clearly see how the proposals made by universities measure up to their actions, and how they serve the public's interests. On a related note, universities that demonstrate effective, transparent stewardship of their public resources might be more attractive to private donors who want to ensure that their gifts are well managed.

Shared governance structures offer opportunity for transparent and accountable budgeting practices in several ways. Faculty governance can ensure greater advocacy on behalf of interests that are widely represented within the university. By virtue of their interactions with students, faculty can speak with passion and clarity regarding departmental and student needs. With a larger body of contributors comes an increased opportunity to critique established procedures that may interfere with meeting changing needs and circumstances. Allowing university actions to mirror institutional needs will make for more meaningful and attainable strategic goals. Strategic goal-setting in both the short and long term demonstrate to the public what the university's priorities are. A budget isn't simply a line-item document listing expenditures and revenues. As Simmons explains, "the budget should be thought of as a plan and . . . this plan should be based on the strategic goals/direction of the university" (Simmons, 2012, p. 6).

While the current research was limited to 67 universities, affiliated with 10 university systems in eight states, the findings are limited. They can best be seen as presenting a snapshot of the wide variation of budgetary practices among public universities and colleges. Some states have multiple public university systems, each with a different approach to budgetary decision-making. Even within systems, institutional autonomy granted to individual campuses would predictably generate considerable diversity in budgetary practices. Comparing systems from within the same state against each other could provide insight into whether discrepancies in the state university systems' budgetary processes and reporting are due to state differences, or institutional differences. Each state's governance, policy, and practices could very well influence state-affiliated universities' methods of budgeting and reporting.

Conclusion and Future Research Questions

The present study provides a useful picture of the variation that exists both between and within public university systems in regard to current budget practices. While there is no established set of best practices for budgeting in higher education, there is an established set of best practices for public institutions that, when applied to public universities, functions quite well in maintaining the accountability that state schools should strive for. Although they vary in location and size, almost all the universities sampled have taken some first steps in implementing processes similar to those described by NACSLB. Some, such as SUNY Fredonia, SUNY Potsdam, and UC Riverside are further along than others in that process. This paints an optimistic picture about the future of transparency and budgetary reform on college campuses. In most cases, there will be a precedent for implementing good practices, which can lead to further refinements and improvements in budgeting practices over time.

However, one should be mindful that budgeting best practices are purely administrative functions. That is, they simply improve actions around the budget process and reporting and hopefully provide a platform for long-range planning. They have no causal link to academic outcomes for students, or overall university performance in terms of ratings and rankings. The hope is that transparent and accountable budgeting practices will produce focused, long- and short-term strategic goals that will positively influence the academics and services accessible to students and thus enhance institutional reputation. Moreover, the degree to which these best practices provide better information to stakeholders and help improve the quality of their engagement in decision-making is uncertain. Research on the link between transparent, participatory budgeting processes and internal stakeholder trust in an institution suggests that when faculty and staff are invited to participate, they feel more trust toward the academic institution (Simmons, 2012). The same conclusion as it applies to the public has not been established. Further research that explores whether members of the public and local community leaders gain trust in institutions and confidence in their stewardship of public resources that are more transparent in their budgeting practices would be warranted.

References

Chabotar, K.J. (1995). Managing participative budgeting in higher education. *Change, 27*(5), 20–29.

American Association of University Professors. (1966). *Statement on government of colleges and universities.* Retrieved from https://www.aaup.org/report/statement-government-colleges-and-universities

Facione, P.A. (2002). The philosophy and psychology of effective institutional budgeting. *Academe, 6*(88), 45–48.

Ferris State University & Public Sector Consultants, Inc. (2003). *Michigan's higher education system: A guide for state policymakers.* Retrieved from http://www.pcsum.org/Portals/0/docs/fsu_heguide2.pdf

Government Finance Officers Association (GFOA) (n.d.). Awards criteria (and explanation of the criteria). Distinguished Budget Presentation Awards Program.

Harris, M.S. (2007). From policy design to campus: Implementation of a tuition decentralization policy. *Education Policy Analysis Archives, 15*(16), 1–18.

Jarzabkowski, P. (2002). Centralised or decentralised? Strategic implications of resource allocation models. *Higher Education Quarterly, 56*(1), 5–32.

Lane, J.E. (2007). The spider web of oversight: An analysis of external oversight of higher education. *Journal of Higher Education, 78*(6), 615–644.

McLendon, M.K. (2003). Setting the governmental agenda for state decentralization of higher education. *Journal of Higher Education, 74*(5), 479–515.

McLendon, M.K., Deaton, R., & Hearn, J.C. (2007). The enactment of reforms in state governance of higher education: Testing the political instability hypothesis. *Journal of Higher Education, 78*(6), 645–675.

Meisinger, R.J., & Dubeck, L.W. (1984). *College & university budgeting: An introduction for faculty and academic administrators.* Washington, DC: National Association of College and University Business Officers.

National Advisory Council on State and Local Budgeting (NACSLB). (1998). *Recommended budget best practices: A framework for improved state and local government budgeting.* Chicago: Government Finance Officers Association.

National Conference of State Legislatures. (2015). *Performance-based budgeting: Fact sheet.* Retrieved from http://www.ncsl.org/research/fiscal-policy/performance-based-budgeting-fact-sheet.aspx

Shakespeare, C. (2008). Uncovering information's role in the state higher education policy-making process. *Educational Policy, 22*(6), 875–899.

Simmons, C.V. (2012). Budgeting and organizational trust in Canadian universities. *Journal of Academic Administration in Higher Education, 8*(1), 1–12.

Tandberg, D.A., & Anderson, C.K. (2012). Where politics is a blood sport: Restructuring state higher education governance in Massachusetts. *Educational Policy, 26*(4), 564–591.

Appendix 6.1
Criteria met by Individual Campuses

University	Operating Budget on Website	Budget Process Outlined		Faculty Role	Student Role	Strategic Plan	Performance Based
		Budget Timeline	*Stakeholders Identified*				
CSHE							
Lincoln University						X	
Penn State	X		X	X		X	
Temple University	X	X	X	X		X	
University of Pittsburgh	X	X	X	X	X		
CUNY							
Baruch College				X	X	X	
Bronx Community College				X	X	X	
Hunter College				X	X	X	
Queensborough Community College	X	X	X	X		X	
TAMU							
Texas A&M University	X			X		X	
Texas A&M University–Commerce	X	X		X		X	
Texas A&M University–Corpus Christi	X	X		X	X	X	
UC							
UC Berkeley	X	X	X	X	X		
UC Davis	X			X			
UCLA				X	X		
UC Riverside	X	X	X	X		X	X

CSU							
CSU Fullerton	X	X	X	X	X	X	
Humboldt State University	X		X	X	X		
San Diego State University	X			X	X	X	
SUSF							
Florida State University	X			X		X	
University of Central Florida	X			X		X	
University of Florida	X			X	X	X	
U of M							
University of Michigan–Ann Arbor	X			X	X		
University of Michigan–Dearborn	X			X	X		
University of Michigan–Flint	X			X		X	
n/a Michigan							
Eastern Michigan University	X			X		X	
Michigan State University	X	X	X	X			
Western Michigan University	X			X	X	X	
UNC							
UNC Chapel Hill	X			X			
UNC Charlotte				X	X		
Winston-Salem State University		X	X	X		X	
UTenn							
University of Tennessee–Chattanooga	X		X	X	X	X	

continued on next page

Appendix 6.1 *(Continued)*

University	Operating Budget on Website	Budget Process Outlined		Faculty Role	Student Role	Strategic Plan	Performance Based
		Budget Timeline	*Stakeholders Identified*				
University of Tennessee–Knoxville	X			X			
University of Tennessee–Martin	X	X		X			
SUNY							
University at Albany				X	X	X	
Alfred State						X	
Binghamton University				X	X	X	
Brockport				X	X	X	
Buffalo State College				X			
University at Buffalo	X			X		X	
Canton	X					X	
Cobleskill		X		X			
College of Agricultural & Life Sciences (Cornell University)						X	
College of Human Ecology (Cornell University)							
College of Industrial and Labor Relations (Cornell University)							
College of Veterinary Medicine (Cornell University)						X	

Cortland						X	
Delhi				X		X	
Empire State College				X	X		
Farmingdale				X			
Fredonia State College	X			X		X	X
Geneseo	X			X	X		
Morrisville State College							
New Paltz	X	X	X	X		X	
New York State College of Ceramics (Alfred State)							
Old Westbury		X	X	X	X	X	
Oneonta				X		X	
Oswego						X	
Plattsburgh				X	X	X	
Potsdam	X	X		X	X		X
Purchase		X	X	X		X	
Stony Brook	X			X	X	X	
SUNY College of Environmental Science and Forestry				X		X	
SUNY College of Optometry				X	X	X	
SUNY Downstate Medical Center				X			
SUNY Maritime				X	X	X	
SUNY Polytechnic Institute				X		X	
Upstate Medical University				X		X	

Appendix 6.2
Faculty and Student Committee Information Breakout

Non-SUNY Schools						
Campus	Faculty Committee	Student Committee	Faculty Committee Membership	Student Committee Membership	Faculty Committee Charge	Student Committee Charge
California State University–Fullerton	Planning Resource & Budget Committee	Same	11 faculty, 8 administrators	2 students	Yes	Same
California State University–Humboldt	University Resources & Planning Committee	Same	4 faculty, 7 staff, 1 provost, 1 dean, 3 VPs	2 students	Yes	Same
California State University–San Diego	Academic Resources & Planning Committee	Same	9 faculty, 1 staff	2 students	Yes	Same
Commonwealth System of Higher Education–Lincoln University	n/a	n/a	n/a	n/a	n/a	n/a
Commonwealth System of Higher Education–Penn State	Budget Subcommittee–General Education Planning and Oversight Task Force	n/a	6 faculty members, 1 staff member, 2 administrators	n/a	Yes	n/a

Commonwealth System of Higher Education–Pittsburgh	Senate Council Budget Policies Committee	Same	14 faculty, 2 staff, 2 administrators	3 students	Yes	Same
Commonwealth System of Higher Education–Temple University	Budget Review Committee	n/a	9 faculty	n/a	Yes	n/a
CUNY–Baruch College	Faculty Senate Committee on Planning & Finance	n/a	5+ faculty, senate vice chair, VP academic affairs, VP administration (last 2–ex officio)	n/a	Yes	n/a
CUNY–Bronx Community College	College Personnel & Budget Committee	n/a	5 members from each department, additional 1 member for each member above 40, president & VPs (ex officio)	n/a	Yes	n/a
CUNY–Hunter College	Committee on the Budget	Same	9 faculty, provost, VP administration	4 students	Yes	Same
CUNY–Queensborough Community College	Personnel & Budget Committee	n/a	For each of the 17 departments on campus: 5 members plus chair of department	n/a	Yes	n/a

continued on next page

Appendix 6.2 *(Continued)*

Non-SUNY Schools						
Campus	Faculty Committee	Student Committee	Faculty Committee Membership	Student Committee Membership	Faculty Committee Charge	Student Committee Charge
Texas A&M University System–Texas A&M University	Budget Information Committee	n/a	10 faculty	n/a	Yes	n/a
Texas A&M University System–Commerce	Budget Committee	n/a	Only 2 faculty listed for 2013–2014 school year	n/a	n/a	n/a
Texas A&M University System–Corpus Christi	Budget Analysis Committee	Student Government, University Strategic Planning & Budget Council, Student Fee Advisory Committee, Chancellor's Student Advisory Board of the Texas A&M University System	At least 3 faculty members	No cap on student involvement set on website	Yes	http://academic affairs.tamucc. edu/Rules_ Procedures/ PDF/13.99.99. C1%20 Students%20 Role%20and %20Participa tion%20in% 20Institutional. pdf

State University System of Florida–Florida State University	University Budget Advisory Committee	n/a	4 appointed faculty, 2 faculty senate officers, president, 7 VPs, budget director	n/a	Yes	n/a
State University System of Florida–University of Central Florida	Budget & Administrative Procedures Committee	n/a	15 faculty, 2 administrators	n/a	Yes	n/a
State University System of Florida–University of Florida	Faculty Senate Budget Council	Same	6 faculty, 4 staff	1 student	Yes	Same
University of California–Berkeley	Budget & Interdepartmental Relations	Committee on Student Fees and Budget Review	12 faculty, 1 nonvoting faculty member, 1 senate analyst	10 to 15	Yes	http://csf.berkeley.edu/csfconstitution.asp
University of California–Davis	Planning & Budget Committee	n/a	13 faculty, 2 advisors, 2 academic federation representatives	n/a	Yes	n/a
University of California–Los Angeles	Council on Planning & Budget	Same	17 faculty, vice chancellor academic planning & budget (ex officio)	4 students (2 undergraduate, 2 graduate)	Yes	Same

continued on next page

Appendix 6.2 *(Continued)*

Non-SUNY Schools						
Campus	Faculty Committee	Student Committee	Faculty Committee Membership	Student Committee Membership	Faculty Committee Charge	Student Committee Charge
University of California–Riverside	Committee on Planning & Budget	n/a	11 faculty	n/a	Yes	n/a
University of Michigan–Ann Arbor	Provost's Advisory Committee on Budgetary Affairs	Student Budget Advisory Committee	9 faculty	No cap on student involvement set on website	Yes	http://www.provost.umich.edu/Student%20Budget%20Advisory%20Committee_background%20information.pdf
University of Michigan–Dearborn	University Budget Committee	Same	6 faculty, 3 staff, provost, VC business affairs	3 students	Yes	Same
University of Michigan–Flint	Chancellor's Advisory Committee for Budget & Strategic Planning	n/a	7 faculty, 1 librarian, chancellor, provost, vice chair administration	n/a	Yes	n/a
University of North Carolina–Chapel Hill	University Priorities & Budget Committee	n/a	Not specified	n/a	Yes	n/a

University of North Carolina–Charlotte	Faculty Academic Planning and Budget Committee	UNCC Budget Council	Past, current, and president-elect, 2 faculty, 1 senior faculty	President and VP of Student Government sit on council	Yes	None
University of North Carolina–Winston–Salem University	Budget Committee	n/a	3 faculty, additional administrators	n/a	Yes	n/a
University of Tennessee–Chattanooga	Budget & Economic Status Committee	University Planning and Resource Advisory Council	Up to 9 faculty, provost (ex officio)	President of the Student Government Association	Yes	http://www.utc.edu/business-financial-affairs/pdfs/2013-2014/budget-instructions-fy-13-14.pdf
University of Tennessee–Knoxville	Budget & Planning Committee	n/a	At least 10 faculty, campus CFO (ex officio)	n/a	Yes	n/a
University of Tennessee–Martin	Budget & Economic Concerns Committee	n/a	Not specified	n/a	Yes	n/a
Michigan State University	University Committee on Faculty Affairs	n/a	17 faculty, 1 librarian, provost, 2 advisors to provost, 2 staff	n/a	Yes	n/a

continued on next page

Appendix 6.2 *(Continued)*

Non-SUNY Schools

Campus	Faculty Committee	Student Committee	Faculty Committee Membership	Student Committee Membership	Faculty Committee Charge	Student Committee Charge
Eastern Michigan University	University Budget Council	n/a	5 faculty	n/a	Yes	n/a
Western Michigan University	Campus Planning & Finance Council	Same	11 faculty, VP finance, associate VP budget & planning, director of campus facilities	2 students	Yes	Same

SUNY Schools

Campus	Faculty Committee	Student Committee	Faculty Committee Membership	Student Committee Membership	Faculty Committee Charge	Student Committee Charge
University at Albany	Resource Analysis & Planning Committee	Same	VP finance ex officio, 6–8 faculty, 1 professional	1 Undergrad	Yes	Same
Binghamton University	Budget Review Committee	Same	9 faculty, VP ex officio	1 undergrad, 1 grad student	Yes	Same
Brockport	Budget & Resource Committee	Same	president, 4 VPs, 5 deans, 6 faculty, 6 other administrators, 2 staff	2 undergrads, 1 grad student	Yes	Same

	Budget & Staff Allocations Committee	Same	faculty, professional staff	Students	Yes	Same
Buffalo State College						
University at Buffalo	Budget Priorities	n/a	not specified	n/a	Yes	Same
Canton	n/a	n/a	n/a	n/a	n/a	n/a
Cobleskill	Fiscal Affairs and Strategic Planning Committee	Same	VP finance ex officio, 8 teaching faculty (1 per school), 5 at-large faculty, 4 professional staff, 1 CSEA, 1 CAS, and 1 at-large staff	1 student	n/a	n/a
College of Agricultural and Life Sciences (Cornell University)	n/a	n/a	n/a	n/a	n/a	n/a
College of Human Ecology (Cornell University)	n/a	n/a	n/a	n/a	n/a	n/a
College of Industrial and Labor Relations (Cornell University)	n/a	n/a	n/a	n/a	n/a	n/a
College of Veterinary Medicine (Cornell University)	n/a	n/a	n/a	n/a	n/a	n/a

continued on next page

Appendix 6.2 *(Continued)*

SUNY Schools						
Campus	Faculty Committee	Student Committee	Faculty Committee Membership	Student Committee Membership	Faculty Committee Charge	Student Committee Charge
Cortland	n/a	n/a	n/a	n/a	n/a	n/a
Delhi	Annual Budget & Planning Committee	n/a	"broad representation"	n/a	n/a	n/a
Empire State College	Program, Planning & Budget Committee	Same	president & his/her appointed reps, senate chair (ex officio), 7 college senate members including at least 1 professional staff member	Students are not mandated to sit on committee, but student members of the college senate may be approved to sit on committee	Yes	Same
Farmingdale State College	Planning & Budget Committee	n/a	8 faculty, 1 librarian, 2 staff, VP academic affairs	n/a	Yes	n/a
Fredonia State College	Planning & Budget Advisory Committee	n/a	5 faculty, 2 staff	n/a	Yes	n/a
Geneseo	Budget Priorities Committee	Same	5 administrators, 3 faculty, 1 staff	1 student	Yes	Same
Morrisville State College	n/a	n/a	n/a	n/a	n/a	n/a

New Paltz	Budget, Goals & Plans Committee	n/a	n/a	n/a	n/a	n/a
New York State College of Ceramics (Alfred University)	n/a	n/a	n/a	n/a	n/a	n/a
Old Westbury	College Wide Allocation Resource & Budget Planning Committee	Same	6 faculty (2 ex officio), 4 administrators (1 is provost, ex officio), 1 librarian (ex officio), 2 staff, 1 union representative	1 student (ex officio–student government president)	Yes	Same
Oneonta	Committee on Academic Planning and Resource Allocation	n/a	5 faculty	n/a	Yes	n/a
Oswego	n/a	n/a	n/a	n/a	n/a	n/a
Plattsburgh	Standing Committee on Resources and Planning	Same	9 faculty, 7 administrators, 1 staff	1 student	Yes	Same
Potsdam	Business Affairs Committee	Same	4 faculty, 6 administrators	2 students	Yes	Same
Purchase	Budget Advisory Committee	n/a	n/a	n/a	n/a	n/a

continued on next page

Appendix 6.2 *(Continued)*

SUNY Schools						
Campus	Faculty Committee	Student Committee	Faculty Committee Membership	Student Committee Membership	Faculty Committee Charge	Student Committee Charge
Stony Brook	Academic Planning & Resource Allocation	Same	11 faculty, 2 professionals, provost	2 students	Yes	Same
SUNY College of Environmental Science and Forestry	Executive Committee	n/a	12 faculty, SUNY senator & SU senators (ex officio)	n/a	Yes	n/a
SUNY College of Optometry	Institutional Research & Planning Committee	Same	5 faculty, 3 staff, director of institutional research & planning	1 student	Yes	Same
SUNY Downstate Medical Center	Committee of Research, Resources, Planning & Budget	n/a	5 members, at least 1 should be professional staff	n/a	Yes	n/a
SUNY Maritime	Budget Committee	Same	5 members (3 voting at any one time)	1 student	n/a	n/a
SUNY Polytechnic Institute	Planning & Budgeting Committee	n/a	6 faculty, 1 nonfaculty	n/a	Yes	n/a
Upstate Medical University	Upstate Affairs Committee	n/a	6 faculty	n/a	Yes	n/a

Part III

Lessons Learned

Governance Leaders Reflect on Their Experiences

7

A Shared Governance Success Story

Joe Hildreth

This chapter provides an overview of the process used at SUNY Potsdam to develop a procedure for faculty review of the three academic deans. It contains information on the process, the final timetable, and the actual review instrument. It should be a useful resource for faculty wishing to conduct such reviews.

Background

For several years, there was disagreement between faculty and the administration in my home campus of SUNY Potsdam over the issue of faculty review of the academic deans. The faculty felt that evaluations needed to be done for their school deans. In fact, several evaluations were done using anonymous surveys over the years. The bylaws in the School of Arts and Sciences even included a timetable for faculty review of the school's dean.

The bylaws' inclusion of the faculty evaluation of the school's dean was not supported by our administration, on the grounds that it was against SUNY policy. In 2005, I was president of the University Faculty Senate when the UFS Governance Committee prepared and presented a report that supported faculty evaluations of senior administrators. The UFS positively received the report and passed a resolution that affirmed the prerogative of local governance bodies to engage in evaluation of administrators. In addition, the resolution urged campuses to engage in this process.

In 2005 John R. Ryan was Chancellor of the State University of New York. He responded to the UFS resolution of support for faculty

163

evaluation of administrators with this statement: "I appreciate the Senate's interest in the evaluation of administrators and believe that such an evaluation is a campus prerogative."

As UFS senator I shared this information with my campus. The faculty of the School of Arts and Sciences voted to support the bylaws' inclusion of faculty evaluation of the school dean. The administration continued to resist this concept on the grounds that only senior administration is responsible for the evaluation of the academic deans. This disagreement lasted until 2010.

The Committee

In 2009 our local governance leader Chris Lanz asked me to lead a committee that would generate an agreement with the administration on the issue of faculty evaluation of academic deans. In addition, the Faculty Evaluation of the Academic Deans Committee was charged with the development of college-wide guidelines for the evaluation process. My committee consisted of representatives from each of our three schools and an academic dean.

It was most important for the process to be viewed as fair, representative of the entire campus, and transparent. To accomplish these goals, I put out a call for faculty representatives from each of our three schools as well as a representative of the campus senior administration. Minutes were recorded during each meeting and these were shared with faculty and the administration. This provided the committee with valuable, timely feedback that influenced the content of our work. I believe that it also prepared both the faculty and the administration to accept the eventual product.

The representatives from the three schools were all volunteers. It must have been luck that all of them were faculty of wisdom, intelligence, experience, and good judgment. They were David Curry, Chair of Philosophy, School of Arts and Sciences; Paul Siskind, composer, Crane School of Music; and Don Straight, Chair of Secondary Education, School of Education and Professional Studies. Bill Amoriell, Dean, School of Education, represented the administration on the committee. Each member of the committee contributed to the development of our objectives, the wording of the guidelines, and the communication of the effort to their respective schools. I will be forever grateful for the opportunity to work with a committee of such high quality.

Research

The resources presented in the UFS report on Faculty Evaluation of Administrators were studied by the committee. The document produced by Sharon Miller and colleagues entitled "Evaluating Administrators: Designing the Process in a Shared Governance Environment" was especially helpful. In addition, each of Potsdam's three schools had conducted a faculty evaluation of the dean in the past. The experiences of those efforts were discussed as well.

Early in the process, the committee met with Potsdam provost Margaret Madden. We wanted to have an in-depth discussion on the reason for the objection to this practice. We found that the word "evaluation" was a major reason. Our provost believes that Potsdam's senior administration has ownership of and the responsibility for the "evaluation" of the deans. Faculty input is desirable, but the administration wanted to retain the ownership and the responsibility for the actual evaluation.

In our discussion, we agreed that if the faculty engaged in a "review" of the deans, this would provide the administration with "faculty input" and provide the reviewed dean with needed performance feedback. This simple agreement provided our committee with the needed pathway forward. Consequently, we changed the name of our committee to the Faculty Review of Academic Dean Committee.

Guidelines and Procedures

The committee worked for over a year developing the guidelines and procedures for faculty review of academic deans. These contained a timetable, the description of a Dean Review Committee, the review procedure, and a review instrument. The basic points of the timetable were the decision to review the dean every five years and to provide a formative review of a newly hired dean in the third year.

Our review instrument (appendix 7.1) provides a common template for use in all three schools. It consists of 31 review items in the four following categories: Academic Leadership, Administration, Budget, and Management Style. It was agreed that each school could add a few additional questions based on particular needs from each evaluation cycle.

The committee agreed that our Office of Institutional Effectiveness would administer the review instrument in such a way that responses are anonymous. The office will then prepare summary statistics and make the data available to the dean, the provost, and the chair of the Dean Review Committee. The dean will report to the faculty of the school on the results of the review and future plans to address the identified issues.

Process Adoption

Following the development of the guidelines and procedures and review instrument, each member of the committee presented the documents to the constituency that they represented. Each school voted to accept the committee's work and the guidelines and review instrument. Dean Amoriell retired and was replaced by the new dean of the School of Education and Professional Studies, Peter Brouwer. He presented the committee's work to the senior administration. After several meetings and additional editing of the guidelines and procedures, the administration agreed to the process outlined in the guidelines.

The final step was the acceptance and endorsement of the guidelines and review instrument by the Potsdam Faculty Senate in the fall 2011 semester. This endorsement was passed with a substantial majority vote.

Conclusion

Our work resulted in the production of the document entitled *Guidelines and Procedures for Faculty Review of the Academic Deans* (appendix 7.2). The review instrument has been used to provide faculty with the opportunity to review the dean of the Crane School. The results provided the dean and the provost with honest, formative feedback. This has helped the dean to continue his development as an academic leader. It enabled faculty to communicate their concerns with their dean. It has provided our provost with a balanced, accurate faculty view of the performance of the Crane School dean. As a result, the campus community has a healthy atmosphere of communication and respect for the roles of faculty and academic administrators.

Following the first implementation of the review instrument, I asked one faculty member for his observations. He believed the faculty review process was useful in providing enhanced communication between faculty and administration. He also stated that "the opportunity to anonymously provide our administration with the faculty perception of their effectiveness is most valuable. This will produce an effective, working relationship that should benefit the entire institution."

My reflection is that the process was fair, balanced, representative, and transparent. The review instrument is an effective tool that has been used to promote a positive relationship between faculty and administration. I believe our guidelines, procedures, and review instrument would be useful on most campuses. I hope other campuses will develop their own process for the faculty review of the academic deans.

Appendix 7.1
SUNY Potsdam Academic Dean Review Instrument

Faculty review of each Academic Dean is to be made according to the Guidelines and Procedures for Schoolwide Faculty Input for Review of Academic Deans. During this process, it is important to at all times observe the professional standards of administrative review. Thus, the following instrument has been carefully constructed for use in this process.

Your candid and responsible participation in the review of the Dean is requested. Responses will be gathered, and a numerical summary will be completed. The Dean will receive this numerical summary of results, as well as the original copies of the evaluation complete with narrative responses; this feedback data will also be reviewed by the three members selected by the Dean from the School's Dean Evaluation Committee, as specified in the Guidelines and Procedures. The desired result is a review of the Dean that will be helpful in recognizing those areas in which perceptions are favorable, as well as those areas requiring more attention; ideally, the latter will be supplemented with constructive suggestions about how improvement may be realized.

The questionnaire divides the Dean's responsibility into four major areas: Academic Leadership, Administration, Budget, and Management Style. Questions are grouped by those categories and numbered sequentially throughout the document.

Each area is identified, followed by a set of questions, each of which is designed to elicit a judgment. Respondents can choose to decline judgment due to a lack of knowledge of the area queried, or to circle a single number on a scale of 1 to 5. The rating "1" is always the lowest score possible and "5" is always the highest score possible. Ratings "2" and

"4" represent somewhat less than or more than average, respectively; "3" indicates an average rating. The instrument gives the opportunity for supportive examples or comments on each question. Narrative responses, illustrations, and other supporting information are encouraged. So too are narrative responses to issues or concerns not included in the instrument; simply attach those responses to the questionnaire when it is submitted. Please note, however, that the Dean will receive all narrative comments, without any editing or redaction.

The last page of the questionnaire lists the subject heading of each question and asks you to mark the ten items you consider most important as well as those ten you consider least important. However, please answer all questions without regard to any differences in relative importance.

Academic Leadership

The Dean is expected to provide leadership in guiding and developing the curricula offered in the School. Responsibilities include evaluating existing major programs, fostering a climate for renewal and change, and organizing the available resources in order to increase the effectiveness of the total curriculum, consistent with the mission of the College.

1. Knowledge of Departments and Majors

> In order to assess the curriculum and to plan for new programs, the Dean must know the strengths, weaknesses, and problems of all existing departments, majors, and programs, as well as their potential for both the short and long range.

> [   ] No basis for judgment.

> 1 = The Dean has a poorly balanced view of departments, majors, and programs, and does not remain adequately informed.

> 5 = The Dean has a very well-balanced view of the departments and majors and is fully informed on the status of all academic programs.

> Rating: 1   2   3   4   5

If you wish to support your rating with a comment, do so here:

____

____

2. Fostering of Academic Climate

The Dean is in a position to encourage and support faculty innovation and contributions in new courses, majors, or other programs.

[   ] No basis for judgment.

1 = The Dean does not encourage new ideas for courses and programs from the faculty.

5 = The Dean highly encourages new ideas for courses and programs from the faculty.

Rating: 1   2   3   4   5

If you wish to support your rating with a comment, do so here:

____

____

3. Consultation with the Faculty

The Dean has responsibility for making a wide range of decisions regarding academic policies of the School, many of which impact the faculty.

[   ] No basis for judgment.

1 = When making academic policy decisions, the Dean does not consult with faculty.

5 = When making academic policy decisions, the Dean consults with faculty.

Rating: 1   2   3   4   5

If you wish to support your rating with a comment, do so here:

____

____

4. Curricular Leadership

Over a period of time, the Dean is responsible for leading the improvement of the overall curricula of the School.

[   ] No basis for judgment.

1 = Over the past several years, the Dean has failed to provide effective leadership in improving the curricula.

5 = Over the past several years, the Dean has provided effective leadership in improving the curricula.

Rating: 1   2   3   4   5

If you wish to support your rating with a comment, do so here:

____

____

5. Faculty Representation

The Dean is responsible for representing the academic needs and interests of the faculty of the School to other administrators, other schools, other colleges, and the outside community.

[   ] No basis for judgment.

1 = The Dean does an inferior job of representing faculty academic needs and interests.

5 = The Dean does a superior job of representing faculty academic needs and interests.

Rating: 1   2   3   4   5

If you wish to support your rating with a comment, do so here:

____

____

6. Influence on Teaching Environment

The Dean can create a favorable environment for good teaching. Promotion of good teaching can be accomplished through such things as direct example, personal contact with faculty, and fostering opportunities for faculty to improve their teaching.

[   ] No basis for judgment.

1 = The Dean does a very poor job in creating an environment for good teaching on campus.

5 = The Dean does an outstanding job in creating an environment for good teaching on campus.

Rating: 1 2 3 4 5

If you wish to support your rating with a comment, do so here:

____

____

7. Fostering Research and Scholarship

The Dean is in a position to foster the research, scholarship, and professional development of the faculty.

[   ] No basis for judgment.

1 = The Dean does a very poor job in creating an environment for, and encouraging the development of, these activities.

5 = The Dean does an outstanding job in creating an environment for, and encouraging the development of, these activities.

Rating: 1 2 3 4 5

If you wish to support your rating with a comment, do so here:

____

____

8. Handling Student Concerns

Part of the Dean's function is to maintain awareness of student academic needs and respond appropriately.

[   ] No basis for judgment.

1 = The Dean is not aware of student academic needs or does not respond appropriately in daily operations and decisions.

5 = The Dean is consistently aware of student academic needs and responds appropriately in daily operations and decisions.

Rating: 1   2   3   4   5

If you wish to support your rating with a comment, do so here:

____

____

9. Fostering Good Advising

The Dean's office has responsibility for creating a structure and climate that encourages good advising for students in the School.

[   ] No basis for judgment.

1 = The Dean does nothing to facilitate a good advising system for students.

5 = The Dean does everything possible to facilitate a good advising system for students.

Rating: 1   2   3   4   5

If you wish to support your rating with a comment, do so here:

____

____

10. Supporting Academic Freedom

The Dean is in a key position to foster the values of academic freedom within the college and beyond.

[   ] No basis for judgment.

1 = The Dean does not provide or protect academic freedom.

5 = The Dean can be relied upon to provide and protect academic freedom.

Rating: 1   2   3   4   5

If you wish to support your rating with a comment, do so here:

____

____

Administration

Much of the Dean's work involves simply dealing with the execution of the routine business of the School. This responsibility includes many details, acting to meet planned deadlines, coping with unexpected problems, and coordinating the activities of several people, all within the framework of the mission of the College.

1. Administrative Management

The Dean performs and oversees many administrative functions. These include course schedules, personnel deadlines, budget administration, and others.

[   ] No basis for judgment.

1 = The Dean is inefficient and ineffective in handling administrative functions.

5 = The Dean is efficient and effective in handling administrative functions.

Rating: 1   2   3   4   5

If you wish to support your rating with a comment, do so here:

____

____

2. Executive Judgment

As an administrator, the Dean is often called upon to make a number of significant policy decisions.

[   ] No basis for judgment.

1 = Most of the time, the Dean makes unsound policy decisions.

5 = Most of the time, the Dean makes sound policy decisions.

Rating: 1   2   3   4   5

If you wish to support your rating with a comment, do so here:

____

____

3. Planning Ability

The Dean is called upon to anticipate future directions for the School and College, and must take them into account when planning.

[   ] No basis for judgment.

1 = The Dean demonstrates no skill or foresight in planning.

5 = The Dean demonstrates great skill and foresight in planning.

Rating: 1   2   3   4   5

If you wish to support your rating with a comment, do so here:

____

____

4. Delegating Authority and Responsibility

The Dean is in a position to delegate authority and responsibility to department chairs and other personnel who report to the Dean.

[   ] No basis for judgment.

1 = The Dean does not appropriately delegate responsibility to others.

5 = The Dean is skillful in appropriately delegating responsibility to others.

Rating: 1   2   3   4   5

If you wish to support your rating with a comment, do so here:

____

____

5. Acting Decisively

The Dean has the obligation to make important decisions, even in absence of complete freedom of movement. The Dean's authority is limited by faculty rights and procedures on one hand, and local and state-wide administration on the other.

[   ] No basis for judgment.

1 = When most of the facts are available and a decision is needed, the Dean is indecisive.

5 = When most of the facts are available and a decision is needed, the Dean acts promptly and decisively.

Rating: 1   2   3   4   5

If you wish to support your rating with a comment, do so here:

____

____

6. Dean's Role as Faculty Representative

The Dean is responsible for representing concerns of the School faculty to the administration.

[   ] No basis for judgment.

1 = The Dean does not represent concerns of the faculty to the administration.

5 = The Dean is perceived to accurately and forcefully represent the concerns of the faculty to the administration.

Rating: 1   2   3   4   5

If you wish to support your rating with a comment, do so here:

____

____

Budget

The overall budgetary responsibilities of the Dean are both important and complex. Stewardship is exercised over all funds allocated to the School.

1. Budgetary Management

The Dean is responsible to wisely manage all funds allocated to the School.

[   ] No basis for judgment.

1 = The Dean manages School funds poorly and unwisely.

5 = The Dean wisely and prudently manages School funds.

Rating: 1   2   3   4   5

If you wish to support your rating with a comment, do so here:

____

____

2. Fairness in Budgeting

The Dean is fair in budgeting the School's allocated funds.
[   ] No basis for judgment.

1 = The Dean does not manage School funds fairly.

5 = The Dean fairly manages the School's funds.

Rating: 1   2   3   4   5

If you wish to support your rating with a comment, do so here:

____

____

3. Budgetary Representation

The Dean must represent the School in competing within the College for budgetary resources. Garnering adequate resources serves to sustain our programs, staffing, teaching, and research.

[   ] No basis for judgment.

1 = The Dean does a very poor job competing internally for budgetary resources.

5 = The Dean does an outstanding job competing within the College for budgetary resources.

Rating: 1   2   3   4   5

If you wish to support your rating with a comment, do so here:

____

____

4. External Resources

The Dean is increasingly responsible for working with the Office of Advancement to secure external sources of revenue for the School.

[   ] No basis for judgment.

1 = The Dean does a very poor job of soliciting external resources for the School.

5 = The Dean does an excellent job of soliciting external resources for the School.

Rating: 1   2   3   4   5

If you wish to support your rating with a comment, do so here:

____

____

Management Style

The Dean's management style is important. A Dean's effectiveness depends in part upon the quality of personal relationships with associates and subordinates.

1. Accessibility

The demands on the Dean's time are many, but responsibility still exists to be available to School personnel for one-on-one consultation and discussion.

[   ] No basis for judgment.

1 = The Dean is inaccessible and avoids talking with School personnel.

5 = The Dean is accessible and welcomes discussion with School personnel.

Rating: 1   2   3   4   5

If you wish to support your rating with a comment, do so here:

____

____

2. Fairness

The Dean must treat all School personnel fairly and equitably and should make this treatment appropriately visible through words and deeds.

[   ] No basis for judgment.

1 = The Dean is neither fair nor equitable in treatment of School personnel.

5 = The Dean is fair and equitable in treatment of School personnel.

Rating: 1   2   3   4   5

If you wish to support your rating with a comment, do so here:

____

____

3. Personal Manner

As an administrator, the Dean should react to difficult situations in a level-headed manner. When difficulties arise, actions should be based upon reason and common sense.

[   ] No basis for judgment.

1 = In response to difficult situations, the Dean responds inappropriately or unreasonably.

5 = In response to difficult situations, the Dean responds in a reasonable manner.

Rating: 1   2   3   4   5

If you wish to support your rating with a comment, do so here:

____

____

4. Skill in Working with Groups

The Dean spends much of his time working with committees and small groups. Most of these groups are engaged in identifying problems and suggesting solutions.

[   ] No basis for judgment.

1 = As a group member or leader, the Dean is ineffective in helping the group identify problems and suggest solutions.

5 = As a group member or leader, the Dean is very effective in helping the group identify problems and suggest solutions.

Rating: 1   2   3   4   5

If you wish to support your rating with a comment, do so here:

____

____

5. Keeping Communication Lines Open

The Dean must facilitate adequate and appropriate communication in the School. While certain accessible information is confidential, the Dean can generally share—and encourage others to share—information that is relevant to the School.

[   ] No basis for judgment.

1 = The Dean does a very poor job of facilitating an environment of open communication within the School.

5 = The Dean does everything possible to facilitate the flow of information among School personnel.

Rating: 1   2   3   4   5

If you wish to support your rating with a comment, do so here:

____

____

6. Listening to Faculty

The Dean can learn little from School personnel unless they are heard. Listening to faculty does not necessarily mean agreeing with them; it does mean trying to understand their perspectives and meanings.

[   ] No basis for judgment.

1 = The Dean seldom listens to School personnel.

5 = The Dean listens very carefully to School personnel and tries to completely understand their perspectives and meanings.

Rating: 1   2   3   4   5

If you wish to support your rating with a comment, do so here:
____
____

7. Honesty and Follow-through

The Dean deals with School personnel on many important matters, and over an extended time period. They should not only be able to have faith in the Dean's good intentions but also to have confidence that stated intentions will be acted upon.

[   ] No basis for judgment.

1 = The Dean is often dishonest or insincere. School personnel cannot rely on what they are told.

5 = The Dean is honest and sincere. School personnel can always rely on what they are told.

Rating: 1   2   3   4   5

If you wish to support your rating with a comment, do so here:
____
____

Personnel and Procedures

A continual concern of the Dean is the maintenance of academic quality throughout the School. The Dean is responsible for ensuring that appropriate standards and procedures are used for recruiting, selecting, and retaining quality School personnel.

1. Role in Personnel Recruitment and Selection

> The recruitment and selection of new School personnel is important to the School. The Dean's participation in this process is important.

> [   ] No basis for judgment.

> 1 = The Dean does a very poor job in the recruitment, selection, or retention of quality School personnel.

> 5 = The Dean does an outstanding job in the recruitment, selection, and retention of quality School personnel.

> Rating: 1   2   3   4   5

If you wish to support your rating with a comment, do so here:

____

____

2. Standards in Personnel Decisions

> Through decisions and recommendations, the Dean is responsible for establishing standards having significant impact upon administrative decisions regarding reappointment, tenure, promotion, and discretionary salary increases.

> [   ] No basis for judgment.

> 1 = The Dean's standards are not clear in the decision-making processes regarding reappointment, tenure, promotion, and discretionary salary increases.

5 = The Dean's standards are very clear in the decision-making processes regarding reappointment, tenure, promotion, and discretionary salary increases.

Rating: 1   2   3   4   5

If you wish to support your rating with a comment, do so here:

____

____

3. Handling Conflicts

The Dean is in a position to be aware of any real or potential conflicts between individuals or factions among School personnel. The Dean's actions should help avoid development of any conflicts, and, as brought to his attention, should also reduce, mediate, and help resolve any existing conflicts that may adversely affect the smooth functioning of the School.

[   ] No basis for judgment.

1 = The Dean does a very poor job of preventing, reducing, mediating, and resolving conflicts between individuals or factions among School personnel.

5 = The Dean does an excellent job of preventing, reducing, mediating, and resolving conflicts between individuals or factions among School personnel.

Rating: 1   2   3   4   5

If you wish to support your rating with a comment, do so here:

____

____

4. Sensitivity to Personnel Concerns

The Dean is in a position to be aware of and understand matters that are of concern to academic departments, offices, or individual School personnel.

[   ] No basis for judgment.

1 = The Dean is insensitive to personnel concerns and is unwilling to become aware of, and to understand, issues and problems.

5 = The Dean is sensitive to personnel concerns and is very willing to become aware of, and to understand, issues and problems.

Rating: 1   2   3   4   5

If you wish to support your rating with a comment, do so here:

____

____

You have reviewed the Dean on the following items. Please place a "+" mark in front of the ten items you regard as the most important, and a "–" indicator in front of the ten items you regard as least important. Thank you for your input!

Academic Leadership

_____   1. Knowledge of Departments and Majors

_____   2. Fostering of Academic Climate

_____   3. Consultation with the Faculty

_____   4. Curricular Leadership

_____   5. Faculty Representation

_____   6. Influence on Teaching Environment

_____   7. Fostering Research and Scholarship

_____   8. Handling Student Concerns

_____   9. Fostering Good Advising

_____   10. Supporting Academic Freedom

Administration

_____ 11. Administrative Management

_____ 12. Executive Judgment

_____ 13. Planning Ability

_____ 14. Delegating Authority and Responsibility

_____ 15. Acting Decisively

_____ 16. Dean's Role as Faculty Representative

Budget

_____ 17. Budgetary Management

_____ 18. Fairness in Budgeting

_____ 19. Budgetary Representation

_____ 20. External Resources

Management Style

_____ 21. Accessibility

_____ 22. Fairness

_____ 23. Personal Manner

_____ 24. Skill in Working with Groups

_____ 25. Keeping Communications Lines Open

_____ 26. Listening to Faculty

_____ 27. Honesty and Follow-through

Personnel and Procedures

_____ 28. Role in Personnel Recruitment and Selection

_____ 29. Standards in Personnel Decisions

_____ 30. Handling Conflict

_____ 31. Sensitivity to Personnel Concerns

Appendix 7.2
School-wide Faculty Input for
Review of Academic Deans Guidelines
and Procedures (Finalized Fall 2011)

I. Definitions

At SUNY Potsdam, the Office of the Provost completes evaluation of Academic Deans on a regular basis. Through the process defined hereby, eligible personnel from each School have a mechanism through which input for this evaluative process is ensured. To distinguish this document from the administrative "evaluation," the word "review" is used throughout.

In this document, the phrase "School governing body" shall refer, respectively, to the Arts and Sciences Council in the School of Arts and Sciences, the Personnel Committee of the School of Education and Professional Studies, and the Crane Faculty Association in the Crane School of Music.

Further, the phrase "Dean Review Committee" shall be defined as follows:

> For the School of Arts and Sciences, the Arts and Sciences Council will appoint a subcommittee composed of five members of the faculty of the School to serve as the Dean Review Committee for the purpose of overseeing the review process.

> For the School of Education and Professional Studies, the Dean Review Committee consists of all (six) members of the School's Personnel Committee.

> For the Crane School of Music, the Dean Review Committee consists of all (five) members of the standing Personnel Committee of the Crane Faculty Association, as elected in accordance with the Crane Bylaws.

In each School, the Dean Review Committee will determine School personnel eligible to participate in this process; inclusion of all stakeholders is encouraged.

Finally, in order to ensure the completeness of data captured, considered, and reported through this process, each Academic Dean shall select three members from the appropriate Dean Review Committee to confidentially review all quantitative and qualitative data.

II. Feedback Process Timetable

In the case of a newly hired Academic Dean, a formative feedback cycle will be carried out in the Dean's third year, modeled on the accompanying instrument. For this cycle, which will be initiated and administered by each School, the Office of Institutional Effectiveness will report the response rate to School personnel, and the Dean will present a reflective acknowledgment in response to the feedback received.

Thereafter, administrative evaluations of the Dean will occur in the fifth year and at subsequent five-year intervals and will incorporate feedback from the School personnel using the accompanying instrument. Naturally, the Provost stands willing to consider concerns expressed by faculty about the performance of the Dean at times other than those specified by this defined cycle.

Each academic year, it will be the responsibility of the College Provost to determine the Academic Dean(s) to be evaluated according to the five-year cycle. The Provost will notify each Dean and the appropriate School governing body and will inform the personnel of the School(s) administered by the Dean(s) to be evaluated. Each School's governing body shall then convene or assemble, as appropriate, its Dean Review Committee and shall select its Chair, who shall be the contact person for the Office of Institutional Effectiveness. Each Dean Review Committee shall oversee the entire feedback process to ensure its integrity. The Chair of the Dean Review Committee will make regular reports on the review process to the appropriate governing body of the School during the evaluation year and shall respond to any nontechnical questions relating to the review instrument during the review implementation. The actual review(s) will be administered in the spring of the designated academic year.

III. Feedback Instrument Elements (adapted from Sharon Miller et al., "Evaluation of Administrators: Designing the Process in a Shared Governance Environment")

For each particular review cycle, minimal appropriate additions to the attached common college template may be made by mutual agreement among the Dean, the Dean Review Committee, and the Provost. The common template provides 31 specific review items in the four following categories:

A. Academic Leadership—The Academic Dean is expected to provide leadership in guiding and developing the curricula offered in the School. Responsibilities include evaluating existing major programs, fostering a climate for renewal and change, and organizing the available resources in order to increase the effectiveness of the total curriculum, consistent with the mission of the College.

B. Administration—Much of the Academic Dean's work involves simply dealing with the execution of the routine business of the School. This responsibility includes many details: acting to meet planned deadlines, coping with unexpected problems, and coordinating the activities of several people, all within the framework of the mission of the College.

C. Budget—The overall budgetary responsibilities of the Academic Dean are both important and complex. Stewardship is exercised over all funds allocated to the School.

D. Management Style—The Academic Dean's management style is important. A Dean's effectiveness depends in part upon the quality of personal relationships with associates and subordinates.

IV. Feedback Collection Procedure

For each review cycle, whether formative or ongoing, the appropriate Dean Review Committee(s) will generate a list of unique ID codes for all of the School personnel eligible to complete the survey; this will permit the removal of duplicate responses and help to validate the data. Respondent anonymity will be preserved, since the Office of Institutional Effectiveness will only be provided with the list of ID codes, and not the names associated with them. Finally, the unique ID codes will be removed after data tabulation takes place.

The Office of Institutional Effectiveness will electronically administer the instrument to all eligible School personnel; hard copies will not be accepted, though printed copies of the instrument will be available for respondent use to facilitate more rapid completion of the online questionnaire. In the introductory section, demographic data of the reviewer, as well as duration of employment and other such details, may be collected at the request of the Dean Review Committee; respective Committees will have discretion to determine these particular items for each implementation, while being careful that any such data maintains individual respondent anonymity. This input, which may be optional, would only be used to disaggregate data for purposes of more meaningful analysis. Upon completion of responses for a five-year review, the Office of Institutional Effectiveness will then prepare summary statistics and make all feedback data available to the Provost, the Dean, and the three individuals selected by the Dean for confidential review. (Refer to previous item II for details of data use from the third-year formative review cycle.)

The Dean will prepare a summary of the findings, which will include a narrative reflection on the conclusions to be drawn and a description of the activities to be undertaken to respond to the issues revealed by the review. The Dean will submit this written summary to the College Provost and will report to the School personnel on the results of the review and future plans to address the identified issues. The Dean is encouraged to make available any data that would give meaningful context to the summary report.

8

Task Forces

A Case Study at SUNY Oswego

Gwen Kay and Joan M. Carroll

This chapter offers a reflection on the success and failure of the task force model as a measure of effective shared governance. Using a decade's worth of task forces on one campus, we offer suggestions to optimize task force work so that the end product approximates the established goals and enables much participation across the faculty, staff, and administration on a given campus.

Task forces can be, by their very nature, efficient or unwieldy, time limited or time delimited. On our campus (SUNY Oswego), task forces have been a positive force for change, helping us grapple with situational rather than long-term issues. On the whole, the process has worked well for us, and we believe it can be a model of shared governance. After analyzing task forces over the past decade, we can articulate what works, and what does not. According to SUNY Oswego's shared governance bylaws,

Article VII—Communication between Faculty and Administration

Section 4. Governance Task Forces

a) The Faculty Assembly and the administration shall concurrently create task forces on issues of college-wide concern and charge them with specific duties in order to enhance communication and consultation among faculty, administration, professional staff, the unions, and the students. Each task force and its charge shall be established by formal written approval of both the Faculty Assembly and the administration. The written charge shall include a deadline for the work to be completed and a detailed description

191

of how the membership shall be determined. A report of the results shall be recorded in the minutes of the Faculty Assembly. Upon reaching its deadline, the task force shall cease to exist, unless otherwise extended by the consent of both the Assembly and the administration.

b) Each task force shall include balanced representation from the faculty, administration, professional staff, unions, and, when appropriate, the Student Association.

c) Members of the Faculty Assembly or the administration shall request the creation of a task force whenever initiatives may require special expertise from among the faculty, the administration, professional staff, the unions, and the students.

d) In situations where governance procedures involving both the faculty and the administration and the College Council are not fully specified in the Policies of the Board of Trustees or in the Faculty Bylaws, a task force may be created to resolve procedural ambiguities.

At SUNY Oswego, our model of shared governance is simultaneously governed by councils through the bylaws of the Faculty Assembly (our campus governing body, equivalent to faculty senate elsewhere) and committees through the Provost's Committee on Committees. The clearest difference, or distinction, between the two is that councils often have actionable items relating to the academic nature of the institution, while committees do other work. In the event that a committee has something that could be considered actionable, the relevant council would bring the issue to the floor of the faculty assembly. As on most campuses, the councils and committees are quotidian.

Periodically, however, an event or issue arises that requires work but will also be time limited (or, so we hope). In the recent past, these issues have included shared governance, grappling with the new General Education guidelines, and trying to resolve some items raised by the Middle States Evaluation. The typical task force emerges out of the Faculty Assembly Executive Board, from discussions with the provost and standing campus councils. Often, the work to be done is beyond the scope of one council. Too, a broader scope of membership would make for a better result.

Task force composition is a key element in the smooth operation of any group. Half of the membership is voted upon by the faculty assembly, frequently with representation across schools; the other half of the membership is administration appointed and includes faculty, staff, and members of administration. This varied constituency ensures that all voices are heard and that different perspectives, and knowledge, will be put to good use. On the other hand, this also means that every task force has a minimum of 8–10 people, and numbers can get (potentially) unwieldy.

What seems to motivate faculty to participate in task forces is that their mission is clear, and the commitment is time limited. Someone with a particular interest in an issue may volunteer to serve and be elected from the floor. Failing that, they may ask administration to be one of their appointed representatives. The time frame for each task force is carefully thought out and is almost always sufficient to accomplish the task at hand. In many cases, the members will meet weekly or biweekly to work through their agenda and fulfill their mission. When the timetable is adhered to, the results are often very positive. When the timetable is ignored, things tend to get bogged down, or delayed unnecessarily because there is no feeling of urgency.

A final important factor in the work of the task force is the efficiency and/or desire of the chair/co-chairs. Administrative support means that secretarial help is readily available, no small aid given the large charges of some task forces. Also, of course, the provost checks in with the task force periodically, as does the faculty assembly.

Chronology

We have had ten task forces in the period from 2003 through 2013. First, an enumeration; then we shall examine what worked, which completed their tasks, which sunsetted and which did not (and what happened to those that did not). Second, we shall offer our recommendation for the ideal task force.

In 2003–2004, we created the College Hour Task Force (April 2004) and the Sexual Harassment & Consensual Relations Policies & Procedures Task Force (April 2004). The former task force was to help answer the following questions: Could a unified hour of no classes, campus-wide, work? Would it benefit students and faculty to have a common open hour? Would meetings be scheduled? Outside speakers? Office hours? And, in the event the answer was "yes," what time would be ideal, and how would that impact the teaching day, balancing labs, seminars, internships, and other unique disciplinary needs.

For the latter, the task force was largely in response to issues that had arisen on other campuses and was driven by a desire to clarify our own language about sexual harassment and consensual relationships. Each of these task forces completed their work within the year. The proposal for college hour was reported out and accepted in May 2005, and the policy on consensual relationships, part of the recommendations of the second task force, was approved in May 2005 as well.

The following year, 2004–2005, saw the creation of the Joint Task Force on Hybrid Courses (November 2004). Many of the issues that were discussed in this task force could have been part of the agenda for the faculty assembly–led council on Distance Learning (now Academic Outreach). This was the early years of course management systems; questions to be addressed included what software to recommend, support for faculty offering these courses and/or incentives to develop these courses (remuneration for course development? a laptop?), how many to offer, the target audience (our own students? students elsewhere?), and the impact on our current students and course offerings (we did not want to cannibalize ourselves).

In 2005–2006, three task forces were created, and one spawned a time-limited committee that should have been properly labeled a task force. The first of the three, the Conflict of Interest and Professional Ethics Task Force (September 2005), focused on integrity, both academic and personal. This task force addressed a combination of issues raised by the Sexual Harassment and Consensual Relationships Task Force and high-profile academic and public figures who were dismissed from their positions because of plagiarism. In the fall (October 2005), the Task Force on Academic Administrative Officer Review was established. This task force was, in part, to align with SUNY system expectations about such reviews. The task force's recommendation (May 2006) to review academic officers on a rotating basis, while approved, came to naught, because of retirements, expected retirements, and departures for new jobs. The third task force, Writing Across the Curriculum, was created to help implement clear writing expectations and aid in assessment (March 2006).

Out of the earlier College Hour Task Force came a committee, the College Hour Committee (March 2006). This signaled that the earlier report had been positive and the assembly was willing to move forward with a trial College Hour, provided all questions could be adequately answered and an assessment of success would occur after the trial semesters, to determine whether to permanently implement college hour. The three-semester pilot would begin in spring 2007, giving the committee a summer and a semester to answer questions and create the template. This time frame allowed for both course scheduling and details of implementation to be worked out in advance, without altering an established semester's worth of courses that spanned the proposed no-class hour.

In 2006–2007, several task forces came to fruition, and several more were created. The Professional Development Center Task Force was created in February 2007. The Writing Across the Curriculum (WAC) Task Force proposals (March 2007) included recommending the creation of a WAC Steering Committee, one that was readily adopted. Ultimately, this task force led to the creation of a standing committee, within the provost's purview, rather than the faculty assembly's, as the issues were not curricular in nature.

Admission to a Major or Change of Major, 2008–2009's task force, was in response to so-called "impacted" majors. These heavily subscribed majors could refuse admission to students who had not entered already having declared that major during the admissions process; the task force was to review the practice of labeling majors as "impacted" and make recommendations about criteria, process, and procedures by which faculty could set requirements to control for enrollment. Created in April 2009, the committee was to issue its report in December 2010.

As important as that task force's work was, and as delayed as it was (by one semester), it was small potatoes compared to the General Education Visioning Task Force, *the* task force of the year 2009–2010. The task force was approved for creation in the fall of 2009, but it took almost another semester before every college had representation on the committee (November to April). General Education had been overhauled earlier in the century, but GE2000, as it was colloquially known, had some difficulties, notably that the courses in one entire classification— "intellectual issues," or classes that were intended to be multi- or interdisciplinary—were required for graduation, but there was a paucity of such classes offered. Further, some majors, particularly those with very high credit-hour requirements (usually the sciences), did not change their requirements, nor did they offer any of the courses themselves—perhaps the result of serving in an impacted major (discussed earlier). This inequity pushed the burden of these courses onto the liberal arts more than the sciences, and these courses serviced students across all three schools (Arts & Sciences, Business, and Education).

Within the year, the General Education Visioning Task Force had created recommendations. These were (electronically) distributed, discussed at the department level, and then discussed on the floor of the faculty assembly in October 2010. Following this discussion, a Task Force on Designing General Education for the 21st Century was created (November 2010) to take the next step. This task force, to tackle GE21, was given one and a half years (November 2010 to August 2012) to examine the current system; identify student competencies, knowledge, and attributes to be gained; and propose one or more plans for general education reform.

In the penultimate year, 2011–2012, a task force on Shared Governance, Committee Structure and Collaboration was created. This task force was a dual-purpose entity, addressing concerns raised by the Middle States Evaluation team as well as those raised internally by the Personnel Policies Council. The committee, created in spring 2012, was to meet regularly and issue its report by December 2012.

Reflections

Our task forces have been a mix of *proactive*, *reactive*, and *progressive*. What we mean by this is that some task forces anticipate, such as those examining hybrid courses and writing across the curriculum. Others have been in response to a situation, on our campus or elsewhere, and these would include the sexual harassment, impacted majors, academic integrity issues, and shared governance. Finally, on occasion the committees were forward looking, and both college hour and (multiple) general education task forces would fit this bill. Further, some of these task forces have led to the creation of standing committees in response to the recommendations of the task force—the Writing Across the Curriculum Committee is an excellent example of this, out of the Writing Across the Curriculum Task Force.

Examining one task force from each category will help illuminate some best practices, or practices to avoid! An excellent example of a task force that "anticipated" would be one that looks at hybrid courses. This task force came out of some questions the provost had, thinking about the future of higher education and the intersection of the internet with our ability to reach larger groups of students. The questions she posed did not fall particularly within any one extant committee, but reached across a broad range, so a task force was convened to identify challenges, software, and/or strategies for future development in that direction. The faculty who served were those in the forefront of educational pedagogy and/or thinking about the possibilities offered by computer technology;

the administration-appointed members included leadership from the office of extended learning, the most likely area to be impacted by these decisions, whatever they may be.

An example of a reactive task force, and one that was less successful, was Shared Governance, Committee Structure and Collaboration. (Perhaps the cumbersome name should have been a clue?!) This task force was a dual-purpose entity, addressing concerns raised by the Middle States Evaluation team as well as those raised internally by the Personnel Policies Committee. The consensus between the faculty assembly Executive Board and the administration, approved by the faculty assembly as a whole, was a task force created in spring 2011. The original time frame was considered, and those who sought seats on the task force, voted by the faculty assembly, committed to working through the summer months, as the report was to delivered fall of 2011. Instead, the committee got off to a slow start, in part because of a delay in filling the mandated constituency from elected faculty, and did not meet fully for the first time until late in 2011. By the time the group met, it was, according to its charge, to have had the final report already submitted. Over the course of the spring, and into the following academic year, the group met a few times, on an irregular basis. The combination of irregular meetings, and diffuse leadership, without incentive or action by the chair to move things forward, did not bode well for the committee. Ultimately, the task force submitted its recommendations a year and a half later than anticipated. In its report, it addressed few of the items in its original charge; most members were so demoralized that it was unclear that they would be willing to continue to serve on a committee to fully address the challenges set before it.

In sharp relief to this somewhat dismal story, we have hope (and success, even) from a progressive orientation, and that would be general education. For the on-campus success of the General Education Visioning Task Force, see the earlier discussion in this chapter. As luck would have it, within the designated period of the task force's work, SUNY standards started to change as well, so the work of the task force, once confined to simple change internally, became much larger, and more prescient, in terms of SUNY systemness and ease of transfer from and across community colleges. This progressive decision stood us in good stead as the general education ground changed beneath our feet, and we were uniquely positioned to be quickly adaptive.

For most of these task forces, the recommendations were heard, and accepted by the body, but not always implemented. Timing issues—when reports were submitted, when action could be taken, when task forces might work on their assignments—impaired or aided success of the mission. For GE discussions, for example, the body voted to reframe our general education offerings, in line with recommendations from the task force(s) and SUNY Trustees, but for those not paying attention, it felt as if the decision to change our plan was pushed from above, rather than arising organically within our midst, and rushed, appended in a meeting late in the semester, not allowing for adequate discussion when in fact each step had had much discussion and broad dissemination.

What made the task forces effective? In our opinion, the best measures for success were transparent guidelines in the task force's charge, a clear and delineated timeline, and a strong leader. Getting a committee to meet can be challenging, particularly if it starts mid-semester, after schedules have been fixed. With advance notice, though, this can be arranged. Some committees met weekly or biweekly. Others utilized electronic exchanges to keep work flowing in off weeks. Because everyone on the task force has already bought in to its concept—they agreed to either be voted onto the committee by the faculty assembly or appointed by administration—leadership is critical.

9

Mentoring the Next Generation of Governance Leaders

Taking Advantage of Routines, Exceptions, and Challenges for Developing Leadership and Succession Planning

Sharon F. Cramer

This chapter explores multiple models for governance as a vehicle for developing future leaders and mentors. Included is a discussion of how crisis circumstances can be used to enable governance members to think differently about their leadership skills. Ways that mentoring as a proactive aspect of governance can be both offered and sought are explored. Comments by governance members and leaders are incorporated into the chapter.

"After meeting with governance leaders from other campuses, I now see how the issues we face on my home campus are aligned with those elsewhere."

"I was greatly influenced toward positions of influence as I have been nurtured by senate officers to become a leader."

"My four years as the chair of our university senate have definitely given me opportunities to not only help our students, my colleagues, and the institution, but helped me to see myself in a different light."

"I am grateful for the opportunities to learn and to grow within governance. And it is that growth that makes being a leader so exciting: to learn new things and new ways of approaching problems."

> —Thoughts from governance members and leaders,
> in reflecting on their service

As members of campus governance units look ahead to the next few years, they will likely see many institution-wide challenges: implementation of a new general education program, adjustment to a budget shortfall, serving in leadership positions during an institution-wide accreditation review (e.g., Middle States), or changes in academic policies, required due to the need for accommodations to new federal or state guidelines. Few experienced governance leaders consider these significant responsibilities without dread. This chapter will encourage campus governance members and leaders to look at these exceptional circumstances in a new way: as greenhouses, within which it is possible to facilitate the development of leadership perspectives, and unique opportunities for mentoring. This chapter has also been designed to be a resource for campus governance members who might consider taking on more responsibilities, eventually evolving into leadership within (and beyond) their own current roles.

Shortly after I received continuing appointment (tenure), a former chairman of my academic department encouraged me to become involved in both campus- and state-wide governance. When I asked him why, he explained that being involved in governance had been one of the most satisfying aspects of his career. And when I specifically asked about serving on a state-wide governance committee, he explained it simply: "In those committees, I worked with the smartest people I ever met." Now, looking back at that invitation, I can say that I completely concur with his observations.

For several decades, governance was a significant part of my life. Campus governance began for me via membership on a standing committee of our college senate in my third year on campus, and continued through my service as parliamentarian of the SUNY University Faculty Senate. I came to appreciate the complexity of leadership, and how to develop, match, or adjust my talents to governance needs. As I look back at my years in governance, at the two awards I received from the SUNY University Faculty Senate, my humility increases. The biggest change is that I became ever more passionate about two aspects of governance: mentoring and succession planning.

Although my experience as a campus senator, leader, and my involvement with the SUNY University Faculty Senate will be my reference points for this chapter, campus governance members as well as leaders and administrators can use the recommendations provided within the chapter during any specific point in an annual cycle. Most members of the campus governance community can make use of the ideas herein for responsibilities that have a start, middle, and end (e.g., oversight of an ad hoc committee that has a specific, finite charge; communication about a new required policy that emerged from governance; oversight of a committee that is working on a specific project).

The focus of this chapter was only very clear in retrospect: work on small or large exceptional projects provides unique opportunities for mentoring. Ideally, there would be a connection between the institution's strategic plan and the annual goals for campus governance committees, as suggested by Kaplan and Norton (2004). The following questions can be used by either the person who will be a mentor, or the person who might consider becoming a leader.

> Question 1: What can a mentor do to create a supportive climate, leading to leadership aspirations and opportunities?

> Question 2: How can new challenges become self-evaluative opportunities?

> Question 3: How does one go from learner to mentor and/or leader?

These questions can serve as starting points for discussion within campus governance, on campus, and within larger units (e.g., the University Faculty Senate or the Faculty Council of Community Colleges). The discussion of each question within this chapter is designed to stimulate conversation; the brevity of the chapter prevents an exhaustive answer to each one.

Ideally, the chapter may also stimulate a commitment to informal mentoring relationships versus formal programs, given the relative scarcity and high cost of formal programs—and the many opportunities for low-cost informal ones. Although not every governance leader can be (or needs to be)[1] an effective mentor, and not every governance member can become a leader, perhaps this chapter will inspire you to think differently about yourself and others with whom you work, in terms of mentoring and leadership.

Mentoring Pragmatics: Giving and Getting

In most cases, campus governance members come to governance via similar routes: someone encouraged them. Governance is an abstract concept until it is personalized—by commitment to a specific issue, admiration of a leader, or a magnetic attraction to the governance climate. Most members have little formal training in governance (or parliamentary procedure); they are usually, at best, well-intentioned volunteers. Faculty members (other than political scientists or economists) likely have little in-depth knowledge of, and experience with, governance. If professional staff members or students are members of the governance body, they may be able to contribute examples about specifics related to institutional needs, based on experiences or tasks in their day-to-day work.

Many professional staff members may have very narrowly defined work responsibilities, which (unless they serve on institution-wide committees) can mean that often their only work contacts are within their own offices.[2] Faculty members who are deeply involved in their academic responsibilities, or research, may be similarly isolated. Thus, for some, serving as a campus senator, or a committee member of a campus or state-wide governance committee, might be one of their few opportunities to interact with others whose disciplines, or professional roles, are different from their own. For some, this is tremendously appealing—like the moment in *The Wizard of Oz* when sepia turns to color. Governance sells itself to some by opening a door. A subset of these people have the potential to become more deeply involved in governance, to the point that they will become mentors and/or leaders.

Although many faculty members have opportunities to more regularly participate in institution-wide initiatives, few think of themselves as potential governance members, or leaders. And yet, when some do participate, they may see themselves and their institutions differently, as shown in the following two reflections:

Personal Reflection

> I never considered myself a leader, though I have assumed various leadership roles—from newspaper editor to department chair to leadership among my peers (as the elected comprehensive college sector representative within the University Faculty Senate). I guess people see things in me that I myself don't recognize.
>
> —Joe Marren
> Professor and Chair, Communication Department
> SUNY Buffalo State; Senator, SUNY University Faculty Senate,
> 2010–2016, and Sector Representative, Comprehensive Colleges,
> SUNY University Faculty Senate

The opportunity to participate in governance provides a perspective that would be nearly impossible to obtain in any other way.

Institutional Reflection

> Prior to my involvement with governance on campus, I tended to react negatively when I heard of new policies and strategies—I disagreed with many (and even wondered where they came from). Becoming involved with campus governance, and eventually becoming a leader in our organization, gave me a "seat at the table." This has led me to a more nuanced understanding of the issues and a comprehension of the process. My voice is now heard during that process, and my opinions can have an impact on important policies and strategic directions on my campus before they are finalized.
>
> —M. Scott Goodman, PhD
> Chair and Professor, Chemistry
> SUNY Buffalo State, SUNY University Faculty Senate, 2011–2017

In considering how to look at both self and the institution, this chapter offers the structure of three questions to enable mentors to look at people with whom they work and encourage future leaders and mentors.

Question 1: What Can a Mentor Do to Create a Supportive Climate, Leading to Leadership Aspirations and Opportunities?

Developing confidence and the ability to problem-solve are essential aspects of leadership. These skills best emerge in a climate of candor and self-reflective examination, to figure out what is working, and what needs to be improved. (For some, this is boiled down to three queries: "What should I stop doing?" "What should I start doing?" "What should remain the same?") The capacity for self-reflection can be learned, as individuals observe others who routinely strive for ways to ensure that the evolving solutions match the problems presented.

When I became a senior faculty member, and chair of our college senate, I made a conscious decision to reach out to members of my campus who I thought had leadership potential. This included members of my committees, or senators whom I encouraged to serve as members or chairs of committees. Years later, many told me that, after my invitation, they began to see themselves in new ways.

Although we had no explicit leadership development plan for our governance organization, several of the governance members were subsequently promoted to leadership positions—either within governance, or promotions within their careers. For some, their governance experiences led to new aspirations, to personal and professional transformations. As they learned more about the interconnections between different parts of the campus, the silos within which they had worked disintegrated. The encouragement they had received in the greenhouse of governance had given them new awareness of possibilities to explore—within themselves, and in the scope of their professional lives. Returning to their departments, at the end of their governance term, these individuals realized that (much like a beloved pair of shoes from a previous season) what had previously been a comfortable fit was no longer right for them. They continued to seek out ways to develop and implement a broader personal and professional vision. Others found that their mentors remained advocates for them long after their service ended.

Reflection on Being Mentored

> I finished my PhD because of the support, reminders, and love bestowed upon me by my mentors in UFS. When I say, "I think one day I would like to be a college president," they always say, "I can see that," and "How can I help you get there?"
>
> —Dr. Noelle Chaddock, Chief Diversity Officer, SUNY Cortland,
> and Chair, Diversity, Equity and Inclusion Committee,
> SUNY University Faculty Senate, 2013–2016; Associate Dean
> of Academic Affairs for Diversity and Inclusivity, Rhodes College

Many governance leaders view their term in office to have been a transformative one:

Reflection on Personal Transformation

> I anticipate that the experience I had as senate chair will help me in every future role, because it made me more confident in many ways—in my ability to be a leader, and my determination to use better communication to improve my institution.
>
> I have learned so much about my institution, and have a more pragmatic view of the people involved at all levels. What an amazing experience!
>
> —Amy McMillan, PhD, Associate Professor,
> Biology, and College Senate Chair, SUNY Buffalo State

Challenges are the machines that crumble the campus silos via governance activities and solutions. During crises, routines vanish. Exceptional circumstances (or short-term leadership assignments) can be opportunities for campus governance specialists to face problems they have never seen before; they will need to learn to adjust to the ambiguity facing them. Suddenly, previously successful strategies do not match the presenting problems. Although not every committee member, or every senator, has the potential to become a leader, all need to be encouraged to rise to their own levels of excellence. It is up to the governance leadership to assist them in striving beyond their reach to take on tasks they might ignore, but (with assistance) could accomplish. Overcoming the apprehension, and becoming adaptive, creative problem-solvers, requires the following on the part of the supervisors/mentors:

- Believe in supervisees; they will gain confidence because they know their mentors believe in them.

- Listen to them as they sound out their thoughts, and provide gentle direction.

- Give them access to resources—on and off campus.

- Create a learning organization (e.g., Mohr & Dichter, 2001) such that shared problem-solving becomes a norm, rather than the exception.

- Provide honest feedback to committee chairs, or individuals with potential for leadership, with the goal of facilitating leadership development.

At a particularly difficult juncture in my career, when I was unsure of my skill at making the financial case for a new initiative in my academic department, I expressed my hopelessness to a campus colleague, whom I considered a mentor. This, coincidentally, happened shortly after a national election. His response was to ask me if I thought that the newly elected president was fully informed about all aspects of running the nation.

He encouraged me to do what the president was likely doing—surrounding himself with smart, thoughtful, articulate people, and reflecting on the information they provided to him, before taking action. This let me know that my mentor was aware of the holes in my knowledge and concurrently had confidence in me to rise above the challenge—and even learn from it. The conversation went a long way toward enabling me to reconsider the problem from new perspectives, after talking with individuals (both on and off campus). The result was that I helped my department move forward, while experiencing my own professional growth.

At crucial points, I recall using different strategies to give our senators opportunities to build their skills. When we came to the challenges of communication regarding work on our strategic plan, I met with committee chairs to talk about what we could do to develop a communication plan. We involved campus experts to design a communications plan and modify our web presence.

Another challenge faced us when two new academic units were added to our organizational structure. We decided to offer several open forums to discuss a possible downsizing of the number of senators representing each unit in the senate (a topic that had been under consideration within the senate for many years). We opened these forums to the entire campus and specifically invited previous senate leaders (several of whom had retired). Those who attended shared personal and historic perspectives unknown to most current senators. A valuable contribution came from a classified staff member who attended an open forum. She presented a well-crafted proposal she and her peers had developed, which called for including classified staff representation within our all-college senate. The results of the forum included no downsizing of membership, representation of one of the two new units (after determining that the members of the second unit were already represented), and a change to bylaws to reflect the addition of a "classified staff" senator. The paradigms and open discussion formats we developed continue to be used (with an upcoming one planned to gain input on the college budget). Participating in the senate (at the campus or at a broader, system level) helps individuals transcend their parochial views.

Reflection on New Perspectives

> Being in the University Faculty Senate has opened my eyes to issues I never thought about, and being the sector representative for the comprehensive colleges has helped me understand the broader aspect of issues. I think things through more clearly now.
>
> —Joe Marren

Prior to participation in the governance process, most governance members (senators and committee members) had viewed complex outcomes as emerging from behind closed doors. People who dine at a sophisticated restaurant experience the presentation of an elaborate entrée; the waiter's flourish gives no hint of what is involved in growing the many ingredients incorporated into each menu item. Deconstructing the process of leadership is a lot like watching HGTV to learn about gardening: certain routines for problem-solving become clear. The more skills are practiced in a supportive environment, the more they become understood, and eventually become routine. Much like learning to prepare soil for growing different types of plants, previously unknown ideas and skills (e.g., discussing SUNY-wide concerns; considering how student fee increase will impact the budget of relevant units, as well as the students; learning the jargon of different campus units) can be demystified when discussed among colleagues. Individuals serving in leadership roles can find themselves rising to, and meeting, the challenges facing them.

Reflection on New Responsibilities

> As senate chair, I was often the only one who had the position to find common ground between two disparate groups (faculty vs. admin or subsets that disagreed); many times, decisions had to be made and I was the only faculty member "in the room." It fell to me to keep in mind not only what *I* thought was right, but what would be right for the hundreds of faculty and professionals here at Fredonia as well as our students. The role amplifies who you are naturally, and since I am the type of person who wants to help others, and wants to fix what needs fixing, my inherent outlook led to development of new skills. The opportunity of serving in this role empowered me to take risks, in order to do what needed to be done.
>
> —Rob Deemer, Chair, University Senate, SUNY Fredonia, 2010–2016; Associate Professor, Music Department, SUNY Fredonia

An example enlightening all was sharing the "End-of-year Annual Reports." Most campus members (governance participants or others) never saw the final reports of standing committees. Usually, they were not finished by the final meeting, and the "promise I'll finish it" reports never materialized. Under my tenure, we established a template for the final report (see appendix 9.1), which was used by all chairs. This gave chairs, and their committee members, a sense of what they had accomplished, as well as prompting a plan for the year ahead. As a result, people who were considering joining a committee could see what the committee's primary work had been.

As chair of the UFS Governance Committee, I recommended that a similar process be followed at the University Faculty Senate level. This final report format, as well as one for committee reports to the body (see appendix 9.2), standardized reporting. Making use of this strategy served as a point of pride for committee chairs, while also making their individual professional annual reports easier to write. These reports also drew open heavy curtains, showing aspects of governance that had previously been hidden.

It should be noted that some committee chairs were not initially enthusiastic about the use of templates—for interim or final reports. They critiqued the use of such models as "heavy handed," "controlling," or "eliminating creativity." An argument in favor of such an approach is that it provides consistency for the readers, and inclusiveness of details that might otherwise be missed. The format eventually becomes second nature to chairs, freeing them up to spend their time and energy on other, more substantive matters. And when new chairs begin, the established norms are continued.

Opportunities to use their knowledge in campus-wide contexts can facilitate increased confidence and practice of emerging skills. Giving individuals titles and the associated responsibilities (e.g., chair of an ad hoc committee, or co-chair of a task force) for specific exceptional circumstances, or for short-term responsibilities, can facilitate the movement toward leadership development. Additional graduated leadership opportunities could include the following:

- Participating in professional development activities (online, on campus, off campus) oriented toward leadership development.

- Serving as "Lead" on a governance subcommittee.

- Giving periodic updates on the work, by presenting at campus, state, and national governance conferences. (Note: funding for sending individuals to conferences, either to learn or to present, must be incorporated into the annual governance budget, either via the campus or the system, if the institution is part of a larger system.)

Ideally, these new experiences will enable governance members to develop more confidence. However, assistance is needed to foster willingness for most individuals to move outside the comfort zone of familiar routines.

Question 2: How Can New Challenges Become Self-Evaluative Opportunities?

As "exceptional circumstances" become seen as incubators for learning, the campus governance members can become increasingly self-reflective. Instead of viewing recommendations for corrections or reconsiderations as criticism or personal attacks, campus governance professionals can recognize the nugget of truth in them, prompting self-improvement. Linking the actions of a committee with the strategic plan of the unit, college, or system can facilitate increased understanding of how campus governance unit actions impact the whole campus.

Bolman and Deal (2013) describe how the crisis serves to highlight a leader's capabilities or insufficiencies:

> Crises are an acid test of leadership. In the heat of the moment, leaders sometimes hesitate until events pass them by. Other times they jump into the fray, making bad decisions. Either way, they look weak, foolish, or out of touch. A deft response to crisis bolsters a leader's credibility. (p. 304)

Depending upon the needs of the moment, a leader could respond to the crisis from one of Bolman and Deal's four frames (structural, human resource, political, or symbolic) and facilitate very different outcomes. Exhibit 15.1 (p. 308) illustrates how "approaching conflict" can be either an opportunity for "maintain[ing] organizational goals" (structural), "confront[ing] conflict to develop relationships" (human resource), "us[ing] power to defeat opponents and achieve goals" (political), or "negotiate[ing] meaning and develop[ing] shared values" (symbolic). The leader's intentionality moves the organization forward when difficulties emerge.

Instead of dreading conflicts, Bolman and Deal would suggest that it is possible to reframe the problems and instead consider these opportunities as chances to develop leadership skills during exceptional circumstances. Bennis and Thomas (2002) make the following observation on the same topic: "the skills required to conquer adversity and emerge stronger and more committed than ever are the same ones that make for extraordinary leaders" (p. 40), making use of the "crucibles of leadership" that, in testing individuals, lead to skill development.

For individuals developing their leadership skills to learn *prior* to the actual challenge taking place, activities such as the following might be considered as opportunities for reflection and discussion:

- Plan on, and hold, an annual conversation with governance chairpersons that can include some or all of the following:
    - Discuss specific difficult events that occurred during the year (in which the individual may or may not have been directly involved), and jointly analyze both process and outcome.

- o Identify specific leadership goals the individual would like to develop in the year ahead, and incorporate specific skills into the plan.

- o Consider upcoming short-term leadership opportunities (e.g., exceptional circumstance) in which the individual might become involved.

- Facilitate participation in state-wide or system-wide governance activities.

- Take ten minutes every Thursday afternoon to ask yourself these questions:

  - o *What did I do to help my leadership candidates to stretch beyond their reach?*

  - o *How did I recognize efforts as well as achievements?*

  - o *What happened this week to show me progress toward my overall, and specific, leadership goals?*

As a governance leader, I would regularly think back on my past (including leadership in my academic department and professional organizations) to help me face the future. Some of those reflections were about the belly flops. Knowing how much I learned from looking closely at what I failed to accomplish, as well as what I actually achieved, I did not pull any punches in my self-analysis. I tried to honestly prepare for (and not duck) major difficulties, and learn from each one.

Of one thing I was certain: I would need multiple resources to meet each seemingly insurmountable encounter. I turned to colleagues, research, and pilot efforts to approach the unexpected, and was enriched by the knowledge that I was not facing the difficulties alone. One of the most challenging, but ultimately profoundly transformative, professional experiences I had was leading a team of enrollment management and technology specialists to implement a new student information system. Although at the outset we differed in almost every way regarding our perspectives about our institution, and our goals, we learned to speak the same language, and to function as a collaborative, respectful team.

An unexpected resource our team used, to get past our old ways of thinking, was *High Five* by Ken Blanchard and colleagues. The book uses a parable to illustrate how teamwork requires not only one or two outstanding talents, but also collaboration leading to improvement of all members. The book provided a lighthearted starting point for discussion.

We used it to highlight how team members could support each other's developing skills, and thereby learn more about themselves. While learning, all members found themselves increasing their confidence as well as their skill set.

I found myself returning to the concepts of that book many times during my governance life, as I thought about enabling all members to contribute more to making our governance organizations honest, proactive, and responsive to the needs of our campus or state system. This simple book enables the reader to gain access to complex ideas that were embedded in it. Blanchard's principles emerged from earlier ideas. Daniel Goleman's classic book *Emotional Intelligence* (1995) and Howard Gardner (in his 1983 *Frames of Mind*) both brought forward the presence of emotional awareness as a vital component of successful encounters. Goleman clarified how self-knowledge, combined with skills in governing emotions, can lead to progress both at home and in the workplace. He contrasted the cost of "emotional illiteracy" (high for individuals as well as for organizations) with the potential benefits of "schooled" emotions that are contained and understood.

Not entirely accepted, Goleman's ideas aroused strong feelings in many (e.g., Antonakis, Ashkanasy, & Dasborogh, 2009) who considered Goleman to be too theoretical. Regardless of whether one agrees entirely with Goleman or not, feelings exist and can be heightened during difficult times. Being astute and capable of managing feelings can enable leaders to be prepared for unintended emotional injury or possibly becoming the unwitting victims of deliberate emotional sabotage or blackmail. New perspectives, via governance roles, can give each member new insights.

Gaining New Perspectives

> I am involved with governance at the SUNY level, which has been quite eye-opening. I now see how the issues we face on my home campus are aligned with those on other campuses. Many times, other SUNY campuses have already tackled problems that we are just starting to grapple with at home. Learning about their approaches and solutions can help to inform our local decision-making process. Being involved at the SUNY level has really changed my perspective—instead of seeing things through a relatively restrictive and narrow lens, I am able to take in the big picture and see how our campus fits into the larger system.
> —M. Scott Goodman

In reflecting on my decades in governance, I am most appreciative of the guidance that I and others have received at times when powerful emotions threatened impartiality. Whether it is the outreach made by a leader facing apparent disloyalty, an insecure member accusing another of unethical behavior, or frustration at the slowness of a policy change, individuals who are caught in an emotional web need help extricating themselves. Colleagues, resources (such as Bolman and Gallos's 2011 publication, *Reframing Academic Leadership*), can enable governance members and leaders to not only learn but grow from highly charged experiences.

Question 3: How Does One Go from Learner to Mentor or Leader?

One aspect of moving from learner to leader involves an increased awareness of, and comfort level with, others on campus. Intentionally encouraging governance members to become involved in campus-wide activities in ways such as those identified as follows can facilitate this process:

- Encouraging participation on broad-based governance committees to examine the potential obstacles and benefits to be derived from accomplishing the committee's goals.

- Serving on a campus committee, outside of governance, that oversees policies relevant to the exceptional circumstance.

Just as becoming a leader is not an option for everyone, becoming a mentor is not realistic for every governance chair or leader. In some cases, there is no capacity for leadership or mentoring. In other cases, there is no interest in the investment of time, self-reflection, or leaving old habits behind.

- If you are a *potential leader*, and you realize that the match between you and the leader of your governance organization is not right for mentoring, consider inviting another resource person to be your mentor.

- If you are a current *governance leader*, and recognize that one of your senators has a capacity for leadership, and you are not the right mentor, explore other ways your campus could provide mentoring to this individual. Candor in recognizing obstacles or lack of fit between self and others can eliminate wasted time and effort.

Being systematic in approaching the possibility of serving as a mentor can be done via a combination of inward reflection and outward observation (Cramer, 2016). The following questions can enable both potential leaders and mentors to consider the transition from learner to leader:

- What capabilities do I currently have that could be the basis of mentoring or leading?

- What aspects of my professional and educational background could be the foundation for further learning in the area of mentoring or leadership? In what areas would I need to develop new frames of reference and depth of knowledge?

- Am I willing and able to participate in self-reflective inquiry, adjustment, and forward thinking, either to develop my leadership skills or to (as a mentor) serve as a role model?

- Who in my professional context could serve as resources for me as I develop my mentoring or leadership skills? In what ways can I be proactive in approaching these individuals, and invite them to assist?

- How can I develop the skill set I need to become the mentor or leader I aspire to be?

- What supports can I put in place, so that I can take reasonable risks in my professional development as a mentor or leader?

Becoming a mentor or leader can enable individuals to see themselves and others very differently.

Finding New Ways to Serve

I discovered that chairing campus governance is like walking a tightrope between administration and the rest of the campus. This role tested my ability to understand issues, listen effectively, communicate fairly and regularly, and make decisions about how to effectively lead the senate:

* I've discovered that leadership is about managing *all* these areas, but not needing to be THE expert; instead, I have come to understand who the experts are, and seek their advice. I take advice, run it through the filters of all I know, and only then do I act.

* I am a conduit for information—taking advice, recommendations, policies, attitudes, different ways of seeing and thinking about the issues, and sharing them as broadly, honestly, and rapidly as possible.

* I want to ensure that there are fewer misconceptions and misunderstandings, and—instead—more shared knowledge about our institution.

—Amy McMillan

Evolving a leadership style can enable a new leader, and those working with him or her, to have confidence that attentive, thoughtful leaders will offer others new avenues of communication. A pragmatic strategy I developed, which served me well, was to resist the urge to give a quick response to a request for something complex, or to a commitment. By saying, "Let me give that some thought, and get back to you in a few days," I prevented myself from many mistakes. Protecting ourselves from ourselves—sometimes that is just what we need to make renewed commitments to our institutions.

Conclusion

At the beginning of this chapter, readers were encouraged to think of exceptional circumstances for campus governance staff members as "greenhouses for facilitating the development of leadership perspectives, and unique opportunities for mentoring." Greenhouses can be both oppressive and nurturing, depending on your perspective. If you are not a plant, the moisture and heat can be oppressive. But if you realize that your time in the greenhouse is short-lived and provides something for you (as it would for the plants) that can be done in no other way, then the discomfort is worth it. The greenhouse offers opportunities for nurturing and joy in achievement: the same is true at the end of a year of governance into which leadership and mentoring is deliberately infused.

To potential leaders: Leadership is not just for other people. Consider what you might contribute to your department, your governance unit, or your campus (or your system, if your institution is part of a larger system). Make use of chances to step forward, and learn if leadership could be a satisfying addition to your career.

To potential mentors: As a mentor, the normal tendency with exceptional circumstances is to hope you can get through the pressures quickly, losing as little skin as possible. Instead, I suggest that these painful times can offer a chance for learning and growth. As future leaders begin to look at their work, campus, and profession in new ways, they begin to consider how they might take on new positions. Others—you—can assist them with this process. As one governance member later said, "I saw through the mirage I'd been in before: there were opportunities in front of me that I'd never previously considered."

Notes

Deepest appreciation is expressed to the governance members who participated in this chapter, those governance members who have informed my judgment over the years, Heather Maldonado, PhD, whose edits improved this chapter, and Louise Lonabocker and Heather Zimar of *College & University (C&U)*, in which a modified version of this chapter was published.

1. For some governance members or leaders, direct service to advance a specific agenda may be the priority. Mentoring, when done well, is a time-intensive activity. Some people may not be able to (or interested in) making a serious commitment to mentoring.
2. Although some professional staff members (e.g., those in residence life, counseling staff, with titles of associate and assistant directors) have responsibilities that require collaborative work across campus, many have in-depth roles that have little to do with others on campus (e.g., enrollment management staff members, IT staff, budget, et al.).

References

Antonakis, J., Ashkanasy, N.M., & Dasborogh, M.T. (2009). Does leadership need emotional intelligence? *The Leadership Quarterly* (20), 271–261.

Bennis, W.G., & Thomas, R.J. (2002). Crucibles of leadership. *Harvard Business Review, 80*(9), 39–45.

Blanchard, K., Bowles, S.M., Carew, D., & Parisi-Carew, E. (2000). *High five: The magic of working together.* New York: William Morrow.

Bolman, L.G., & Deal, T.E. (2013). *Reframing organizations: Artistry, choice and leadership*, 5th ed. New York: John Wiley & Sons.

Bolman, L.G., & Gallos, J.V. (2011). *Reframing academic leadership.* San Francisco: John Wiley & Sons.

Cramer, S.F. (2016). Giving back: Mentoring others as you were mentored. *C&U (College & University), 91*(4), 37–40.

Goleman, D. (1995). *Emotional intelligence.* New York: Bantam.

Kaplan, R.S., & Norton, D.P. (2004). Keeping score on community investment. *Leader to Leader* (33), 13–19.
Mohr, N., & Dichter, A. (2001). Building a learning organization. *Phi Delta Kappan, 82*(10), 744–747.

Appendix 9.1
Template for Final Report for Committees (Buffalo State)

(name) Committee
Final Report: 20xx–20xy
Members:
Charge:
Name of chair submitting report:
Anticipated vacancies for upcoming year:
List of meetings held by committee:
Report:
    Old business from previous year (description and outcome):
    Items postponed from previous year (description and outcome):
    New business (description and outcome):
Goals for upcoming year:

Appendix 9.2
Template for Committee Reports of the UFS

(name) Committee
Report Date:
Presented at: xxxx 20xy UFS Plenary
Charge:
Current Committee members (names, institutions, contact information)
Chair (name, institution, contact information)
Committee Goals for 20xx–xy:
Committee meeting dates (include type of meeting):
Committee accomplishments since previous UFS Plenary:
Requests to UFS senators from committee:
Anticipated upcoming actions/accomplishments:

10

Reframing Leadership Development through Shared Governance

Heather D. Maldonado

Institutions of higher education in the United States have used shared governance as a means of engaging constituents in campus operations since the 1900s. Leadership development for faculty and professional staff has become more intentional in recent decades, but shared governance is often an overlooked means of achieving development goals. This chapter uses Bolman and Deal's (2013) organizational frames and interpretations of shared governance experiences to explore the leadership development potential of such service. Recommendations to diversify those engaging in service roles and to maximize the leadership development though shared governance are provided.

The study of leadership in higher education has experienced increased attention in the past few decades. This research is often grouped around positional leadership (Bryman, 2007; Isaac, Behar-Horenstein, & Koro-Ljungberg, 2009), leadership competencies (Smith & Wolverton, 2010; Turner, Norwood, & Noe, 2013), or identity and leadership (BlackChen, 2015; Davis & Maldonado, 2015; Haake, 2009). What these bodies of research do not address are the opportunities institutional service—particularly in the form of participating in shared governance—can play in the development of faculty and staff members' leadership abilities.

This chapter employs Bolman and Deal's (2013) organizational frames as a means of understanding and maximizing the effectiveness of shared governance. Their frames are explained and then illustrated, using my experiences with shared governance at the campus and system levels. Bolman and Deal's frames are then applied to my experiences in shared governance with SUNY Buffalo State's College Senate and the State University of New York's (SUNY) University Faculty Senate. Shared governance—the

217

collaborative decision-making between the institution executives and academic governing bodies—consists of processes employed by US colleges and universities since the 1900s (Crellin, 2010) and allows for broad engagement in higher education's administrative practices and progressions. My shared governance examples are then generalized for leadership development strategies for shared governance leaders, supervisors, and individuals interested in professional growth.

A Model of Shared Governance and Leadership Development

SUNY Buffalo State's current shared governance model was designed in 1971, when it "replaced what had been a tripartite system of governance that consisted of a Faculty Council, a Student Council and an Administrative Council" (SUNY Buffalo State College Senate Handbook, 2012, p. 4), to be inclusive of different campus constituencies. Further, since I began my tenure on campus, the inclusivity has gone deeper than simply representation, due to the relationships established between campus administration and leaders of the college senate. Our college senate is comprised of faculty, professional staff, classified staff, and students with our current bylaws requiring faculty be in the majority over all other groups combined. Our college senate is a recommending body to our college president. SUNY Buffalo State is part of the State University of New York (SUNY) system and, as a result, also participates in the shared governance of the SUNY system through the University Faculty Senate (UFS). Our campus has two UFS seats, two UFS alternate seats, and multiple representatives serving on UFS committees. Involvement and engagement with the academic processes addressed by campus and system shared governance provide varied opportunities for leadership and professional development.

My career journey has taken me from Student Affairs to Academic Affairs, and shared governance has provided invaluable insight and professional growth for me. A brief summary of the positions I have held and the major committee accomplishments are illustrated in table 10.1. In addition to the shared governance experiences I have had at SUNY Buffalo State, I have also participated in the SUNY University Faculty Senate (UFS) for several years (see table 10.2).

The importance of these shared governance experiences—at both the campus and system levels—cannot be understated. While many in higher

Table 10.1. Campus-Level Shared Governance as Leadership Development

Campus Position	SUNY Buffalo State College Senate Position	Committee Service	Major Accomplishments
Assistant to the dean & director of academic standards	At-large senator, two three-year terms	Instruction and Research: three years; co-chaired committee for one year and chaired committee for two years Standards for Students: three years, chaired committee for three years	Revisions to the academic misconduct policy Academic calendar development Modification of general education requirements Graduate thesis grading policy Thesis continuation policies Revisions to academic standing policies
Assistant dean & director of academic standards	Professional staff senator, two three-year terms	Standards for Students: four years (plus upcoming year), chaired committee for four years (plus upcoming year)	Priority registration for students receiving military benefits Freshmen admissions policy CAS Self-Study on academic advisement across campus Recommendations to improve advising

Table 10.2. System-Level Shared Governance as Leadership Development

University Faculty Senate Service	Major Accomplishments
Operations Committee: three-year term, committee member	Faculty composition study System-wide policy database
Committee on Ethics and Institutional Integrity: one-year term, committee member	Civility on campus
Operations Committee: two-year term, committee member	Performance metrics Online journal funding
Operations Committee: one-year term, committee chair	To Be Determined
Alternate UFS senator for SUNY Buffalo State	To Be Determined

education have studied long hours to delve deeply into their disciplinary or professional specialties, most have not spent much time studying organizational development or institutional power systems. This deficiency can be overcome through purposeful self-reflection, personal development, and intentional practice (Hempsall, 2014; White, 2012). It has been my experience that, when done well, shared governance provides the perfect laboratory setting to engage in transformative professional development opportunities while serving one's campus or higher education system.

Bolman and Deal (2013) offer a way to make sense of complex organizations by using a variety of lenses—structural, human resources, political, and symbolic. I will apply these four frames to highlight the types of professional growth that can occur through involvement in shared governance. The model does not imply that all four frames are used equitably—organizations likely use all the frames simultaneously, but to varying degrees. Individuals within organizations will have a natural preference for some of the frames, as well as differing levels of comfort with each type. From my perspective, the important point is to become familiar with the frames, and to become skilled at working within them as the need to do so arises.

Structural Frame

Bolman and Deal (2013) note that the structural frame is has its roots in industrial psychology and sociology, and that it is defined by two key assumptions within organizations: how to divide work (differentiation) and how to coordinate work once it has been divided (integration). The clear delineation of responsibility found in well-defined structures enables people to focus on tasks, maximizes the utilization of their expertise, and provides clear channels for decision-making. It is a frame well suited for processes, analysis, and problem-based work. The structural frame depends on vertical coordination (which includes establishing lines of authority, rules and policies, and planning and control systems) and lateral coordination (which includes formal and informal meetings, task forces, influential relationships to synchronize roles, matrix structures wherein people have more than one supervisor, and technological and interorganizational networks). As Bolman and Deal (1991) argue:

A structure is more than boxes and lines arranged hierarchically on an official organization chart. It is an outline of the desired

> patterns of activities, expectations, and exchanges among execu-
> tives, managers, employees, and customers or clients. The shape
> of the formal structure very definitely enhances or constrains what
> an organization is able to accomplish. (p. 46)

As much as this description resonates with higher education's structural administration frames, it also rings true for the structural frames of shared governance in institutions of higher education in the United States.

My experiences with shared governance on my campus and within our state system have been exemplars of the structural frame. Both entities have clear differentiation and vertical coordination as evidenced by the specific roles of the governance leader, elected senators, committee chairs, and committee members. Both entities also have clear integration due to the specific systems and lateral coordination that is deployed to ensure progress is being made by the organization. Organizational bylaws and the parliamentary procedures defined by *Robert's Rules of Order*, both of which are utilized by SUNY Buffalo State's College Senate, are examples of the vertical coordination needed for effective shared governance in the structural frame. New member orientation, planning meetings, and liaisons to important constituencies are examples of essential practices of lateral coordination and can be seen through SUNY's UFS new committee chair orientation and networking opportunities, multiday summer and fall planning meetings, and regular interactions with SUNY System Administration. Institutions or campus governance bodies wishing to improve their effectiveness should assess the current differentiation and integration in their structure, modify these elements as needed, and identify way to enhance vertical and lateral coordination to improve organizational outcomes.

Human Resource Frame

Bolman and Deal (2013) state that those who first articulated the notion of the human resource frame "argued that people's skills, attitudes, energy, and commitment are vital resources that can make or break an enterprise" (p. 117). The human resource frame highlights the importance of "fit" between an organization and the individuals who form the organization. The frame emphasizes motivation and the factors (such as needs, motives, and personality) that can enhance or stunt a person's motivation at work. To develop the best possible mutually beneficial relationship, individuals must feel they are engaged in meaningful work for their organization so the organization can benefit from the full talent and potential of its members.

Serving as a committee chair for SUNY Buffalo State's College Senate has allowed me ample opportunity to work within the human resource frame. While some people dread the idea of chairing a committee because they fear being "stuck" with a large amount of work and little commitment from the group members, I have never had that experience as a committee chair. Perhaps it was just good luck, but—if theory is to be believed—I think my effectiveness as a committee chair has come from my recognition that the heart of SUNY Buffalo State (including our college senate and the committees I have chaired) is our people. We have deeply talented people at our institution who want the best for our students and work to fulfill our institutional mission. As a committee chair, I have tried to consistently do two things for my committees: (1) run efficient, meaningful meetings, including crafting consequential agendas, providing necessary information and data for substantial discussion, being goal/outcome oriented, and sharing information—including committee meeting minutes and college senate updates—in a timely fashion, and (2) "encouraging the heart" (Kouzes and Posner, 1999) of my committee members, which includes "setting clear standards, expecting the best, paying attention, personalizing recognition, telling the story, celebrating together, and setting the example" (p. 18). These two strategies have resulted in the SUNY Buffalo State College Senate committees I chaired having highly involved members who engage in significant service for the institution, generally resulting in more actions (in the form of resolutions or recommended policy changes) than most of my peers. Smith and Wolverton (2010) identify competency in areas such as analytical thinking, communication, and interpersonal behaviors as hallmarks of successful leadership—and the use of such competencies as a campus leader prevent creating campus frustration with fruitless service obligations. Being aware of the human resource frame and adopting practices that support individuals engaging in meaningful and rewarding work is a fairly simple (and low-cost) way for campus leaders to achieve positive results within their organization.

Political Frame

Understanding organizations through the political frame means putting aside emotional reactions to the term "political" based on personal reactions to organized government processes and actions to understand a less loaded definition of the term. Conceptualizing politics as "the realistic process of making decisions and allocating resources in a context of scarcity and divergent interests" (Bolman & Deal, 2013, p. 184) enables the exploration of the political frame as a means for successfully fulfilling higher education goals. The assumptions of the political frame characterize organizations as coalitions of constituencies with diverse interests that compete over scarce resources and arrive at decisions through bargaining and negotiation. The political frame is concerned with power because—from the point of view of those employing this frame—power is what is used to arrive at decisions to benefit one's constituency. However, power in the political frame can be broader than authority, since power also capitalizes on networks of influence. Thus, power (in its many forms) in the political frame should simply be viewed as a way to achieve group goals and create the aspirational organizational reality.

Bolman and Deal identify authorities and partisans as the two main players in the political frame, with authorities being the "officers in charge" of decision-making, and partisans potentially being the "voice of the other" in the organization. It is because of these innately contentious relationships (due to structure and scarcity) that conflict will always be present in political frames. What is essential is quickly recognizing when the political frame is activated, and adeptly handling political conflict constructively so the organization can advance. Making use of these skills often differentiate the aspiring from the effective leader.

My shared governance experience has provided an in-depth case study of the political frame during our most recent general education review. Perhaps one of the most central features of a college senate is faculty oversight of the college curriculum, and the curriculum is also often a vigorously fought political contest with competing interests from multiple constituencies. Our most recent review in the college senate resulted in the recommendation of a nearly thirty-credit reduction of our liberal arts college's general education curriculum. This happened through the successful negotiation of a particular coalition that adeptly created rules for the new general education program that privileged some disciplines. SUNY Buffalo State is about to undertake our next general education review, and coalitions have already begun politicking to try to regain some of what they perceive was lost in the last review. SUNY Buffalo State's general education review case study highlights the importance of awareness of the political frame, knowledge and comfort in using political tools such as coalition building and influence, and recognizing when and how to use various forms of power to achieve organizational goals.

Symbolic Frame

The symbolic frame is perhaps the most overlooked way of making sense of organizations, yet it can be exceptionally powerful for those who are interested in maintaining a system or inspiring change of the system. Leaders should be aware that an action (or inaction) internalized by members of an organization may be something different than it appears, and be self-reflective about their choice of action in order to provide the inspirational and symbolic meaning needed to shape the organizational culture. As Bolman and Deal (2013) state, "culture is both a product and a process. As a product, it embodies wisdom accumulated from experience. As a process, it is renewed and re-created as newcomers learn the old ways and eventually become teachers themselves" (p. 263). It is important to note that people will create their own symbols and meaning when facing uncertainty. A strong organizational culture will help unite the people within the organization and best position them to achieve the organization's goals.

One of my earliest memories of my involvement with the SUNY Buffalo State College Senate was becoming embroiled in our college senate discussion about revising our bylaws to provide appropriate shared governance representation across campus due to the reorganization of the institution. The reorganization dissolved the organizational units of academic faculties and created four academic schools plus a university college and a graduate school led by administrative deans. The college senate discussion included questions about the size of the body, the number of representatives from each school, if representation from the university college and the graduate school should be included, and the need for a faculty majority over all other combined constituencies (i.e., staff, students, at-large seats).

These matters were hotly debated by the impacted constituencies. However, representation for the university college and the graduate school were quickly voted down. Additionally, the need to maintain a faculty majority at all times—even when a professional staff member was elected to an at-large position that was intended to represent all constituencies— was approved. While the new college senate bylaws certainly belong in the structural frame that was discussed earlier in this chapter, the speed of the discussion and the dismissal of concerns sent a very clear symbolic message about the lack of acceptance of the newly created university college and graduate school structures and the secondary role professional staff are perceived to have at the institution. The reverberations of these symbolic gestures continue to be perceived on campus today.

A similar symbolic battle was fought over SUNY Buffalo State's interpretation of UFS bylaws and the eligibility of professional staff to be elected UFS senators or serve on UFS committees. Professional staff were being prohibited from running for UFS seats and not being notified of the opportunity to serve on UFS committees (even though the UFS committees include areas of focus directly related to some professional appointments' areas of expertise, such as Equity, Inclusion, and Diversity; Operations; and Student Life). It took contacting the UFS about the issue—which was discussed in the UFS Governance Committee, a resolution crafted, and campuses were notified—to allow professional staff to engage with the UFS shared governance opportunities. This incident was another example of something happening (or, in this case, *not* happening) that led to a particular symbolic interpretation of the value of professional staff within the campus culture. The two examples of the symbolic frame being applied to interpret shared governance events are meant to illustrate the need for awareness of acts, symbols, and stories as indicators of institutional culture and values, thereby assisting leaders to engage intentionally, in both word and act, with their organization.

Recognizing the Value of Shared Governance in Leadership Development

Shared governance offers a unique opportunity for motivated campus faculty and, if allowed, staff to engage in meaningful service to the institution in ways that broaden their awareness about college- and system-wide issues, expand their collegial network, and improve understanding among divergent constituencies. As a bonus, these opportunities come at a low cost to the institution since often the only cost to the campus is release time for governance work and snacks (sometimes) at the monthly governance meeting. However, the return-on-investment can be stunning if people emerge from their shared governance experiences feeling more connected to their institutions due to having meaningful interactions where their voices—and the voices of those they represent—have been heard by colleagues and administrators in their efforts to improve their institutions. Intentionally developing the leadership skills of emerging campus leaders and purposefully developing a healthy shared governance process are essential acts needed to engage individuals and improve the organization.

Participating in shared governance is not, however, without its problems. First, particularly for professional staff, not all supervisors support their employees' participation in out-of-office activities. Gaining permission to take on shared governance service may be a delicate matter that requires patience and strategizing to be actualized. Second, sexism and racism may emerge in shared governance just as in other areas of society and higher education (Maldonado & Draeger, 2017; Stanley, 2006). Females have reported overt acts of sexism in relation to their running for senate positions. People of color have reported racist microaggressions during committee meetings. Women and people of color still can find themselves the lone representative of their group in their shared governance circle. Increasing the diversity of representation within shared governance systems will help warm the chilly climate for underrepresented groups' participation and help ensure a more comprehensive dialogue to improve the work of shared governance bodies.

I am fortunate to work at an institution that goes beyond valuing diversity through a sentence in a mission statement; instead, there is evidence that members of campus truly value diversity through representation of all campus constituencies in the shared governance process. This commitment to diversity has allowed me the opportunity to serve on both our institution's college senate and with the system's University Faculty Senate. While I have participated in excellent intensive leadership development cohorts, such as SUNY Buffalo State's Achieving Success through Leadership program and HERS Wellesley's Women in Higher Education Leadership Program, these types of programs often lack the same essential element: *doing* the leadership that has been studied over an extended period of time in the program. Shared governance provides repeated opportunities to hone the leadership skills that are often cited in performance plans, academic journals, and business trade books. Campuses that allow professional staff to serve as members of their shared governance body should encourage supervisors to guide staff to use shared governance as professional development opportunities, so staff can expand their knowledge, skills, and network. Governance leaders should remember that, in addition to the important administrative skills and positional knowledge, today's professional staff are often highly credentialed and sometimes scholarly experts in their disciplines, with important voices that should be sought out in the shared governance of an institution.

This chapter discussed structural, human resources, political, and symbolic frames as ways to understand how organizations operate in US colleges and universities. Shared governance experiences were provided to illustrate these frames and highlight the ways in which shared governance operates. Reframing leadership development as something that can be accomplished by working within a shared governance organization is an excellent way to simultaneously engage in professional development and service. Acquiring an awareness of organizational frames is essential for faculty and professional staff desiring to lead their campuses in achieving institutional outcomes.

References

BlackChen, M. (2015). To lead or not to lead: Women achieving leadership status in higher education. *Advancing Women in Leadership, 35,* 153.

Bolman, L.G., & Deal, T.E. (1991). *Reframing organizations: Artistry, choice, and leadership.* San Francisco: Jossey-Bass.

Bolman, L.G., & Deal, T.E. (2013). *Reframing organizations: Artistry, choice, and leadership (5th ed.).* San Francisco: Jossey-Bass.

Bryman, A. (2007). Effective leadership in higher education: A literature review. *Studies in Higher Education, 32*(6), 693–710.

Crellin, M.A. (2010). The future of shared governance. *New Directions for Higher Education* (151), 71–81.

Davis, D.R., & Maldonado, C. (2015). Shattering the glass ceiling: The leadership development of African American women in higher education. *Advancing Women in Leadership, 35,* 48.

Haake, U., Pedagogiska institutionen, Umeå universitet, & Samhällsvetenskapliga fakulteten. (2009). Doing leadership in higher education: The gendering process of leader identity development. *Tertiary Education and Management, 15*(4), 291–304.

Hempsall, K. (2014). Developing leadership in higher education: Perspectives from the USA, the UK and Australia. *Journal of Higher Education Policy and Management, 36*(4), 383–394.

Isaac, C.A., Behar-Horenstein, L.S., & Koro-Ljungberg, M. (2009). Women deans: Leadership becoming. *International Journal of Leadership in Education, 12*(2), 135–153.

Kouzes, J.M., & Posner, B.Z. (1999). *Encouraging the heart: A leader's guide to rewarding and recognizing others.* San Francisco: Jossey-Bass.

Maldonado, H., & Draeger, J. (2017). Identifying, understanding, and responding to sexism in academia. In K. Cole & H. Hassel (Eds.), *Surviving sexism in academia: Strategies for feminist leadership.* (pp. 5–12). New York, NY: Routledge.

Smith, Z.A., & Wolverton, M. (2010). Higher education leadership competencies: Quantitatively refining a qualitative model. *Journal of Leadership & Organizational Studies, 17*(1), 61–70.

Stanley, C.A. (2006). Coloring the academic landscape: Faculty of color breaking the silence in predominantly white colleges and universities. *American Educational Research Journal, 43*(4), 701–736.

SUNY Buffalo State College Senate Handbook (2012). Retrieved from http://collegesenate.buffalostate.edu/sites/collegesenate.buffalostate.edu/files/uploads/Documents/SENATE%20MINUTES/SENATE%20ROSTER%20AND%20SENATE%20LISTING/COLLEGESENATEHANDBOOKrevisedBillRaffel July12.pdf

Turner, P.K., Norwood, K., & Noe, C. (2013). A woman with a plan: Recognizing competencies for ascent to administration in higher education. *NASPA Journal about Women in Higher Education, 6*(1), 22–47.

White, J.S. (2012). HERS institutes: Curriculum for advancing women leaders in higher education. *Advances in Developing Human Resources, 14*(1), 11–27.

Contributors

Martha J. Asselin, PhD, proudly served Schenectady County Community College for over 25 years. She retired in 2017 as Vice President of Student Affairs at the college, having previously served for 17 months as Acting President of Schenectady County Community College. Dr. Asselin has more than 30 years of professional experience in higher education overall. She has had a diverse career with progressive increases in position and level of responsibilities.

Dr. Asselin was instrumental in securing various grants for Schenectady County Community College, most notably was the Gates Foundation grant in collaboration with Schenectady City Schools to open the Schenectady Smart Scholars Early College High School, serving 500 students in Schenectady High School in grades 9 through 12. Dr. Asselin has been appointed by the SUNY chancellor to serve on various working groups for policy design and strategic planning, including: the SUNY Work Group for Developing System Policies for Sexual Violence, the SUNY Work Group for Development of Practices and Protocols for Addressing Ebola, and two SUNY Chancellor's Task Forces: One on Social Media Responsibility and the other on Addressing Mental Health at College Campuses.

Dr. Asselin has been active in her profession through professional affiliations and memberships, her campus through committee memberships and activities, and her community through her board work. She has been a member of the American Council on Education Women's Network, SUNY Community College Chief Student Affairs Officers Association, SUNY Council on Assessment Advisory Board, SUNY Campus Safety Advisory Board, and more. She has served as a mentor for women through the American Council on Education of NENY and for the *Albany Business Review*'s Women Mentorship program.

Dr. Asselin holds a Bachelor's of Science in Psychology and Sociology from SUNY–Oswego and a Master's of Science and a Doctor of Philosophy in Educational Administration and Policy Studies from the University at Albany. In 2012, Dr. Asselin published her dissertation, *Utilizing Social Networks in Times of Crisis: Understanding, Exploring and Analyzing Critical Incident Management at Institutions of Higher Education.*

Steven C. Bahls has been president of Augustana College (Illinois) since 2003. He received his JD from Northwestern University School of Law and his BBA from University of Iowa. He has served as dean of Capital University Law School in Columbus, Ohio; associate dean and professor of University of Montana School of Law; and as a practicing lawyer in Milwaukee. He taught corporate law and has published many scholarly articles about corporate governance. He has written extensively about higher education and shared governance in *Trusteeship, Chronicle of Higher Education,* and *Inside Higher Ed.* He is the author of the book *Shared Governance in Times of Change: A Practical Guide for Universities and Colleges,* published in 2014 by AGB Press. President Bahls is serving on or has served on the boards of several national organizations, including the Council of Independent Colleges, National Association of Independent Colleges and Universities, Lutheran Education Conference of North America, and University of Montana School of Law Board of Visitors.

Joan M. Carroll, MS, CPA, retired after 36 years of service as an associate professor of accounting in the School of Business at SUNY Oswego. She earned BS and MS degrees in Accounting at Clarkson University, where she also captained their first women's ice hockey team. At Oswego, she was involved in campus governance throughout her career, chairing the faculty assembly 2012–2017 after serving as assembly vice chair and chair of the Personnel Policies Council 2003–2012.

Sharon F. Cramer, PhD, SUNY Distinguished Service Professor at Buffalo State College, was a faculty member from 1985 to 2011. During her career, she served as an academic leader in roles that included department chair (1995–1999), chair of the college senate (2007–2010), and chair of the Governance Committee of the SUNY University Faculty Senate (2007–2010). She was an officer, or on the Board of Directors, of four professional and governance organizations and received the highest award from each of them. From the SUNY University Faculty Senate, she received the Ram Chugh award in 2011 and the Senator Emerita award in 2015. From 2011, anticipated through 2019, she served as parliamentarian for the SUNY University Faculty Senate.

Dr. Cramer has given over 100 presentations and keynotes in 23 states and two provinces in Canada. She completed her PhD studies at New York University, and earned an MAT degree from Harvard University and a BA from Tufts University. Her publication record includes three books (one co-authored with Jan Stivers); 28 scholarly articles; 23 reflective, personal articles in the *Buffalo News*; nine academic chapters, as well as serving as the editor of two volumes published by SUNY Press, which focus on shared governance (2017). She is listed in *Who's Who in America* (2006–present), *Who's Who in American Education* (2006–present), and *Who's Who in American Women* (2008–present).

Rob Deemer was a 2016–2017 American Council on Education (ACE) Fellow at Baldwin Wallace University and is currently Head of Music Composition in the School of Music and Assistant to the President at the State University of New York at Fredonia. His works have been commissioned and performed by the Buffalo Philharmonic Orchestra, the President's Own Marine Band, the U.S. Army Orchestra (Pershing's Own), the wind ensembles at the University of Texas and the University of Missouri at Kansas City, contemporary chamber ensembles such as the Rasçher Saxophone Quartet, loadbang, Akropolis Quintet, Great Noise Ensemble, American Contemporary Music Ensemble, and Gaudete Brass. As an author, Deemer has become well known for his writings for *Music Educators Journal, NewMusicBox, Sequenza21*, and the *New York Times*. He is a founding member and chair-elect of the NAfME Composition Council, serves as the chair of the New York State School Music Association Composition & Improvisation Committee, and was selected to be a member of the National Coalition for Core Arts Standards Composition/ Theory Standards Subcommittee. He served for five years on the composition faculty at the Interlochen Summer Arts Camp and is the composer-in-residence with the Buffalo Chamber Players and Harmonia Chamber Singers. In his second of four years as chair of the University Senate, Fredonia was the first winner of the SUNY Shared Governance Award.

Debra Sabatini Dwyer is a research associate professor in the Department of Technology and Society at Stony Brook University. She earned a BS in Economics from Queens College (CUNY) and an MS/PhD from the School of Industrial and Labor Relations in Labor and Health Economics from Cornell University. Dr. Dwyer went on to complete a one-year postdoctoral position in the Maxwell School of Public Policy at Syracuse University. Her areas of expertise are policy studies of the health and labor market. Her work informs social security, labor, and health policy. In addition, she has made significant contributions in the measurement and use of survey data in empirical research.

Prior to coming to Stony Brook University, Dr. Dwyer was Senior Economist in the Division of Economic Research, Office of Research Evaluation and Statistics, at the Social Security Administration in Washington, DC. She worked as part of the disability project team that focused on the disability components of the social security system. Through that work, she developed a model for simulating eligibility for disability insurance and supplemental security income in the general population.

In addition to her teaching responsibilities in economics and public policy, Debra advises and mentors undergraduate and graduate students (MA, PhD) in a number of areas within public policy research. She serves on many academic and community service committees and as a referee for several peer-reviewed journals and books in the areas of health and labor economics. Her research projects and interests include information in the health market, obesity, adolescent risky behavior, work and health, technology and society, and Medicaid reform.

Norman Goodman is SUNY Distinguished Teaching Professor and SUNY Distinguished Service Professor of Sociology at Stony Brook University. He was the first person in New York State to be awarded two distinguished professorships. Goodman received his BA in Sociology from Brooklyn College (CUNY) and his MA and PhD in Sociology from New York University. He has been a Visiting Scholar at the London School of Economics and Political Science and the City University of London.

Goodman is an accomplished scholar. He is author or editor of nine books and over 20 articles in professional journals or book chapters. He has also presented papers at major disciplinary conferences. His academic specialties are in social psychology (especially issues of identity and socialization) and marriage and family life.

Goodman has extensive governance experience at both his campus and the SUNY system. He was chair of his department for 20 years and, at Stony Brook University, he was vice president and then president of the Arts and Sciences Senate and twice president of the University Senate. He has served as a member or chair of most of the standing committees of these two governance organizations. He currently co-chairs the University Senate's Committee on Academic Planning and Resource Allocation in addition to serving on the University Senate's Undergraduate Council and its Student Life Committee. Goodman has also worked collaboratively with administrators at Stony Brook University to establish, maintain, and teach in a number of interdisciplinary undergraduate academic and co-curricular programs, such as the Residential College Program Federated Learning Communities and Living/Learning Centers.

He has been involved in state-wide governance since 1990. He was vice president/secretary of the SUNY University Faculty Senate for six years and a member of its governance, student life, graduate and research, and undergraduate academic policies and program committees, serving as chair twice for the last one. He was also a co-chair of the state-wide Task Force on General Education and is on the Executive Committee of the SUNY Distinguished Academy. He was named the first SUNY University Faculty Senate Fellow, now called the Carl P. Wiezalis University Faculty Senate Fellow. He is the editor of the *SUNY University Faculty Senate Bulletin*, as has been the case for more than a decade.

Joe Hildreth, Art Curator for the SUNY Art Exhibition Series, is Distinguished Service Professor Emeritus in the Art Department at SUNY Potsdam. In addition to his responsibilities as art curator, he was the head of the printmaking program at Potsdam. Mr. Hildreth also serves as the artistic director for the SUNY Thayer/Ross Fellowship program. He has served as Art Department chair, president of the Potsdam faculty senate, and president of the University Faculty Senate. He is a practicing print-maker with numerous exhibitions. Mr. Hildreth most recently designed, implemented, and installed the *SUNY Abstraction* exhibition now open at the SUNY Global Center in midtown Manhattan.

Virginia Horvath, President of the State University of New York at Fredonia since 2012, formerly served as Vice President for Academic Affairs at Fredonia. She previously was at Kent State University as a professor of English, Dean of Academic and Student Services, and Assistant to the President for Strategic Planning. A recipient of Kent State's Distinguished Teaching Award, she has academic specialties in medieval literature, British literature, children's/young adult literature, writing, and poetry. She continues to teach one course every year. She has presented and consulted across the country and beyond on documenting and evaluating faculty and staff work, leadership and professional development, community engagement, service learning, and strategic planning. Horvath earned a BA in English from the University at Buffalo and an MA and PhD in English from Kent State University. She was a visiting professor at Shimane University (Japan) and an American Council on Education Fellow.

She served on the national board of the American Association of State Colleges and Universities (AASCU) and the Steering Committee for the Millennium Leadership Initiative. She is a member of the faculty for the AASCU New Presidents Academy and serves as a member of the advisory council of Auronya College in Pondicherry, India. She also serves on several regional boards of trustees/directors: Brooks Memorial Hospital, the Buffalo Seminary, Chautauqua County Chamber of Commerce, Girl Scouts of Western New York, and the Unitarian Universalist Congregation of Northern Chautauqua. She is a member of the Executive Committee of the Western New York Consortium of Higher Education and co-chair of the Western New York Regional Economic Development Council.

Gwen Kay is a professor of history and director of the Honors program at SUNY Oswego. She was vice chair of the faculty assembly and chair of the Personnel Policies Council, a former faculty senator to the University Faculty Senate, immediate past vice president and secretary, now president of the SUNY University Faculty Senate and member of the SUNY Board of Trustees.

Peter L.K. Knuepfer is Associate Professor of Geological Sciences and Environmental Studies at Binghamton University. From July 1, 2013 through June 30, 2017, he served as president of the Faculty Senate and member of the SUNY Board of Trustees. Professor Knuepfer received his BS and MS degrees in geology from Stanford University and his PhD in geosciences from the University of Arizona. A member of Binghamton's faculty since 1986, he specializes in the study of processes operating at the Earth's surface, particularly rivers and flood hazards. He has taught undergraduate courses in environmental studies and both undergraduate and graduate courses in geology, as well as courses in the Binghamton Scholars program and freshmen seminars. He has been principal advisor to 11 master's and four PhD students, as well as serving on numerous master's and doctoral committees.

Professor Knuepfer has served Binghamton, SUNY, and the public in many ways during his time at Binghamton. He served as director of the Environmental Studies program at BU for more than a decade, has chaired several committees on campus, been a member of senior administrative search committees, and a member of SUNY-wide committees on system-wide assessment as well as University Faculty Senate committees on undergraduate education, graduate education and research, and academic integrity. He has also presented several talks to groups in the

Binghamton area on flood hazards and assessment and has been a member of the advisory board to the Union-Endicott Educational Foundation. He also serves as a church musician. He received the Chancellor's Award for Excellence in Faculty Service in 2005.

Dr. Knuepfer's research has ranged from the study of earthquake hazards (including part of a team that assessed earthquake potential for the proposed Yucca Mountain nuclear waste repository), to analysis of mountain growth in Taiwan and New Zealand, to the glacial history of New York, to the assessment of past and potential future flooding in the Susquehanna River basin. He has authored or co-authored more than 40 scientific papers and 100 professional presentations, as well as co-edited three books. His current project focuses on the magnitude and frequency of prehistoric flooding of the Susquehanna River as well as changes in the frequency of large flooding throughout the Northeast United States in recent decades. He has received many federal grants in support of his research.

Ronald Labuz is a SUNY Distinguished Teaching Professor Emeritus and was a professor of art at Mohawk Valley Community College for 35 years. After working in Columbus, Ohio, as an advertising executive, editor, and president of a publishing firm, he returned home to Utica, New York, to teach at his first alma mater. A graduate of Mohawk Valley Community College, SUNY Oswego, the Ohio State University, and Syracuse University, he has earned master's degrees in philosophy, humanities, and art history and a PhD in humanities. The author of 14 books and over 120 articles, he served as head of the Art Department for 17 years before returning to the faculty to enjoy what he loves most: teaching. He served as the coordinator of art at MVCC and as the college's delegate to the Faculty Council of Community Colleges. As an art historian and a lover of art and history, he has traveled widely, including annual trips to Italy and France. Dr. Labuz has been recognized in many ways for his teaching and scholarship. He has received several MVCC awards for scholarship and collegiality and is the recipient of three State University of New York Chancellor's Awards for Excellence for Scholarship and Creative Activities, Professional Service, and Faculty Service. In 2015, the SUNY Board of Trustees named him SUNY Distinguished Teaching Professor, the first from Mohawk Valley Community College.

Mark Maciulaitis is Associate Vice President for Budget at Stony Brook University. He has worked at Stony Brook University since 1985, initially as a financial analyst. He is an alumnus of Stony Brook University with a BA in psychology, after which he received an MA in Psychology from Kean University, a graduate certificate in business from Long Island University, before receiving an MBA in Finance from Indiana University.

Maciulaitis has served as secretary, then chair, of the SUNY-wide Budget Committee, and he also chaired the SUNY Committee on Dormitory Rehabilitation Financing. At Stony Brook University, he has been a member and chair of numerous committees, including the Lapsing Fund Committee, the EEO Committee, the Campus Budget Model (CBM) Implementation Committee, as well as many others. Recently, he has served as the chair of the campus's Finance and Budget Committee and the IDC and Royalties Allocation Team. The former was charged with developing a new overall budgeting model/process for the university, and the latter with a new model for distributing the campus's IDC and royalty revenues—both of which were included as part of the white paper on budgeting, which was presented to the campus administration last year. He currently serves on the University Council, the campus's Operational Excellence Committee, as well as chairing and serving on a number of committees associated with the latter initiative.

Heather D. Maldonado currently serves as Assistant Provost for Academic Success and teaches in the Higher Education and Student Affairs graduate program at SUNY Buffalo State. Dr. Maldonado's research interests include issues surrounding women in higher education, students' decision-making, and leadership development. She has received the SUNY Chancellor's Award for Excellence in Professional Service and is a graduate of the national HERS Wellesley women's leadership development institute. Dr. Maldonado also has past professional experience in residence life and new student orientation at Rutgers College and Clarion University of Pennsylvania. Dr. Maldonado earned her BA in Political Science from SUNY Geneseo, MA in Higher Education and Student Affairs from The Ohio State University, and PhD in Social and Philosophical Foundations in Education from the University at Buffalo.

Lori Mould is a nontraditional student who graduated from Genesee Community College (GCC) with two degrees, one in Communications and Media Arts and one in Fine Arts. She was active in Phi Theta Kappa, holding the positions of public relations officer, vice president, and president and served on the 2009–2010 New York Regional Officer Team as Historian. she also held positions within the GCC SGA as public relations, campus center representative, and student trustee.

She transferred to SUNY Empire State College (ESC) where she earned her Bachelors of Art in Photojournalism and Documentary Production. She has held various positions within the ESC student government and also the college. She served as a 2013–2014 university/college representative, the acting vice president, and was elected as the 2014–2015 president of the Student Assembly of the State University of New York (SUNYSA) and a trustee for the SUNY Board of Trustees and the NYS Higher Education Services Corp (HESC) Board of Trustees.

She is currently working on her Master of Arts in Adult Learning with concentrations in Higher Education and Veteran Services at SUNY ESC. She is scheduled to graduate in June 2017. Her thesis will include a creative photojournalistic/documentary regarding the causes of the suicide rates of our female military veterans.

The personal growth that she has achieved through her service on each of her campuses, Phi Theta Kappa, SUNYSA, SUNY, and through service learning and community service projects has been life-altering. Lori strongly believes that there is more to education than what you can learn in a classroom.

Chelsea Reome is a recent graduate of the Master of Public Administration program at Binghamton University. At Binghamton University, she served as a graduate research assistant to Professor Thomas A.P. Sinclair. She currently works at the Broome County Health Department. Her research interests are wide-ranging and include topics in public health, community and economic development, and governance. She is a member of Pi Alpha Alpha and an AmeriCorps alumna.

Erin Severs is an Assistant Professor of English at Mohawk Valley Community College. She has been teaching for over twelve years with a heavy focus on teaching developmental writing. In addition to her Master's degrees in English and Women's Studies from the University of Maine, she holds a graduate certificate in Developmental Education from the Kellogg Institute at Appalachian State University, and she is a Freedom Writer Teacher thanks to having had the opportunity to attend The Freedom Writers Institute in California. At MVCC, she is a placement test reader, a SafeSpace trainer, and she chairs the Professional Development All-Campus committee, among other things. She also has been a writer and reviewer for numerous publishing companies including McGraw Hill Higher Education where she currently is a contributor to the online *Connect* products. In addition, Erin is among the first graduating class from MVCC's Leadership Academy, a program through which she has worked on designing a Gender Studies degree program for the college. During Spring, 2018, she anticipates a Sabbatical, during which she will write a textbook for MVCC's developmental writing courses.

Thomas A.P. Sinclair is an associate professor in the Department of Public Administration at Binghamton University. Professor Sinclair's varied research interests focus on democratic governance, from the capacities of small municipal governments principally managed by voluntary boards and their methods for providing needed services to mechanisms for enhancing the transparency and accountability of administrative systems in public universities. He has served in numerous faculty governance leadership roles.

Andrea I. Stagg serves as Deputy General Counsel at Barnard College. Previously, she advised the SUNY Colleges at New Paltz, Oneonta, and Plattsburgh on all legal matters, and was the system-wide expert in Title IX compliance, state authorization, and intercollegiate athletics. Andrea collaborated with the working group that wrote SUNY's sexual and interpersonal violence prevention and response policies, which formed the basis for New York Education Law Article 129-B. She is the author of two peer-reviewed NACUA Notes and a co-author on a book review in the *Journal of College and University Law*. Andrea graduated Phi Beta Kappa with high honors from Rutgers University and received her law degree from the George Washington University, where she was an intern in the Office of General Counsel. Before law school, Andrea worked in federal higher education lobbying on behalf of Rutgers University.

Joseph Storch is Associate Counsel in the State University of New York Office of General Counsel and chair of its Student Affairs Practice Group. He concentrates his practice on student affairs, intellectual property, and compliance with the Clery Act and Title IX. Joe provides technical guidance to higher education institutions and organizations as well as members and staff of the US Senate, House of Representatives, and New York State Legislature on campus violence prevention legislation. Joe co-coordinated SUNY's 2014 university-wide sexual violence prevention policies with stakeholders from inside and outside the SUNY system, and in 2015 he served as a technical advisor developing comprehensive legislation enacted as 129-B of the Education Law. Joe has trained several thousand higher education professionals on compliance with the Clery Act, Title IX, and related obligations, including conference or college presentations in more than two dozen states. In 2014, he received the Commissioner's Award from the State University Police for contributions to safety on campus, and in 2015, NACUA awarded him its First Decade Award, recognizing the member who makes the greatest contribution within their first ten years of practice. Joe graduated summa cum laude from SUNY Oswego where he served as Student Association vice president, from the University at Albany with a master's of Public Policy, and from Cornell Law School where he served as Moot Court Board Chancellor. After law school, he clerked for the New York State Appellate Division, 3rd Department.

Nina Tamrowski is the president of the Faculty Council of Community Colleges and has been a member of the Board of Trustees since July 2015. She recently received the Chancellor's Award for Excellence in Faculty Service in spring of 2015, in recognition of her service in many arenas, including her campus and the Faculty Council of Community Colleges (FCCC).

Tamrowski has served as delegate to the FCCC from Onondaga Community College since 2009 and was a member of its Governance Committee. She also served as secretary of the FCCC from 2011 to 2013, and as vice president from 2013 to 2015. She was also the Faculty Council liaison to the University Faculty Senate's Governance Committee for five years.

Tamrowski currently serves as a member of the Search Committee for the SUNY Chancellor and served on the Search Committee for the SUNY Provost in 2014.

Tamrowski has been a professor of political science at Onondaga Community College since 1993. At Onondaga, she has regularly taught American National Politics, State and Local Politics, Comparative Politics, and Women and Politics. Tamrowski served for four years as the chair of the Social Sciences and Philosophy Department. She has been a member of Onondaga's Faculty Executive Committee since 2009. She was a founding co-chair of OCC's Service-Learning Committee and served in that role for seven years. From 1999 to 2002, Tamrowski was the executive director of OCC's Student Government Organization. In that capacity, she taught leadership skills to students and managed the student government leaders and their affairs.

She earned a Master of Arts degree in Political Science from Syracuse University and completed her PhD coursework in political science as well. Tamrowski's BA degree in Spanish and Political Science is from SUNY College at Brockport.

Index